Secret Gospels

Secret Gospels

Essays on Thomas and the Secret Gospel of Mark

Marvin Meyer

To Jim,
best wishes,
Marv

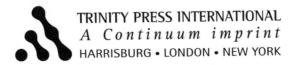

TRINITY PRESS INTERNATIONAL
A Continuum imprint
HARRISBURG • LONDON • NEW YORK

Trinity Press International
A Continuum imprint
P.O. Box 1321, Harrisburg, PA 17105

Cover image: *Gospel of Thomas,* Nag Hammadi Codex II, page 51: The conclusion of the *Gospel of Thomas,* with the title. Courtesy of the Institute for Antiquity and Christianity, Claremont, California.

Cover design: Wesley Hoke

The following images are used by permission of the Institute for Antiquity and Christianity, Claremont, California: *Gospel of Thomas,* Nag Hammadi Codex II, page 32, and *Gospel of Thomas,* Nag Hammadi Codex II, page 39.

The following images are used by permission of Charles W. Hedrick: Clement of Alexandria, Letter to Theodore, pages 2 and 3.

Scenes 1–9, Villa of the Mysteries, frescoes in the triclinium, are used by permission of Scala/Art Resource, N.Y. Scene 10, Villa of the Mysteries, fresco in the triclinium, is used by permission of Alinari/Art Resource, N.Y.

Library of Congress Cataloging-in-Publication Data

Meyer, Marvin W.
    Secret Gospels : essays on Thomas and the secret Gospel of Mark / Marvin Meyer.
        p. cm.
    Includes bibliographical references and index.
    ISBN 1-56338-409-4 (pbk.)
    1. Apocryphal Gospels. I. Title.
    BS2851 .M49 2003
    229'.8 – dc21   2002012306

Printed in the United States of America

03   04   05   06   07   08   10   9   8   7   6   5   4   3   2   1

Contents

Acknowledgments

I am pleased to express my appreciation to some of the people and organizations that helped to bring this book to fruition. These essays have been prepared and published over the past two decades, and during that time numerous colleagues and students have offered advice and counsel, for which I am grateful. I thank Gawdat Gabra, Girgis Daoud Girgis, Samiha Abd El Shaheed, among others at the Coptic Museum, for their kindness and generosity in giving me access to the Coptic *Gospel of Thomas* over the years. I am pleased that the several publishers have given permission to reprint the essays included in this book, and I thank Charles W. Hedrick for providing new photographs of the letter of Clement of Alexandria and the Institute for Antiquity and Christianity for providing photographs of the *Gospel of Thomas*. I acknowledge the support of several grants that have aided in my research on the *Gospel of Thomas* and the *Secret Gospel of Mark,* and in particular I acknowledge the support of the Griset Chair in Bible and Christian Studies at Chapman University. I thank Henry Carrigan for the invitation to publish these essays with Trinity Press International, and the editorial staff at Trinity Press International for their industry and professionalism. I also thank Linden Youngquist for his help with issues of formatting. Finally, I salute the patience and support of my wife and children, who for many years have endured a scholar frequently preoccupied with secret gospels, and who have shown me in countless ways what wisdom truly means.

Introduction

This book, *Secret Gospels,* consists of ten essays that address themes in the *Gospel of Thomas* and the *Secret Gospel of Mark,* two gospels that may be considered secret gospels. These gospels also present two early and compelling versions of the good news of Jesus of Nazareth.

Secret Gospels

Since the discovery of the Nag Hammadi library and the publication of the texts in the library, the *Gospel of Thomas* has assumed a prominent and oftentimes controversial place in the study of the historical Jesus, Christian origins, and early Christian literature. The *Gospel of Thomas* is given its traditional title (literally, "The Gospel According to Thomas") in the manuscript of the Nag Hammadi edition of the Coptic text, at the very end of the text. What is most likely an earlier version of the title of the work is given in the incipit, or opening prologue of the text, where reference is made to hidden sayings of Jesus: "These are the hidden sayings that the living Jesus spoke and Judas Thomas the Twin recorded."[1] The *Gospel of Thomas,* then, is designated as a collection of hidden sayings of Jesus, and the hidden sayings (in Coptic, *ⁿšaje ethep;* in Greek, reconstructed for P. Oxy. 654, *hoi logoi hoi [apokryphoi]*[2]) may also be understood as secret sayings, from a secret gospel.

A similar incipit with an interest in hidden or secret sayings of Jesus is to be found in the *Book of Thomas* (or, *Book of Thomas the Contender*), another Nag Hammadi text, which resembles the *Gospel of Thomas* in several respects but offers a more vigorously ascetic perspective. In the *Book of Thomas,* the opening also indicates that the book is primarily a collection of hidden or secret sayings, and the collection is said to derive from a discussion overheard on a stroll with Jesus and Judas Thomas: "The hidden sayings that the savior spoke to Judas Thomas, which I, Mathaias, in turn recorded. I was walking, listening to them speak with each other."[3]

1

An equally vivid description of the composition of such secret gospels and secret books is presented in yet another Nag Hammadi text, the *Secret Book of James,* a work that uses *apokryphon,* the same word of Greek origin as in the reconstructed incipit of the Greek *Gospel of Thomas,* in the opening sentences of the text. As a result, the text is commonly referred to as the *Apocryphon of James* in the scholarly literature. While this description may hardly be taken as an exact account of how Christian gospels were composed, it does indicate a popular understanding of such compositional moments. In a manner somewhat reminiscent of imaginative accounts, especially Markan, of Jesus teaching in parables openly and giving allegorical interpretation in secret,[4] the *Secret Book of James* also distinguishes between what Jesus revealed openly and what he revealed secretly: "The twelve followers [were] all sitting together, recalling what the savior had said to each of them, whether in a hidden or an open manner, and organizing it in books." James the Just, the brother of Jesus and the pseudonymous author of the document, then adds, "[And] I was writing what is in [my book]."[5]

But this fanciful understanding of how Christian gospels and other Christian books were written on the basis of secret or open conversations with Jesus is not the real reason for considering a text like the *Gospel of Thomas* a secret or hidden gospel. As I propose in the essays below, the sayings of the *Gospel of Thomas* are wisdom sayings, hidden, obscure, secret wisdom sayings. What characterizes these wisdom sayings is that they are all hidden, but they are capable of interpretation and even demand interpretation if they are to be understood. The need for such interpretation is underscored in the hermeneutical principle articulated in the first saying of the gospel: "Whoever discovers the interpretation (*hermēneia*) of these sayings will not taste death." The *Gospel of Thomas* is a hidden or secret gospel with which readers may creatively interact, and through the interaction with and interpretation of the hidden sayings of Jesus, the gospel proclaims, the hidden is revealed, death is overcome, and life is transformed.

The *Secret Gospel of Mark* has been known to scholars since the time of the discovery of the letter of Clement of Alexandria to Theodore in the Mar Saba monastic library and the publication of the text by Morton Smith. Since then this secret gospel has generated both heat and light in scholarly discussions. According to the letter of Clement that contains the fragments of the *Secret Gospel of Mark,* Mark composed an original gospel book, and, after the martyrdom of Peter, a second, "more spiritual gospel" that he edited in Alexandria, Egypt, with additional material from his own notes and Peter's.[6] Clement calls this more spiritual edition of Mark's gospel a *mystikon euangelion,* which may be translated as "secret" or "spiritual" or "mystical gospel."[7] The title *Secret Gospel of Mark* was used by Morton Smith, and it has stuck as the usual way of referring to the gospel.

The more spiritual edition of Mark may be considered secret or spiritual or mystical in slightly different ways. The Greek words *mystikon, mystērion,* and related terms are used in the Greco-Roman mystery religions. The mystery religions come up more than once in the essays below, and thus they merit some attention here (and later) in the introduction. In the mystery religions, these Greek words indicate what is to be closed and subsequently opened. The mystery religions emphasize the lips and the eyes. In the mystery religions, if the lips are closed, the mystery is kept secret, and if the eyes are closed (and then opened), the mystery is eye-opening, enlightening. In Clement's letter the *mystikon euangelion* is explained with terms from the mystery religions, so that the *mystikon euangelion* may well be understood in that context as the secret or spiritual or mystical gospel that should be kept secret but that enlightens those who read it. Clement maintains that the more spiritual gospel was to be read "only by those being initiated into the great mysteries."[8] He goes on to say that there is a further edition of the Gospel of Mark, a Carpocratian gospel, but Clement has little good to say about it. He calls the doctrine of Carpocrates blasphemous, carnal, and filthy, and charges that this gospel edition is full of lies. But Clement seems to consider the *mystikon euangelion* to be an authentic version of the gospel in the Markan tradition.

These two secret gospels, the *Gospel of Thomas* and the *Secret Gospel of Mark,* offer two distinctive proclamations of the good news of Jesus. The *Gospel of Thomas* offers a gospel of wisdom. The Gospel of Mark, including the *Secret Gospel,* offers a gospel of the cross, but a gospel of the cross, I shall maintain, that is chiefly concerned with the life of discipleship.

Gospel of Wisdom

The *Gospel of Thomas* is a gospel of the wisdom of Jesus and the hidden wisdom sayings of Jesus, which readers are to encounter, interpret, and understand. According to the *Gospel of Thomas*, it is through the encounter with the wisdom of Jesus and the discovery of the meaning of the hidden sayings of Jesus that people are saved. In the *Gospel of Thomas*, Jesus does not die for the sins of people. Rather, Jesus speaks sayings of wisdom for the insight of people, and they "will not taste death." In saying 3 he offers words that recall the Delphic maxim, "Know yourself," as he recommends knowledge as the path leading to an understanding of self and God: "When you know yourselves, then you will be known, and you will understand that you are children of the living father." Or, as *Gos. Thom.* saying 13 puts it, Jesus, as the bartender, tends the bubbling spring of wisdom, but it is up to his followers to take the brew, drink for themselves, and live.

It is easy to see how the *Gospel of Thomas*, as a gospel of wisdom with a commitment to knowledge and understanding, resembles aspects of gnostic texts. Nonetheless, the *Gospel of Thomas* lacks features typically associated with gnosis — for instance, a gnostic Sophia myth, an account of wisdom's fall from the glory of the pleroma ("fullness" of the divine) and the subsequent story of the creation of the world by the demiurge, with a remarkable reinterpretation of Genesis. The *Gospel of Thomas* proclaims wisdom in a more general way. Wisdom is not personified in *Thomas* as a divine figure in a tragic drama, as she is in gnostic texts, and the more modest reflections upon Genesis in the *Gospel of Thomas* can hardly be compared with the radical gnostic versions of the creation story. Today scholars are even debating what gnosis is and whether gnosis and Gnosticism are adequate categories for description and classification. The *Gospel of Thomas* does not fit precisely into our scholarly categories, and it raises more taxonomic questions than it answers. All in all, a more qualified approach to the classification of the *Gospel of Thomas* seems necessary. When the essay "Making Mary Male: The Categories 'Male' and 'Female' in the *Gospel of Thomas*" was originally published in 1985 on the basis of presentations given before, I was already hesitant about how to classify the *Gospel of Thomas*. In the essay I place the *Gospel of Thomas* on "the periphery of Christian Gnosticism," and I describe the *Gospel of Thomas* as "a gnosticizing gospel." Over the years I have become more hesitant. Today I prefer to describe the *Gospel of Thomas* as a gospel with only an incipient gnostic perspective.[9]

Unlike the New Testament gospels (or, for that matter, the *Gospel of Peter* and the *Gospel of the Savior*), the *Gospel of Thomas* as a gospel of wisdom has no particular interest in the cross or the crucifixion of Jesus. The death of Jesus plays no role in the *Gospel of Thomas*, and the only reference to the cross is in saying 55, which uses the theme of the cross metaphorically as a feature of an ultimate commitment to the life of discipleship: "Jesus said, 'Whoever does not hate father and mother cannot be a follower of me, and whoever does not bear the cross as I do will not be worthy of me.' " This saying is paralleled in Q and the Synoptic Gospels, for example Mark 8:34, where Mark, like Thomas, connects the theme of the cross to the life of discipleship.

Also unlike the New Testament gospels, the *Gospel of Thomas* has no interest in the resurrection of Jesus as conventionally understood. As indicated in the essays below, there is no empty tomb of Jesus, there is no tomb whatsoever, in the *Gospel of Thomas*, and Jesus is not said to have risen from the dead. He is called "the living Jesus" in the prologue to the gospel, but there is nothing to link this epithet in any way to a resurrection of the body. In the *Gospel of Thomas*, Jesus is called the living one, but God is also called a living one, as are followers of Jesus. According to saying 37, Jesus said to his followers, "When you strip without being ashamed and you take your clothes and put them under your feet like little children and trample them, then [you] will see the child of the living one and you will not be afraid." And, according to saying 114, Jesus said of Mary, in an infamous utterance, "Look, I shall guide her to make her male, so that she too may become a living spirit resembling you males. For every female who makes herself male will enter heaven's kingdom." Jesus, God, and the followers of Jesus all may be considered living ones, and in the *Gospel of Thomas* Jesus the living one appears to live through his sayings. Such a vision of the living one carries us far beyond the New Testament story of the empty tomb and the resurrection of the body.

The *Gospel of Thomas* is not only a sayings gospel, with hidden wisdom sayings of Jesus, but arguably it is an early sayings gospel, and an early date for the *Gospel of Thomas* may have implications for its impact upon the study of the historical Jesus and early Christianity. I am convinced there are good reasons to propose a first-century date for some version of the *Gospel of Thomas*, and I rehearse some of the arguments below. Here I cite one piece of evidence. In 1 Cor 2, in his discussion of wisdom Christians in Corinth, Paul uses language that is familiar from wisdom, gnosticizing, and gnostic texts: *mystērion tou theou* (mystery of God), *sophia* (wisdom), *archontes tou aiōnos* (rulers of this age, or aeon), *ta batha tou theou* (the depths of God), *psychikos* (psychical person, or natural person), *pneumatikos* (spiritual person). Some of these terms become technical terms in Sethian, Valentinian, and other gnostic texts. In the middle of all this, Paul cites a text that must have been of great value to the wisdom Christians with whom he disagrees:

> What no eye has seen,
> nor ear has heard,
> nor has it arisen in the human heart,
> what God has prepared for those who love him.[10]

We now know that a version of this text is also presented as a wisdom saying of Jesus in *Gos. Thom.* 17. Hence, a saying from the *Gospel of Thomas* may have been known already in the middle of the first century among the wisdom Christians of Corinth.

The *Gospel of Thomas* may very possibly be an early sayings gospel, but not all scholars concur, and as a result it is understandable why the *Gospel of Thomas* has assumed a prominent if controversial place in scholarly discussions. As I indicate in the introduction to *The Gospel of Thomas*, scholars have offered three basic explanations to account for the relationship among the *Gospel of Thomas*, Q, and the New Testament Synoptic Gospels: (1) Some have suggested that the *Gospel of Thomas* is dependent upon the Synoptic Gospels, and thus is a secondary collection of sayings derived from the New Testament; (2) others have proposed that the *Gospel of Thomas* is essentially independent of the Synoptic Gospels and is related to traditions similar to the sayings gospel Q; and (3) still others have offered a more complex intertextual model of various moments of interaction between the *Gospel of Thomas* and other texts. As time passes and research continues, I believe it is becoming more and more difficult to marginalize the *Gospel of Thomas* as secondary and late. It seems more and more obvious that the *Gospel of Thomas* is a primary text in the early Christian tradition and contains forms of previously known sayings of Jesus that antedate the canonical gospels and newly discovered sayings of Jesus that are not in the canonical gospels. I am fundamentally in agreement with the second explanation, but I still leave open possibilities that the textual history of the multiple editions of the *Gospel of Thomas* — perhaps better termed Gospels of Thomas — may be more complicated than is usually assumed.[11]

In large part because of research on the *Gospel of Thomas,* along with the sayings gospel Q, the paradigm of the historical Jesus as a Jewish teacher of wisdom has become a leading option in the continuing quest for the historical Jesus. If Albert Schweitzer's apocalyptic Jesus dominated the past century, the image of Jesus the Jewish sage is increasingly attractive inside and outside the academy today. Schweitzer himself seems to have been moving, in his own lifetime, to the conviction that Jesus was, in a foundational way, a Jewish teacher of wisdom and advocate of love. Schweitzer concluded that Jesus was a person who, like Schweitzer himself, taught and lived reverence for life, for "the ethic of reverence for life is the ethic of love widened into universality."[12] Schweitzer believed that his ethic of reverence for all of life — human life, animal life, plant life — resembles the ethic of Jesus and of Buddha, and Schweitzer was convinced that one of the most sublime statements supporting reverence for life is to be found in the Sermon on the Mount, in the sayings of Jesus the Jewish teacher of wisdom.[13]

Gospel of the Cross

The *Secret Gospel of Mark* is a text in the complex Markan gospel tradition that encompasses several identifiable texts that may be understood as editions of the Gospel of Mark: *Secret Mark,* canonical Mark, Matthew, Luke, and Carpocratian Mark. In all these editions, the Gospel of Mark proclaims a gospel of the cross.

The gospel of the cross appeared early in Christianity, with Paul and his predecessors, and the proclamation of the cross has proved to be resilient and dominant in the history of Christianity. To this day the most recognizable symbol of Christianity may be the cross, the most significant piece of furniture in church sanctuaries the altar, and the most familiar popular confession of Christian faith that Christ died for the sins of people. Dominant as it has been, the proclamation of the cross is not without its theological detractors, and scholars and others have suggested that the doctrine of atonement by the blood of Christ reflects an outmoded and unacceptable position that God is an angry deity who must be pacified by the sacrifice of his own son.

The present book may provide the occasion to reexamine formulations of the gospel of the cross in the light of such critiques.

In 1 Cor 15, Paul quotes an early Christian creed to highlight the essence of the gospel — the gospel of the cross — as he understands it: Christ died, Christ was raised.[14] Like devotees of the mystery religions, Paul proclaims a dying savior who, in some sense, rises, and in the balance of 1 Cor 15, he employs themes familiar to devotees of the mystery religions, for example the Eleusinian mysteries of Demeter and Kore. The resurrected body, he emphasizes, is like a seed of wheat or some other grain that dies and then rises. For the initiates into the Eleusinian mysteries, this cycle of grain was dramatized in the death and new life of Kore and, by extension, the initiates into the mysteries. For the early Christians envisioned by Paul, this cycle of grain was used as a metaphor for the death and resurrection of Christ as the firstfruits of the resurrection of Christians.[15]

Some scholars have maintained that while Paul, Mark, and others proclaim a gospel of the cross and a dying and rising Christ, comparisons with the mystery religions do not convince. Some have argued that the theme of the dying and rising gods and goddesses in the mystery religions is mistaken, and that these deities in the mystery religions do not actually rise as Jesus is said to have risen. They may indeed die, like Jesus, but thereafter they stay where they belong, that is, dead.

Such a critique of dying and rising deities may well be motivated by apologetic concerns designed to maintain the uniqueness of the resurrected Christ. In fact, the deities in the mystery religions provide ample evidence for the proclamation of the continuation of life and the manifestation of new life in the mysteries. Here a few examples must suffice. Like the grain, Kore returns mythically to the land of the living from her yearly sojourn in the realm of Hades, in the Eleusinian mysteries. In the mysteries of Isis and Osiris, Osiris exists in the realm of the dead as the ruler of that realm, and the "grain Osiris" proclaims the growth or rebirth of grain and of Osiris. When Lucius is initiated into the mysteries of Isis, according to Apuleius's *Metamorphoses,* he undergoes a nocturnal death experience by passing through the realm of death, the realm of Osiris, and emerging, dressed like the rising sun, to celebrate his initiation, after the manner of a birthday, in the morning. Archeological monuments of the mysteries of Mithras show the Mithraic bull also anticipating new life, and heads of grain grow from the dying bull.

The Mithraic inscriptions from Santa Prisca, Rome, include references to one that "is piously reborn and created by sweet things." In the mysteries of the Great Mother Cybele and Attis, Attis too provides a hint of new life after his death: his body does not decay, his hair continues to grow, and his little finger (his penis?) remains in motion. During the spring the death of Attis is observed on the Day of Blood, and new life may be celebrated in the Hilaria.

Deities die and rise, and so do their followers, in the mystery religions. It is no wonder that Clement of Alexandria, of *Secret Gospel of Mark* fame, can say that Christianity may be taken as a mystery religion — the only true mystery, he hastens to add, with a Christian perspective on the evaluation of the mysteries.[16] At least in part, he may be right.

The Gospel of Mark, with its proclamation of the cross, is a part of this tradition of deities and their followers who die and rise. In the Gospel of Mark, including the *Secret Gospel of Mark,* however, the gospel of the cross is proclaimed in a distinctive manner, with little interest in sacrifice and blood atonement and more interest in the cross and the life of discipleship. When in Mark 10:45 Jesus states that even the son of man or child of humankind — that is, Jesus himself — "did not come to be served but to serve, and to give his life (*psychēn*) as a ransom (*lytron*) for many," he is speaking in the context of discipleship as a life of service and a life for others. Later church theologians would read the doctrine of the atonement by Christ the redeemer in this passage, but Mark has nothing quite like that in mind. According to Mark, if Jesus lives a life of service and gives his life for others, so should his followers. Further, while the resurrection and the tomb of Jesus are very important in the Gospel of Mark, the abrupt and open-ended conclusion of the gospel raises questions about how the reality of the resurrection is to be realized among Jesus' followers. Besides, at the conclusion of the Gospel of Mark the tomb is not really empty. It is occupied by a *neaniskos,* a youth who is dressed in a white robe and who, as a follower of Jesus, identifies with and even resembles him.

Jesus in the *Gospel of Thomas* calls upon his followers to bear the cross, and in the Gospel of Mark he does so as well, only with more insistence and in a more focused way. The Gospel of Mark is centrally committed to preaching the life of discipleship in the light of the cross. It is a historical fact that the historical Jesus was crucified by the Romans, and for Mark the crucial significance of this event is what it means for followers of Jesus and the life of dying and living with Christ. The vicissitudes of the life of discipleship are well documented in the Gospel of Mark, and Mark will not settle for easy discipleship — hence Mark's use of the messianic secret, another secret in the Gospel of Mark, in order to stifle the easy applause that may come from the apparent success of Jesus the wonder-worker. The fragments of the *Secret Gospel of Mark* help to clarify the message of Mark on discipleship by clarifying the place of the elusive *neaniskos,* or youth, in the Markan story. I believe a very good case can be made that the fragments of *Secret Mark* are authentic fragments in the Markan tradition (recall Clement of Alexandria), and early fragments, which reflect an edition of the Gospel of Mark that antedates the canonical version of Mark. I attempt to make that case in the essays below. I then turn to a reading of the *Secret Gospel of Mark* and the story of the *neaniskos* within Mark, and I suggest that there is a subplot featuring the *neaniskos* as a literary figure who exemplifies what it means to be a follower or disciple of Jesus. At the conclusion of the Gospel of Mark I suggest it is this same *neaniskos,* in white, calling the women to discipleship from the tomb of Jesus the crucified one: "[H]e is going before you to Galilee."[17] And those who follow Jesus into the Galilee of their lives discover how to take up the cross and live the life of discipleship.

Such a reading may produce a fresh perspective on the proclamation of the cross and the life of discipleship in the Gospel of Mark. It may shed significant light on Lazarus and the Beloved Disciple in the Gospel of John. It may also make the call to discipleship all the more urgent in our own day.

Essays on Secret Gospels

The ten essays on the *Gospel of Thomas* and the *Secret Gospel of Mark* presented here represent a variety of approaches to these gospels — papyrological, textual, historical, redactional, literary, artistic, homiletical. Nine of these essays have appeared elsewhere; one is published here for the first time. A few photographs of the texts and artwork from Pompeii are reproduced, including new photographs of the letter of Clement of Alexandria with the fragments of the *Secret Gospel of Mark.*[18]

The first six essays deal with the *Gospel of Thomas.* The opening essay, "Albert Schweitzer and the Image of Jesus in the *Gospel of Thomas,*" is based on a paper presented at an international conference on "Images of Jesus" at Chapman University and published in *Jesus Then and Now: Images of Jesus in History and Christology*, edited by Marvin Meyer and Charles Hughes.[19] In this essay I evaluate the figure of Jesus as depicted in the *Gospel of Thomas* and relate this image of Jesus to the work of Albert Schweitzer. The second essay, "The Beginning of the *Gospel of Thomas*," was published in *Semeia 52: How Gospels Begin*, edited by Dennis E. Smith.[20] Here I examine the incipit and opening sayings of the *Gospel of Thomas* in order to ascertain how the opening of the gospel anticipates its overall character. The third essay, "Seeing or Coming to the Child of the Living One? More on *Gospel of Thomas* Saying 37," appeared in *Harvard Theological Review*.[21] This brief study addresses the issue of ink traces on the papyrus of Nag Hammadi Codex II, at *Gos. Thom.* 37, and illustrates once again that the devil is in the details. Tiny ink traces may have large implications. The fourth essay, " 'Be Passersby': *Gospel of Thomas* Saying 42, Jesus Traditions, and Islamic Literature," is to be published in a volume of essays on the *Gospel of Thomas*, edited by Jon Ma. Asgeirsson and Risto Uro.[22] In this work I interpret the shortest and possibly the most enigmatic saying in the *Gospel of Thomas*, and I trace the motifs of the saying through additional literature, especially Islamic literature. The fifth essay, "Making Mary Male: The Categories 'Male' and 'Female' in the *Gospel of Thomas*," was published in *New Testament Studies*.[23] In this essay I survey how the *Gospel of Thomas* uses sexual themes and gender categories in general, and I analyze the use of gender symbolism in the last saying of the *Gospel of Thomas* in particular. The sixth essay, "*Gospel of Thomas* Saying 114 Revisited," was published in *For the Children, Perfect Instruction: Studies in Honor of Hans-Martin Schenke on the Occasion of the Berliner Arbeitskreis für koptisch-gnostische Studien's Thirtieth Year*, edited by Hans-Gebhard Bethge, Stephen Emmel, Karen L. King, and Imke Schletterer.[24] This essay continues the discussion of the previous essay and brings greater clarity and methodological precision to the study of saying 114 and the *Gospel of Thomas* as a whole.

The next four essays deal with the *Secret Gospel of Mark*. The seventh essay, "The Youth in the *Secret Gospel of Mark*," appeared in *Semeia 49: The Apocryphal Jesus and Christian Beginnings*, edited by Ron Cameron.[25] In this essay I introduce the *Secret Gospel of Mark*, summarize some of the scholarly research on the text, and present my own thesis of the subplot with the *neaniskos* as paradigmatic follower or disciple of Jesus. I apply observations from this essay to the Gospel of John and the Johannine Beloved Disciple in the eighth essay, "The Youth in *Secret Mark* and the Beloved Disciple in John." This study was originally published in *Gospel Origins and Christian Beginnings: In Honor of James M. Robinson,* edited by Jack T. Sanders, Charles W. Hedrick, and James E. Goehring.[26] The ninth essay is published in this book for the first time, although I have given academic papers on the topic. Entitled "The Naked Youths in the Villa of the Mysteries, Canonical Mark, and *Secret Mark,*" this essay compares and contrasts naked youths in Homeric and Markan texts and Pompeian artwork, and finds that the similarity among them stems from the fact that all the youths are described as initiates and followers of divine mysteries, Homeric, Markan, and Dionysian. The tenth essay, "Taking Up the Cross and Following Jesus: Discipleship in the Gospel of Mark and *Secret Mark,*" was initially presented as a scholarly meditation at a convocation in honor of three professors of New Testament studies, now all retired, at Calvin Theological Seminary: Andrew Bandstra, David Holwerda, and Bastiaan Van Elderen. Subsequently the paper was published in a special issue of *Calvin Theological Journal.*[27]

The previously published essays have been lightly edited for this book to bring a degree of uniformity of style to the collected essays, and they have been updated.

Notes

1. The translations included here are my own. For the *Gospel of Thomas,* see Marvin Meyer, *The Gospel of Thomas: The Hidden Sayings of Jesus* (San Francisco: HarperSanFrancisco, 1992).
2. The manuscript of P. Oxy. 654 actually has an instance of dittography here: *hoi [hoi] logoi hoi [apokryphoi].*
3. NHC II 138, 1–4.
4. Mark 4:1–20, on parables for those on the outside and "the mystery (or, secret, Greek *mystērion*) of God's kingdom" for those on the inside.
5. NHC I 2, 7–16. This quotation is discussed below in chapter one.
6. Clement of Alexandria, Letter to Theodore 1,21–22.
7. Clement of Alexandria, Letter to Theodore 2,6; 2,12.
8. Clement of Alexandria, Letter to Theodore 2,2.
9. On gnosis, Gnosticism, and the *Gospel of Thomas,* see Michael A. Williams, *Rethinking "Gnosticism": An Argument for Dismantling a Dubious Category*

(Princeton: Princeton University Press, 1996) and Willis Barnstone and Marvin Meyer, *The Gnostic Bible* (Boston: Shambhala Publications [forthcoming]).

10. 1 Cor 2:9. For additional occurrences of this saying in Jewish and Christian literature, as well as a variant in Plutarch, see Meyer, *The Gospel of Thomas*, 76.

11. See Meyer, *The Gospel of Thomas*, 10–17, and the essays below. On the *Gospel of Thomas*, the canonical gospels, and Q, see most recently John Dominic Crossan, *The Birth of Christianity: Discovering What Happened in the Years Immediately After the Execution of Jesus* (San Francisco: HarperSanFrancisco, 1998) and Stephen J. Patterson, *The Gospel of Thomas and Jesus* (Foundations and Facets; Sonoma, Calif.: Polebridge, 1993).

12. Albert Schweitzer, *Out of My Life and Thought: An Autobiography* (trans. Antje Bultmann Lemke; Baltimore: Johns Hopkins University Press, 1998), 235.

13. For further discussion of Schweitzer and Jesus, see Marvin Meyer, "Affirming Reverence for Life," in *Reverence for Life: The Ethics of Albert Schweitzer for the Twenty-First Century* (ed. Marvin Meyer and Kurt Bergel; Albert Schweitzer Library; Syracuse: Syracuse University Press, 2002), 22–36, along with other essays in the volume.

14. 1 Cor 15:3–8: "Christ died for our sins according to the Scriptures, he was buried, he was raised on the third day according to the Scriptures, he appeared to Cephas,...to the twelve,...to five hundred,...to James,...to all the apostles,...to me...."

15. On the discussion of and examples from the mystery religions, see Marvin Meyer, *The Ancient Mysteries: A Sourcebook of Sacred Texts* (Philadelphia: University of Pennsylvania Press, 1999, revised 2002), especially pp. 252–54, "Epilogue: Dying and Rising in Christianity and the Other Mysteries."

16. Clement of Alexandria, *Protreptikos pros Hellenas (Exhortation to the Greeks)* 12.118–23, with a citation of 1 Cor 2:9.

17. Mark 16:7. In the following, final verse of the gospel, the immediate response to this call to discipleship is the flight of the female followers of Jesus, who up until this point had shown more courage and loyalty than the male followers. Only the implied hearer or reader, I propose, can resolve this tension at the end of the gospel.

18. See also Charles W. Hedrick, with Nikolaos Olympiou, "Secret Mark: New Photographs, New Witnesses," *The Fourth R* 13 (2000): 3–11 and 14–16.

19. Marvin Meyer, "Albert Schweitzer and the Image of Jesus in the Gospel of Thomas," in *Jesus Then and Now: Images of Jesus in History and Christology* (ed. Marvin Meyer and Charles Hughes; Harrisburg, Pa.: Trinity Press International, 2001), 72–90.

20. Marvin Meyer, "The Beginning of the Gospel of Thomas," in *Semeia 52: How Gospels Begin* (ed. Dennis E. Smith; Atlanta: Scholars, 1990), 161–73. Reprinted with the permission of the Society of Biblical Literature.

21. Marvin Meyer, "Seeing or Coming to the Child of the Living One? More on *Gospel of Thomas* Saying 37," *HTR* 91 (1998): 413–16. Reprinted with the permission of Cambridge University Press.

22. Marvin Meyer, " 'Be Passersby': *Gospel of Thomas* Saying 42, Jesus Traditions, and Islamic Literature," in essays on the *Gospel of Thomas* (ed. Jon Ma. Asgeirsson and Risto Uro; Leiden: E. J. Brill, forthcoming). Reprinted by permission.

23. Marvin Meyer, "Making Mary Male: The Categories 'Male' and 'Female' in the *Gospel of Thomas*," *NTS* 31 (1985): 544–70. Reprinted with the permission of Cambridge University Press.

24. Marvin Meyer, "*Gospel of Thomas* Logion 114 Revisited," in *For the Children, Perfect Instruction: Studies in Honor of Hans-Martin Schenke on the Occasion of the Berliner Arbeitskreis für koptisch-gnostische Studien's Thirtieth Year* (ed. Hans-Gebhard Bethge, Stephen Emmel, Karen L. King, and Imke Schletterer; Nag Hammadi and Manichaean Studies 54; Leiden: E. J. Brill, 2002), 101–11. Reprinted with the permission of Brill Academic Publishers, Leiden, The Netherlands.

25. Marvin Meyer, "The Youth in the *Secret Gospel of Mark*," in *Semeia 49: The Apocryphal Jesus and Christian Beginnings* (ed. Ron Cameron; Atlanta: Scholars, 1990), 129–53. Reprinted with the permission of the Society of Biblical Literature.

26. Marvin Meyer, "The Youth in Secret Mark and the Beloved Disciple in John," in *Gospel Origins and Christian Beginnings: In Honor of James M. Robinson* (ed. Jack T. Sanders, Charles W. Hedrick, and James E. Goehring; Sonoma, Calif.: Polebridge, 1990), 94–105. Used by permission.

27. Marvin Meyer, "Taking Up the Cross and Following Jesus: Discipleship in the Gospel of Mark," *CTJ* 37 (2002): 230–38. Reprinted by permission.

Part One

GOSPEL
OF THOMAS

These are the hidden sayings that the living Jesus spoke and Judas Thomas the Twin recorded.

¹And he said, "Whoever discovers the interpretation of these sayings will not taste death."

²Jesus said, "Let one who seeks not stop seeking until one finds. When one finds, one will be troubled. When one is troubled, one will marvel and will rule over all."

³Jesus said, "If your leaders say to you, 'Look, the kingdom is in heaven,' then the birds of heaven will precede you. If they say to you, 'It is in the sea,' then the fish will precede you. Rather, the kingdom is inside you and it is outside you.

"When you know yourselves, then you will be known, and you will understand that you are children of the living father. But if you do not know yourselves, then you dwell in poverty, and you are poverty."

³⁷His followers said, "When will you appear to us and when shall we see you?"

Jesus said, "When you strip without being ashamed and you take your clothes and put them under your feet like little children and trample them, then [you] will see the child of the living one and you will not be afraid."

⁴²Jesus said, "Be passersby."

¹¹⁴Simon Peter said to them, "Mary should leave us, for females are not worthy of life."

Jesus said, "Look, I shall guide her to make her male, so that she too may become a living spirit resembling you males. For every female who makes herself male will enter heaven's kingdom."

I

Albert Schweitzer and the Image of Jesus in the *Gospel of Thomas*

I know of no evidence that Albert Schweitzer, the theologian, philosopher, musician, and medical doctor, knew about or commented on the *Gospel of Thomas,* though he might have done so late in his life.[1] It is my conceit to suspect that if he had commented on it, he would have agreed that the *Gospel of Thomas* is a valuable text for our knowledge of the Jesus tradition. After all, Schweitzer based his research on the historical Jesus upon the Gospel of Matthew as well as the Gospel of Mark, and that may have been his way of incorporating Matthean sayings material, from what we now prefer to designate the sayings gospel Q, into his portrait of Jesus.[2] Schweitzer's profound interest in the Sermon on the Mount shows how he valued sayings of Jesus, and this interest led him to declare that the teachings of Jesus on love may be equated with Schweitzer's own ethic of reverence for life, now widened, as he stated, into a universal concern for the will to live of humans, animals, and plants.[3] In 1905, in a sermon he preached on November 19 in St. Nicolai's church, Schweitzer anticipated the *Gospel of Thomas,* particularly in its opening, with its presentation of the living Jesus who lives through his sayings. Schweitzer's words from that sermon call out powerfully over the years and remind us of "the hidden sayings that the living Jesus spoke," according to Thomas: "What kind of a living person is Jesus? Don't search for formulas to describe him, even if they be hallowed by centuries. I almost got angry the other day when a religious person said to me that only someone who believes in the resurrection of the body and in the glorified body of the risen Christ can believe in the living Jesus.... Let me explain it in my way. The glorified body of Jesus is to be found in his sayings."[4]

So I affirm my conviction concerning the significance of the image of Jesus in the *Gospel of Thomas* for our knowledge of Jesus traditions and our investigation of the historical Jesus. As I do so, I wish to advance three suggestions that will guide this discussion of the *Gospel of Thomas*.

Three Initial Suggestions

1. I suggest that a very reasonable though probably not compelling case can be made for a first-century date for a version of the *Gospel of Thomas*.[5] The manuscript evidence for the *Gospel of Thomas* includes the Coptic text of the *Gospel of Thomas* (almost certainly from a Greek original) in the fourth-century Nag Hammadi library, and three Greek Oxyrhynchus papyrus fragments (1, 654, 655) now housed at Oxford, the British Library, and Harvard. These Greek fragments have been dated, most recently by Harold W. Attridge, to just after 200, around 250, and between 200 and 250, respectively, dates that correspond fairly well to the dates assigned by Grenfell and Hunt.[6] Recall that they calculated that the original document, which was composed not in Egypt but in Syria, must be dated at least half a century earlier, and so they placed the *terminus ad quem,* or latest date of composition, at 140.[7] *Gospel of Thomas* materials are also cited in the church fathers, especially in the account of the Naassene gnostics in Hippolytus of Rome (early third century.)[8] The manuscript tradition for the *Gospel of Thomas* thus rivals that of any other gospel, including the canonical gospels. Furthermore, the *Gospel of Thomas* illustrates features that we commonly identify with first-century issues — quarrels over apostleship, uncertainty about James the Just, the brother of Jesus, use of sayings collections, and so on. Some aspects of *Thomas* and the forms of sayings in *Thomas* seem clearly to antedate the canonical gospels — for example, the use of parables without allegorical amplification, as we shall note below. Gos. Thom. saying 17 presents a saying of Jesus — "I shall give you what no eye has seen, what no ear has heard, what no hand has touched, what has not arisen in the human heart" — which sounds strikingly like Paul's characterization of the wisdom Christians with whom he disagrees in Corinth in the mid-first century.[9]

2. I suggest that we do well to think of multiple editions of the *Gospel of Thomas,* even Gospels of Thomas, rather than a single *Gospel of Thomas.* In the pre-Gutenberg world of antiquity, texts typically went

through substantial changes and modifications as they were copied and recopied. In a way, each copy of a text was a new edition. Helmut Koester has shown how different editions of the Gospel of Mark (including *Secret Mark,* canonical Mark, Matthew, Luke, and Carpocratian Mark) may represent a continuously developing Markan tradition.[10] Such may also be said of editions of the *Gospel of Thomas.* The Coptic text, Greek fragments, and testimonies of the church fathers all differ from one another and may represent different versions of the *Gospel of Thomas.* The fluidity of the textual tradition of the *Gospel of Thomas* may be more pronounced on account of its genre as a sayings gospel. As a collection of sayings, the *Gospel of Thomas* was open to easy modification. The *Gospel of Thomas* exhibits a loose-leaf character so that sayings could be added, deleted, or rearranged with little difficulty, particularly since no overall organizational scheme seems operative in the *Gospel of Thomas,*[11] but only specific points of linkage supplied by *Stichwörter* (catchwords) and small subcollections of parables and other sayings.[12] The limited evidence of the Coptic manuscript and the Oxyrhynchus papyrus fragments supports these possibilities of modification.

3. If there were different editions of the Gospel, or Gospels, of Thomas, then I suggest we shall need to address the likelihood of multiple editors with different perspectives, points of view, literary styles, and theologies in the versions of the *Gospel of Thomas.* It has sometimes been popular to delineate the theology of the *Gospel of Thomas.*[13] We may be forced to abandon such naiveté, and instead acknowledge multiple theological perspectives in a gospel text that was subjected to editorial modification as it was copied and translated. I do not hesitate, therefore, to identify very early Jesus traditions and much later gnosticizing elements in the same Coptic text.

With these three suggestions in mind, let us begin to explore the image, or, perhaps, the images, of Jesus in the *Gospel of Thomas.*

Jesus the Jewish Sage

We begin our quest for the Jesus of Thomas by observing what is most prominent regarding *Thomas*'s Jesus. In the *Gospel of Thomas* Jesus is a Jewish sage, a wise fellow who utters sayings that are described as hidden or secret sayings. The *Gospel of Thomas* is thus a sayings gospel, with little narrative but numerous sayings presented as life-giving sayings of the sagacious Jesus. In the words of the unnamed speaker of saying 1, most likely Jesus, but possibly his twin Judas Thomas, "Whoever discovers the interpretation of these sayings will not taste death." As a sayings source, the *Gospel of Thomas* has much in common, in terms of form and content, with the synoptic sayings source Q, and it also recalls another possible text that is sometimes connected with Q, Papias's logia of the master compiled in Aramaic, according to Papias, by Matthew.[14] In this regard we should also mention the parable and sayings collection in Mark, the sayings of Jesus in the *Didache,* and other extracanonical sayings of Jesus, sometimes called *agrapha.*[15] Within the early decades of the Jesus movement there was an expressed interest in *mnēmoneuein ton logon tou kyriou Iēsou,* as the Acts of the Apostles and *1 Clement* put it, "remembering the sayings of the lord Jesus."[16] Or, as James in the *Secret Book of James* imagines the scene, "The twelve followers [were] all sitting together, recalling what the savior had said to each of them, whether in a hidden or an open manner, and organizing it in books. [And] I was writing what is in [my book]" — a Hebrew book in fact, the text maintains.[17]

Early in the Jesus movement there is this special interest in sayings of Jesus and sayings gospels, but this interest is also to be found much later, in a world of religious thought too often neglected by scholars of early Christianity, the world of Islam.[18] In Muslim sources Jesus (*'Isa* in Arabic) is portrayed as a prophet of God, the messiah and servant and spirit and word of God, the son of Mary, who spoke words of wisdom, performed mighty deeds, and died — if in fact he truly died; perhaps he only seemed to die — at the end of a remarkable human life. In the Qur'an there are relatively few sayings of Jesus, but in other Islamic sources Jesus is featured as preeminently a teacher of wisdom. One Muslim author who collected and edited sayings of Jesus is Abu Hamid Muhammad al-Ghazali. Al-Ghazali was an eleventh- and twelfth-century Muslim professor, theologian, and mystic who wrote voluminously, and the greatest of his books is *Ihya' 'ulum al-din, The Revival of the Religious Sciences.* In this book al-Ghazali presents Jesus as a sage whose sayings often recall sayings of Jesus in Q, the New Testament gospels, and the *Gospel of Thomas.* Thus, in al-Ghazali Jesus says, "Whoever knows and does and teaches will be called great in heaven's kingdom." In a manner that recalls Jewish and Christian wisdom and a passage in Mark, and its parallels, this Jesus says, "Do not offer wisdom to those who are not worthy of it, or you might harm it, and do not withhold it from those who are worthy of it, or you might harm them. Be like a gentle doctor who puts medicine on the diseased spot." As in Q and the *Gospel of Thomas*, Jesus in al-Ghazali contrasts his lot in life with that of a wild beast so as to indicate that he himself, unlike the beast, has no resting place. Jesus offers his greeting of *as-salaam 'alaykum* to a pig so that his tongue will not grow accustomed to speaking evil, and when his followers express disgust about the stinking carcass of a dog, Jesus replies, "How white are its teeth!"[19]

A Gospel of Wisdom

The *Gospel of Thomas*, like these other sources, offers an image of Jesus as a Jewish sage. I hesitate to call him a teacher of wisdom here, since Jesus explicitly denies being a teacher in saying 13, but more on that saying below. The portrait of Jesus the sage in *Thomas* is a remarkable portrait, with stunning differences from the portraits of Jesus in other gospels, especially New Testament gospels. I reiterate what I have written elsewhere: Jesus in the *Gospel of Thomas* performs no physical miracles, reveals no fulfillment of prophecy, announces no apocalyptic kingdom about to disrupt the world order, and dies for no one's sins.[20]

Jesus in the *Gospel of Thomas* is not named the Christ or the Messiah, he is not acclaimed master or lord, and when he refers to himself as the son of man, or the child of humankind, once in the gospel, he does so in the generic sense of referring to any person or simply to himself. This is in saying 86, a saying paralleled, as we have noted, in al-Ghazali: "[Foxes have] their dens and birds have their nests, but the child of humankind has no place to lay his head and rest." And if in the *Gospel of Thomas* Jesus is a child of humankind, so are other people called the children of humankind.[21] Jesus in the *Gospel of Thomas* is not presented as the incarnate and unique son of God, and nothing is said of a remarkable birth. The only saying that might conceivably refer to his birth at all is something of a scandal. *Thomas* 105 reads, "Jesus said, 'Whoever knows the father and the mother will be called the child of a whore,' " and it is possible (though not certain) that this might be an oblique reference to the tradition, known from Celsus in Origen and other sources, that Jesus' mother was seduced or raped by a Roman soldier named Pantera.[22] Recent speculation in this regard has focused upon the gravestone of

a Sidonian archer named Tiberias Julius Abdes Pantera, who was sta-
tioned in Palestine around the time of the birth of Jesus.[23] In the *Gospel
of Thomas* Jesus has nothing remarkable recorded about his childhood.
Of course, except for a single legend in the Gospel of Luke about young
Jesus in the temple, no early gospel discusses the young life of Jesus.[24]
This point should be mentioned here, however, because later the *Infancy
Gospel of Thomas* seems to pick up themes from the *Gospel of Thomas* —
for example, the old person asking a little child about life in saying 4 —
and creates stories about young Jesus. The *Infancy Gospel of Thomas*
has Zacchaeus the teacher say about his young pupil Jesus, "Friends, I
think on my shame that I, an old man, have been overcome by a child."[25]

In the *Gospel of Thomas* a cross is mentioned only one time, in saying 55, and in what seems to be a metaphorical manner, having to do with
bearing a burden and maintaining a commitment against all odds. The
saying echoes what we know from Q and the Synoptic Gospels: "Jesus
said, 'Whoever does not hate father and mother cannot be a follower of
me, and whoever does not hate brothers and sisters and bear the cross as I
do will not be worthy of me.'"[26] In any case, there is no thought of a cross
with saving significance here. In the *Gospel of Thomas* there is no empty
tomb — there is no tomb at all — and Jesus is nowhere portrayed as having
risen from the dead. In P. Oxy. 654 there is a clause about what is buried
being raised that is not a part of the Coptic text of *Gos. Thom.* saying 5.
It might refer to what is hidden away being uncovered, but it should be
noted that this statement about being raised is also preserved on a Christian burial shroud from Oxyrhynchus.[27] In *Thomas* Jesus is called "the
living Jesus," *Iēsous etonh*, but if Jesus is a living one, so is God, and so are
the followers of Jesus.[28] It is most likely meant that the living Jesus of the
Gospel of Thomas lives through his sayings — even as Albert Schweitzer
proclaimed in Alsace many centuries after the *Gospel of Thomas*.

What sort of a portrait of Jesus the Jewish sage do we find, then, in the
Gospel of Thomas? Here I wish to highlight, in more positive terms, five
distinctive features of Jesus that will help to clarify the image of Jesus in
the *Gospel of Thomas*.

Seeking and Finding

First, in *Thomas* Jesus encourages people to seek and find, to search and
discover: *šine auō tetnačine,* "Seek and you will find." This encourage-

ment is given in different forms throughout the *Gospel of Thomas*,[29] but it is presented in a programmatic way in saying 2: "Jesus said, 'Let one who seeks not stop seeking until one finds. When one finds, one will be troubled. When one is troubled, one will marvel and will rule over all.' " Versions of this familiar saying are also known from the *Gospel of the Hebrews* and the *Book of Thomas;* P. Oxy. 654 adds an additional stage in the program of seeking and finding: "[A]nd having ruled, one will rest."[30] The stages enumerated for seeking and finding illumine what it means to discover and learn, and this description of the learning process rings true to the present day. Seeking, searching, learning, the *Gospel of Thomas* suggests, is to be undertaken with commitment, and while the way to discovery may be upsetting, it is also marvelous, and people will attain the end of their journey — here identified as the reign and rest of God — if only they persevere. Jesus' words to his followers on seeking and finding are partially paralleled in Q, the Synoptic Gospels, and the Gospel of John, as an essay in the volume *From Quest to Q* discusses,[31] but this saying has a particular focus, prominence, and even urgency in the *Gospel of Thomas*. In *Thomas* the exhortation to seek and find sets the tone for the entire gospel, which is a gospel of wisdom that may be comprehended by those who seek and find.

What is to be sought and found? This question is not easily answered, and Jesus in *Thomas* may seem at times to assume only a general posture of recommending seeking and finding. The end of the search in the particular saying under scrutiny is the reign and rest of God, the kingdom of God. The following saying, saying 3, goes on to discuss the reign or kingdom of God with a couple of Jesus jokes, in reference to the Delphic maxim *gnōthi sauton,* "Know yourself," and a declaration that the kingdom is within and without but is not to be localized in heaven or in the underworld: "Jesus said, 'If your leaders say to you "Look, the kingdom is in heaven," then the birds of heaven will precede you. If they say to you, "It is in the sea" [the Greek has "under the earth"], then the fish will precede you. Rather, the kingdom is inside you and it is outside you. When you know yourselves, then you will be known, and you will understand that you are children of the living father. But if you do not know yourselves, then you dwell in poverty, and you are poverty.' " Yet, while such may be the goal of the quest, what is specifically to be sought and discovered is clarified in saying 1: "Whoever discovers the interpretation (*hermēneia*) of these sayings will not taste death." The Jesus of

Thomas asks his followers, his students, to seek the interpretation of his sayings, to complete his thoughts, and in this search for meaning life is to be found.

In his recent study on the *Gospel of Thomas*, Richard Valantasis appears to me to be moving in the right direction when he recognizes the need for hearers or readers of Jesus' hidden sayings to encounter the sayings creatively and to add their our interpretive meaning to the sayings.[32] Valantasis calls the theology of the *Gospel of Thomas* "a performative theology," and he asserts that "the theology emerges from the readers' and the hearers' responses to the sayings and their sequence and their variety."[33] I agree with Valantasis' analysis. Only when readers and interpreters encounter the sayings of the *Gospel of Thomas* with insight is the meaning of the sayings uncovered.

Seek and you will find, says Jesus in *Thomas* and in other gospels. I suggest that the oftentimes elusive sage Jesus of *Thomas* is not remarkably different from the oftentimes elusive sage Jesus of Q and the New Testament gospels — though, as we shall observe, some sayings of Jesus in *Thomas* are certainly more cryptic and riddle-like. I also suggest that the Jesus of *Thomas*, like the Jesus of Q and some portions of the New Testament gospels, invites his followers and his listeners to engage his sayings, to find their meaning, and to think his thoughts after him. To this extent, like the Buddha in Theravada Buddhism, Jesus points the way, but it is up to us to labor at the interpretive task.

Telling Stories about the Kingdom

Second, in *Thomas* Jesus tells stories or parables that have an ambiguous quality but that are narrated to help explain, among other things, the kingdom.[34] As in Q and the Synoptic Gospels, Jesus in *Thomas* is wonderfully vague in his references to the kingdom or reign of God and refers to the kingdom in aphorisms and metaphors. According to the *Gospel of Thomas*, Jesus says that the kingdom is within and without; people who are like nursing babies will attain the kingdom, when they are transformed, and children will know the kingdom, but business people and merchants will not get in; women can get in — that's the good news — if they become male — that's the bad news; the kingdom is not an apocalyptic phenomenon, but rather it is spread out upon the earth and people do not see it; and, Jesus says, in a saying also given elsewhere and now known, in a slightly different form, in the so-called *Gospel of the Savior,* "Whoever is near me is near the fire, and whoever is far from me is far from the kingdom."[35] Jesus is vague in these statements, but he describes the kingdom more vividly when he employs the techniques of a storyteller. There are also some stories or parables in *Thomas* that are not told with the kingdom specifically in mind; for example, saying 8, the story of the smart fisherman who keeps the big one but throws the small fry back, is said to be about humankind, in Coptic *prome.*

Thus Jesus tells his illustrative stories in *Thomas.* Some are familiar, some are not. Heaven's kingdom "is like a mustard seed. [It] is the smallest of all seeds, but when it falls on prepared soil, it produces a large plant and becomes a shelter for birds of heaven" (saying 20). "The father's kingdom is like a person who had [good] seed. His enemy came at night and sowed weeds among the good seed. The person did not let them pull up the weeds, but said to them, 'No, or you might go to pull up the weeds and pull up the wheat along with them.' For on the day of the harvest the weeds will be conspicuous and will be pulled up and burned" (saying 57). "The father's kingdom is like a merchant who had a supply of merchandise and then found a pearl. That merchant was prudent; he sold the merchandise and bought the single pearl for himself" (saying 76). "The kingdom is like a shepherd who had a hundred sheep. One of them, the largest, went astray. He left the ninety-nine and sought the one until he found it. After he had gone to this trouble, he said to the sheep, 'I love you more than the ninety-nine'" (saying 107). "The kingdom is like a person who had a treasure hidden in his field but did not know it. And [when] he died, he left it to his [son]. The son [did] not know [about it]. He took over the field and sold it. The buyer went plowing, [discovered] the treasure, and began to lend money at interest to whomever he wished" (saying 109). "The father's kingdom is like [a] woman. She took a little yeast, [hid] it in dough, and made it into large loaves of bread" (saying 96). "The [father's] kingdom is like a woman who was carrying a [jar] full of meal. While she was walking along [a] distant road, the handle of the jar broke, and the meal spilled behind her [along] the road. She did not know it; she had not noticed a problem. When she reached her house, she put the jar down and discovered that it was empty" (saying 97). "The father's kingdom is like a person who wanted to put someone powerful to death. While at home he drew his sword and thrust it into the wall to find out whether his hand would go in. Then he killed the powerful one" (saying 98). And that is what the kingdom is like.

A few observations should be made about these kingdom stories of Jesus in the *Gospel of Thomas*. They are stories that compare the kingdom to features of everyday life in Palestine, stories about the kingdom ... and seeds and weeds, and farming and herding and buying and selling, and discovering hidden treasure out in a field, and carrying meal and baking bread and assassinating the strong man. Often they are stories with a surprising twist, or even godly foolishness, as with the merchant who cashes in his or her entire inventory for a single pricey stone, or the shepherd who abandons his or her entire flock for a single recalcitrant sheep. In *Thomas*, as elsewhere, Jesus intimates that God's reign is to be recognized in the events, at time the surprising events, of everyday life happening all around us. Unlike some parables of Jesus in the Synoptic Gospels, *Thomas*'s stories do not have allegorical interpretations added to them, and it is not clear that these stories themselves have the sorts of allegorical elements within the stories that we may identify in the synoptic versions. Consider *Gos. Thom.* sayings 64 and 65, for instance, the stories of the feast to which people are eventually invited off the street and the vineyard that becomes a site of murder and mayhem.[36] Further, unlike some parables of Jesus in the Synoptic Gospels, *Thomas*'s parables do not have overtly apocalyptic elements, and as Stephen Patterson rightly reminds us, "one must be careful not to read into *Thomas* a note of apocalypticism based upon sayings whose synoptic parallels are given an apocalyptic interpretation in the synoptic tradition."[37] Such is the case in the story of the planted weeds, as we have just read it. In that story the place of God's kingdom around us is uncertain and unclear, but the growth of wheat and weeds will elucidate what is good and what belongs to God, and that will triumph.

Living an Alternative Lifestyle

Third, in *Thomas* Jesus advocates a radical lifestyle, an alternative lifestyle that actively questions the polite amenities, political loyalties, and religious observance of ordinary folks. In saying 42 Jesus says, "Be passersby," *šōpe etet*^{e}*n*^{e}*rparage*, apparently advocating a homeless life of wandering.[38] The closest parallel I know to this saying is a saying of Jesus in an inscription from a mosque at Fatehpur Sikri, India: "This world is a bridge. Pass over it, but do not build your dwelling there." The same basic saying is cited by the medieval author Petrus Alphonsi.[39] In saying 86, quoted above, Jesus observes that he, unlike some animals, has no den or nest or place to rest and call home. In saying 14 Jesus similarly assumes an itinerant, wandering life for his followers, and he advises that they eat whatever is served and return whatever act of gratitude they can provide to those who are kind enough to take them in for the night: "When you go into any region and walk through the countryside, when people receive you, eat what they serve you and heal the sick among them. For what goes into your mouth will not defile you; rather, it is what comes out of your mouth that will defile you."[40] The aphoristic saying on what goes in and what goes out is *Thomas*'s version of a well-known saying. However, the gospel writers could not seem to figure out precisely what bodily exit Jesus had in mind as the one that can make you dirty, and Mark has Jesus simply say that what comes out of a person will defile him. My guess is that Jesus, with a twinkle in his eye, might have kept it ambiguous, leaving it to the people around to contemplate their orifices.

In *Thomas* Jesus tells his followers to reject mundane family ties and family values and identify with a new order of family. This new family of Jesus consists of the women and men together who are followers of Jesus, with no special twelve singled out for apostolic attention — "Those here who do the will of my father are my brothers and my mother. They are the ones who will enter my father's kingdom" (saying 99). These people are the poor, and they are declared fortunate for being poor. They are the beggars who, when they get some money, give it away. Jesus himself may demand his due too, as a panhandler, if Patterson is correct in his understanding of *Thomas* saying 100, where Jesus says, "Give Caesar the things that are Caesar's, give God the things that are God's, and give me what is mine."[41] These people of Jesus do not worry about food or fashion, for what is truly necessary will be provided. As Jesus puts it in saying 36, in words that remind us of Q, "Do not worry, from morning to evening and from evening to morning, about what you will wear." Or, in the Greek version, "[Do not worry] from morning [to evening nor] from evening [to] morning, either [about] your [food], what [you will] eat, [or] about [your clothing], what you [will] wear. [You are much] better than the lilies, which do not card or [spin]. As for you, when you have no garment, what [will you put] on? Who might add to your stature?

That is the one who will give you your garment."[42] These people, the poor ones of Jesus, are declared fortunate for their concern to feed the hungry: "Fortunate are they who are hungry, that the stomach of the person in want may be filled" (saying 69). They are not impressed with the rich and the powerful, and they are not impressed by religious observance. In *Thomas* Jesus has nothing good to say about fasting, praying, tithing, and observing food laws or getting circumcised — if circumcision were really important, would not baby boys be born circumcised, Jesus asks — except that Jesus suggests a more symbolic or spiritual observance: fasting from the world, keeping the sabbath as a sabbath, being circumcised in spirit.[43] Most important, Jesus maintains, is integrity, honesty, authenticity: "Do not lie, and do not do what you hate, because all things are disclosed before heaven" (saying 6). "Do not do what you hate" is the negative formulation of the golden rule, the ethical principle of reciprocity, which Schweitzer used as the basis of his ethic of reverence for life. This saying in *Thomas* may be compared to the command to love one's neighbor, given in a distinctive form in *Thomas* 25: "Love your brother [*pekson;* or, your brother and sister, your sibling] like your soul [*tekpsukhē;* or, your life, yourself], protect that person like the pupil of your eye." Show reverence and respect and love for another life, said Schweitzer, just as you show reverence and respect and love for your own life.[44]

These sayings promoting an alternative lifestyle cannot easily be spiritualized away under the assumption that the author or authors and the readers of the *Gospel of Thomas* were people who cared not for lifestyle but only for mental and spiritual reflection and meditation. Rather, today we might say that the *Gospel of Thomas* portrays Jesus and his followers as street people, people like those invited off the street to the feast in Jesus' parable, with a rejection of everyday mores and a fresh sense of a community of love and mutuality. We might further say that Jesus resembles a Jewish street preacher, a peasant preacher whose insights and stories provide a glimpse of a dramatically different way of living together in God's reign.

Being Transformed

Fourth, in *Thomas* Jesus announces that the wholeness to be experienced by those who find the meaning or interpretation of the sayings promises transformation. One of the most common verbs employed in the *Gospel of Thomas* is *šōpe*, "become," and this verb (and other grammatical constructions) may be used to describe the transformation of those who respond to and follow Jesus. Thus Jesus says that the followers become a single one (*oua ouōt*), and they stand alone (*monakhos*), with a Greek word, used as a loan word in the Coptic, which eventually takes on the meaning of "monk."[45] This word must in fact have been understood in precisely this way by the fourth-century Pachomian monks, at Pabau, who copied and stored the *Gospel of Thomas* in their library. Jesus says that the lion that people eat becomes human.[46] Jesus says that once people became two, but now they may become one again.[47] The followers of Jesus may enter the kingdom when they are completely transformed: "When you make the two into one, and when you make the inner like the outer and the outer like the inner, and the upper like the lower, and when you make male and female into a single one, so that the male will not be male nor the female be female, when you make eyes in place of an eye, a hand in place of a hand, a foot in place of a foot, an image in place of an image, then you will enter [the kingdom]" (saying 22). Mary of Magdala, and any female for that matter, may be transformed and become a living spirit when she makes herself male (saying 114). This statement of transformation, put in strikingly misogynist terms, most likely uses common sexist symbolism from antiquity to depict what is heavenly and imperishable as male and what is earthly and perishable as female. Parallels to this saying are numerous in the literature of antiquity and late antiquity; the parallels in the Hellenistic Jewish thinker Philo of Alexandria are particularly noteworthy. We still sometimes use this symbolism to the present day in speaking of God as the father who is in heaven and of the earth as mother earth or mother nature. We can guess the sort of interpretive spin those Pachomian monks reading the *Gospel of Thomas* may have put on this saying. And some women who chose the ascetic life of self-denial took these symbols of gender quite seriously, and assumed the trappings of maleness by cutting their hair, putting on men's clothing, and looking like males.[48]

An additional kind of transformation is described in the *Gos. Thom.* saying 108. Jesus says, "Whoever drinks from my mouth will become like me; I myself shall become that person, and the hidden things will be revealed to that person." In this saying Jesus announces mystical transformation: one will become like Jesus, and Jesus will become that one. The reference to drinking from the mouth of Jesus recalls the imagery of drinking from divine wisdom in Jewish Wisdom literature and the *Odes of Solomon.*[49] Elsewhere in the *Gospel of Thomas,* in saying 13, Jesus also alludes to drinking: "I am not your teacher [he says to Thomas]. Because you have drunk, you have become intoxicated from the bubbling spring that I have tended." Jesus denies that he is a teacher because his followers must take the initiative and drink for themselves — compare what we observed above about seeking and finding. He is the tender of the spring, the bartender who tends the bubbling spring of wisdom and dispenses the intoxicating spiritual brew. When Jesus goes on to tell Thomas three things, to speak three sayings to Thomas, those three sayings are never disclosed — a coy but effective way of reiterating the need for the reader to seek and find.[50]

One more statement of transformation is of interest in this regard. In *Gos. Thom.* saying 77 Jesus articulates a vision of a transformed cosmos. All comes from Jesus, all attains to Jesus, and Jesus is all and in all. Here Jesus is made to speak in "I am" statements, aretalogical self-predications, so that he sounds like the voice of the divine; and he uses language that is pantheistic or panentheistic: "I am the light that is over all things. I am all: from me all has come forth, and to me all has reached. Split a piece of wood; I am there. Lift up the stone, and you will find me there." In the Greek Oxyrhynchus fragment 1 this saying is combined with a version of another, nearly inscrutable saying: "Where there are [three], they are without God, and where there is only one, I say, I am with that one."[51] While this powerful statement is at home with the description of wisdom, in the Wisdom of Solomon, which permeates and penetrates and renews everything, it is also similar to Johannine and Pauline formulations, and later this sort of saying seems to find a natural form of expression in gnostic and Manichaean mystical texts.[52]

Speaking in Cryptic Sayings

Fifth, in *Thomas* Jesus speaks in hidden sayings throughout the gospel, but some of the sayings are particularly cryptic, riddle-like, and esoteric. Bentley Layton describes all the sayings of Jesus in *Thomas* as obscure, and writes, "Without recognition of their hidden meaning, Jesus' sayings are merely 'obscure.'"[53] He is right, but some of Jesus' sayings are more obscure than others. Consider the following: "Jesus said, 'This heaven will pass away, and the one above it will pass away. The dead are not alive, and the living will not die. During the days when you ate what is dead, you made it alive. When you are in the light, what will you do? On the day when you were one, you became two. But when you become two, what will you do?' " (saying 11). "The followers said to Jesus, 'Tell us how our end will be.' Jesus said, 'Have you discovered the beginning, then, so that you are seeking the end? For where the beginning is the end will be. Fortunate is one who stands at the beginning: that one will know the end and will not taste death' " (saying 18). "Jesus said, 'Fortunate is one who came into being before coming into being. If you become my followers and listen to my sayings, these stones will serve you. For there are five trees in paradise for you; they do not change, summer or winter, and their leaves do not fall. Whoever knows them will not taste death' " (saying 19). "Jesus said, 'If they say to you, "Where have you come from?" say to them, "We have come from the light, from the place where the light came into being by itself, established [itself], and appeared in their image." If they say to you, "Is it you?" say, "We are its children, and we are the chosen of the living father." If they say to you, "What is the evidence of your father in you?" say to them, "It is motion and rest" ' " (saying 50).

How may these and other esoteric sayings in the *Gospel of Thomas* be understood? Stevan Davies sees these sorts of sayings in the *Gospel of Thomas* in the general context of ancient wisdom traditions, and there is good evidence to support his perspective.[54] In this essay we have seen that Jesus is a Jewish sage in *Thomas*, and that traditions placed on his lips are often quite similar to what may be read in other Jewish, Hellenistic Jewish, and Christian wisdom texts. Bentley Layton, conversely, sees the key to understanding these sayings in the ancient myth of the soul, *psychē*, often depicted as a female entity whose career is tied up with the uncertainties of the human experience. As Layton reminds us, a version of the myth of the soul is to be found prominently in the Thomas tradition in the "Hymn of the Pearl" within the *Acts of Thomas*.[55] Other scholarly commentators on the *Gospel of Thomas* seek the meaning of the obscure sayings in gnostic mythology, for example the gnostic myth presented in a famous document of Sethian gnostic spirituality, the *Apocryphon* or *Secret Book of John*. In the case of the last saying cited above, saying 50, the destiny of the people of the light may be paralleled, it is said, in the gnostic concern for the origin of gnostics in the light and their return to the light, which becomes manifest in this world in the image of the divine, and is empowered to move and is destined to rest.[56] I myself doubt whether there is necessarily a single, comprehensive explanatory key that may unlock the meaning of all the sayings in a text like the Gospel of Thomas, which was subject to editorial changes and modifications as it went through multiple editions.

Jesus, Thomas, and Schweitzer

If these are five of the leading features of Jesus in the Gospel of Thomas, what may we conclude about the image of Jesus in this text? I propose three conclusions.

1. The image of Jesus in the Gospel of Thomas presents us with an alternative kerygma to the proclamation that dominates the New Testament gospels. This alternative kerygma is simply another among the several kerygmata that characterized the diversity of proclamation in early Christianity. In this alternative proclamation Thomas resembles Q to an extent. Like Q, the Gospel of Thomas is not a gospel of the cross. Thomas proclaims a nonapocalyptic Jesus who utters life-saving words, and those who follow Jesus and respond to his words will not taste death. Thomas's Jesus is not the incarnate son of God, he is not the sacrifice for sin, he is not the firstfruits of the resurrection, he is not the Messiah, the Christ, the anointed one of God. Whether the Gospel of Thomas should even be considered a specifically Christian text remains a question — the same question we have with Q — but chiefly a scholarly question about taxonomy. Whether this sort of gospel of wisdom remains a viable gospel for today and for the future also remains a question, but a much more interesting question to consider.

2. As we have seen, the image of Jesus in the Coptic Gospel of Thomas from the Nag Hammadi library contains not only early Jesus traditions but also other themes, probably later themes, that are more developed, more esoteric, more riddle-like. These more esoteric themes have prompted some scholars to classify the Gospel of Thomas as a gnostic gospel, and this classification sometimes has been used polemically in order to marginalize the gospel. I am not convinced by those who wish to classify Thomas as a gnostic gospel. To begin with, we scholars continue to struggle with what Gnosticism actually was, and to this day there is no consensus whatsoever. Michael Williams proposes that

we dismantle the category of Gnosticism altogether, a category that he considers dubious, and he suggests that we contemplate replacing it with what he calls "biblical demiurgical traditions."[57] Besides, the *Gospel of Thomas* rarely uses the word *gnōsis* (only once, in saying 39, and then negatively in the context of the Pharisees), and when it reflects upon knowing oneself, it is indebted to discussions of the Delphic maxim (as in, for instance, saying 3). Unlike the *Secret Book of John* and other gnostic or biblical demiurgical texts, the *Gospel of Thomas* presents no narrative of the biblical creation story in order to show the origin of mystical insight and enlightenment in the face of the megalomaniacal creator of the world. Indeed, the *Gospel of Thomas* contains very little that ancient heresiologists and modern scholars are inclined to consider gnostic in some specific sense of the word.

For these reasons many scholars, and I am one of them, do not classify the *Gospel of Thomas* as a gnostic gospel without considerable qualification. The Coptic version of the gospel is an esoteric piece of wisdom, to be sure, but many of us tend to resort to qualifying adjectives to describe the Coptic *Gospel of Thomas*. We call it gnosticizing or proto-gnostic, we identify gnostic proclivities, and we find other subtle ways to nuance our words. The fact is that the Coptic *Gospel of Thomas* contains elements that illustrate how primitive first-century Jesus traditions, with a wisdom orientation, could be read and revised in a second- and third-century early Christian world that was exploring new ways of wisdom and new ideas of gnosis. Here the work of Helmut Koester and James Robinson is helpful, especially Robinson's essay "LOGOI SOPHON," which traces the trajectory from Jewish Wisdom literature to Q and *Thomas* and to gnostic discourses of the risen lord with his followers.[58] The Coptic *Gospel of Thomas* may not fit neatly into our scholarly categories. And if that calls into question our scholarly categories and our reconstructions, so much the better.

3. I propose that the image of Jesus in the *Gospel of Thomas* contains primitive Jesus traditions that may bring us a bit closer to the historical Jesus. In *Thomas* Jesus is a Jewish sage who uses stories, aphorisms, and other utterances to tell of God's presence and God's reign. The manifestation of God's presence may not be readily apparent, but it is all around, and sometimes it startles and surprises. Those who seek to respond to Jesus and his sayings may adopt a counterculture lifestyle that embodies the life of love and mutuality. It is, in a way, a secular life, not a life of

religious piety, but while it is in the world, it is not worldly. It is a life that runs counter to the world and the ways of the world. And it is a life that transforms.

With this image of Jesus, the *Gospel of Thomas* may bring us close to aspects of the historical Jesus. *Thomas* may, in significant respects, have gotten it right.

Which brings us back, at last, to Albert Schweitzer. As we all know, Schweitzer emphasized that Jesus was a Jewish apocalyptic figure who was profoundly committed to his vision but was fundamentally mistaken. Jesus' was a thoroughgoing eschatology. Jesus finally threw himself upon the wheel of the world, but he was crushed, mangled, destroyed.[59] Yet Schweitzer was also deeply interested in the sayings of Jesus, as we noted at the opening of this study, and this interest affected his thinking, his preaching, and his life. In his 1950 preface to *The Quest of the Historical Jesus,* Schweitzer goes so far as to suggest that Jesus' sayings and his teachings on love may actually have transformed and overcome the apocalyptic vision: "It was Jesus who began to spiritualize the idea of God's kingdom and the messiah. He introduced into the late-Jewish conception of the kingdom his strong ethical emphasis upon love, making this, and the consistent practice of it, the indispensable condition of entrance. By so doing he charged the late-Jewish idea of God's kingdom with ethical forces, which transformed it into the spiritual and ethical reality with which we are familiar."[60] Finally, then, Schweitzer may look, with us, to Jesus the Jewish sage, the Jesus we identify in the Sermon on the Mount, Q, and *Thomas,* as the Jesus whose words and sayings may impart life.

Notes

1. On Albert Schweitzer, Jesus, and reverence for life, see my essay, "Affirming Reverence for Life," in *Reverence for Life: The Ethics of Albert Schweitzer for the Twenty-First Century* (ed. Marvin Meyer and Kurt Bergel; Albert Schweitzer Library; Syracuse: Syracuse University Press, 2002), 22–36. On Schweitzer and Jesus, see also the essay by James M. Robinson, "The Image of Jesus in Q," in *Jesus Then and Now: Images of Jesus in History and Christology* (ed. Marvin Meyer and Charles Hughes; Harrisburg, Pa.: Trinity Press International, 2001), 7–25.

2. Albert Schweitzer, *The Quest of the Historical Jesus: A Critical Examination of Its Progress from Reimarus to Wrede,* trans. W. Montgomery (Baltimore: Johns Hopkins University Press, 1998).

3. Albert Schweitzer, *Out of My Life and Thought: An Autobiography* (trans. Antje Bultmann Lemke; Baltimore: Johns Hopkins University Press, 1998), 235.

4. Albert Schweitzer, *Reverence for Life* (trans. Reginald H. Fuller; New York: Irvington/Harper & Row, 1969), 65 (slightly revised).

5. Compare Patterson, *The Gospel of Thomas and Jesus*, 113–20; Patterson, "Understanding the *Gospel of Thomas* Today," in *The Fifth Gospel: The Gospel of Thomas Comes of Age* (ed. Stephen J. Patterson, James M. Robinson, and Hans-Gebhard Bethge; Harrisburg, Pa.: Trinity Press International, 1998), 40–45.

6. Harold W. Attridge, "The Greek Fragments," in vol. 1 of *Nag Hammadi Codex II,2–7 Together with XIII,2*, Brit. Lib. Or. 4926(1), and P. Oxy. 1, 654, 655* (ed. Bentley Layton; Nag Hammadi Studies 20; Leiden: E. J. Brill, 1989), 95–128. See n. 7 for Grenfell and Hunt.

7. B. P. Grenfell and A. S. Hunt, *Logia Iesou: Sayings of Our Lord* (London: Henry Frowde, 1897), 16. Now Søren Giversen, "The Palaeography of Oxyrhynchus Papyri 1 and 654–55" (paper presented at the annual meeting of the SBL, Boston, November 1999), suggests earlier dates for the Oxyrhynchus papyrus fragments on palaeographical grounds.

8. Hippolytus, *Refutatio omnium haeresium* 5.7.20–21; 5.8.32.

9. 1 Cor 2:9. The translation of this and other sayings in the *Gospel of Thomas* is taken from Meyer, *The Gospel of Thomas*. For parallels to this saying, see Meyer, *The Gospel of Thomas*, 76; Michael E. Stone and John Strugnell, trans., *The Books of Elijah: Parts 1–2* (Society of Biblical Literature Texts and Translations 18; Pseudepigrapha 8; Missoula, Mont.: Scholars, 1979), 41–73.

10. Helmut Koester, "History and Development of Mark's Gospel (From Mark to Secret Mark and 'Canonical' Mark)," in *Colloquy on New Testament Studies: A Time for Reappraisal and Fresh Approaches* (ed. Bruce Corley; Macon, Ga.: Mercer University Press, 1983), 35–57.

11. Note the efforts of Stevan L. Davies, *The Gospel of Thomas and Christian Wisdom* (New York: Seabury, 1983); also John Dart, *The Jesus of Heresy and History: The Discovery and Meaning of the Nag Hammadi Gnostic Library* (San Francisco: Harper & Row, 1988). Elaine H. Pagels, "Exegesis of Genesis 1 in the Gospels of Thomas and John," *JBL* 118 (1999): 481–82, suggests seeking and finding as the organizational principle upon which the *Gospel of Thomas* is based — on which principle I elaborate below.

12. Compare Patterson, *The Gospel of Thomas and Jesus*, 94–110.

13. For example, Bertil Gärtner, *The Theology of the Gospel of Thomas* (trans. Eric J. Sharpe; London: Collins/New York: Harper, 1961).

14. In Eusebius, *Historia ecclesiastica*, 3.39.16.

15. On the *agrapha* see Alfred Resch, ed., *Agrapha: Aussercanonische Schriftfragmente* (2d ed., Texte und Untersuchungen zur Geschichte der altchristlichen Literatur 15,3–4; Leipzig: J. C. Hinrichs/Darmstadt: Wissenschaftliche Buchgesellschaft, 1967); Marvin Meyer, *The Unknown Sayings of Jesus* (San Francisco: HarperSanFrancisco, 1998).

16. Acts 20:35; 1 *Clem.* 13:1–2; 46:7–8.

17. *Secret Book of James* (NHC I,2), 2,8–16; the reference to the Hebrew letters (-ⲅⲉⲃⲣⲁⲓⲟⲥ) occurs at 1,16.

18. Compare Geoffrey Parrinder, *Jesus in the Qur'an* (New York: Oxford University Press, 1977); Marvin Meyer, "Did Jesus Drink from a Cup? The Equipment of Jesus and His Followers in Q and al-Ghazzali," in *From Quest to Q: Festschrift James M. Robinson* (ed. Jon Ma. Asgeirsson, Kristin De Troyer, and Marvin W. Meyer; Bibliotheca Ephemeridum Theologicarum Lovaniensium 146; Leuven: Peeters/Leuven University Press, 1999), 143–56.

19. These quotations are taken from Meyer, *The Unknown Sayings of Jesus*, 144–56.

20. Meyer, *The Gospel of Thomas*, 10.

21. *Gos. Thom.* sayings 28, 106.

22. Origen, *Contra Celsum*, 1.28; 32; also rabbinic traditions on Ben Panthera/Pantera/Pandera and Ben Stada.

23. Compare John J. Rousseau and Rami Arav, *Jesus and His World: An Archaeological and Cultural Dictionary* (Minneapolis: Fortress, 1995), 223–25.

24. Luke 2:41–52.

25. *Inf. Gos. Thom.* 7:3.

26. Compare Matt 10:37–38 (Q); Luke 14:26–27 (Q); Matt 16:24; Mark 8:34; Luke 9:23. Other parallels are known from *Gos. Thom.* saying 101; Manichaean Psalm Book 175, 25–30; *Liber Graduum* 3.5.

27. Meyer, *The Unknown Sayings of Jesus*, 139.

28. *Gos. Thom.* prologue, sayings 3, 11, 37, 50, 52, 59, 111, 114.

29. *Gos. Thom.* sayings 2, 18, 24, 38, 76, 92, 94.

30. *Gos. Heb.* 4a, 4b; *Book of Thomas* (NHC II,7), 140,40–141,2; 145,8–16; Papyrus Oxyrhynchus 654.5–9.

31. Harold W. Attridge, " 'Seeking' and 'Asking' in Q, *Thomas*, and John," 295–302 in *From Quest to Q: Festschrift James M. Robinson* (ed. Jon Ma. Asgeirsson, Kristin De Troyer, and Marvin W. Meyer; Bibliotheca Ephemeridum Theologicarum Lovaniensium 146; Leuven: Peeters/Leuven University Press, 1999).

32. Richard Valantasis, *The Gospel of Thomas* (New Testament Readings; London and New York: Routledge, 1997); compare also John Kloppenborg, *The Formation of Q: Trajectories in Ancient Wisdom Collections* (Studies in Antiquity and Christianity; Philadelphia: Fortress, 1987), 305–6, on Pythagorean sayings.

33. Valantasis, *The Gospel of Thomas*, 7.

34. Compare Karen L. King, "Kingdom in the Gospel of Thomas," *FF Forum* 3 (1987): 48–97.

35. *Gos. Thom.* saying 82. See Meyer, *The Gospel of Thomas*, 99–100; Charles W. Hedrick and Paul A. Mirecki, *Gospel of the Savior: A New Ancient Gospel* (California Classical Library; Santa Rosa, Calif.: Polebridge, 1999), 40–41 (in the *Gospel of the Savior* the saying ends "is far from life").

36. Compare Matt 22:1–10 (Q); Luke 14:16–24 (Q); Matt 21:33–41; Mark 12:1–9; Luke 20:9–16. In the parable of the vineyard (saying 65) the owner of the vineyard may be identified as "a [good] person" or "a creditor," depending on the restoration of the Coptic. In the first instance a good person may be interpreted as the victim of violent tenant farmers; in the second an abusive creditor may be understood as opposed by the victimized poor.

37. Patterson, *The Gospel of Thomas and Jesus*, 230 n. 57.

38. Saying 42 may also be translated "Be wanderers." Less likely translations include "Come into being as you pass away" and "Be Hebrews," that is, "migrants."

39. See Meyer, *The Gospel of Thomas*, 87; on the inscription from Fatehpur Sikri, see also Meyer, *The Unknown Sayings of Jesus*, 178.

40. Compare Matt 10:8 (Q); Luke 10:8–9 (Q); 1 Cor 10:27; Matt 15:11; Mark 7:15.

41. Patterson, *The Gospel of Thomas and Jesus*, 68–69, 137–38, 236.

42. Oxyrhynchus Papyrus 655 col. i.1–17. Compare Matt 6:25–33 (Q), 34; Luke 12:22–31 (Q), 32; al-Ghazali, *Revival of the Religious Sciences* 4.190: "Consider the birds: they do not sow or reap or gather into barns, yet God sustains them day by day. If, however, you say, 'But we have a bigger belly than they have,' then I say to you, consider the cattle, how God has provided their sustenance for them" (in Meyer, *The Unknown Sayings of Jesus*, 159).

43. Sayings 27, 53.

44. See Albert Schweitzer, *The Philosophy of Civilization*, trans. C. T. Campion (Buffalo: Prometheus, 1987), 307–29, on reverence for life ("Ethics consist, therefore, in my experiencing the compulsion to show to all will-to-live the same reverence as I do to my own," 309).

45. Compare Aelred Baker, "Fasting to the World," *JBL* 84 (1965): 291–94; M. Harl, "A propos des Logia de Jésus: Le sens du mot *monachos*," *REG* 73 (1960): 464–74; A. F. J. Klijn, "The 'Single One' in the Gospel of Thomas," *JBL* 81 (1962): 271–78.

46. *Gos. Thom.* saying 7; Howard M. Jackson, *The Lion Becomes Man: The Gnostic Leontomorphic Creator and the Platonic Tradition* (Society of Biblical Literature Dissertation Series 81; Atlanta: Scholars Press, 1985).

47. Sayings 4, 11, 22, 23, 48, 106.

48. See Meyer, "Making Mary Male," 554–70.

49. Sir 24:21; *Odes Sol.* 30:1, 5.

50. On some of the efforts — most likely misguided — to find a specific identification of the three sayings or words, see Meyer, *The Gospel of Thomas*, 74–75.

51. Oxyrhynchus Papyrus 1 (horiz.) 23–27 (reconstruction by Harold W. Attridge); compare *Gos. Thom.* saying 30.

52. Wis 7:24–30; John 8:12; Rom 11:36; 1 Cor 8:6; Manichaean Psalm Book 54,19–30.

53. Bentley Layton, *The Gnostic Scriptures* (Garden City, N.Y.: Doubleday, 1987), 376.

54. Davies, *The Gospel of Thomas and Christian Wisdom*.

55. Layton, *The Gnostic Scriptures*, 359–79; also see Gilles Quispel, *Makarius, das Thomasevangelium und das Lied von der Perle* (Novum Testamentum, Supplement 15; Leiden: E. J. Brill, 1967).

56. Patterson, *The Gospel of Thomas and Jesus*, 200; Ernst Haenchen, *Die Botschaft des Thomas-Evangeliums* (Theologische Bibliothek Töpelmann 6; Berlin: Töpelmann, 1961), 39–41, 44; compare Meyer, *The Gospel of Thomas*, 89–90.

57. Williams, *Rethinking "Gnosticism,"* 51–53, 263–66.

58. James M. Robinson, "LOGOI SOPHON: On the Gattung of Q," *Trajectories Through Early Christianity* (ed. James M. Robinson and Helmut Koester; Philadelphia: Fortress, 1971), 71–113.

59. Schweitzer, *The Quest of the Historical Jesus*, 370–71.

60. Cited in Henry Clark, *The Ethical Mysticism of Albert Schweitzer: A Study of the Sources and Significance of Schweitzer's Philosophy of Civilization* (Boston: Beacon, 1962), 88–89 (slightly revised).

2

The Beginning of
the *Gospel of Thomas*

To the sayings (or, words) of the wise incline your ear,
and hearken to my word (or, saying);
apply your heart,
that you may know that they are excellent.
— Prov 22:17 (LXX)[1]

Introduction:
Q and *Thomas* as Sayings Gospels

In contrast to the four canonical gospels, Q and the *Gospel of Thomas* are often considered to be sayings gospels. While the canonical gospels are narrative texts, scholars have noticed that Q and *Thomas* preserve sayings of Jesus with little or no concern for narrative framework. The fate of these two sayings gospels was that they were hidden from the gaze of readers until recent times. In the case of Q, Q was employed as a source by Matthew and Luke and thus assumed its place within those narrative gospels. In the case of the *Gospel of Thomas*, *Thomas* was embraced by Christians with esoteric and probably gnostic interests and eventually found itself buried with other such documents near the foot of the Jabal al-Tarif near Nag Hammadi — or, as was the case with the three Greek fragments of *Thomas*, they were lost, even more ignominiously, in a rubbish heap at Oxyrhynchus, Egypt.

Several of these quick and fairly typical statements about Q and *Thomas* deserve more precise elaboration, and chief among these may be the statements concerning the gattung of Q and *Thomas*. For while even James M. Robinson considers it appropriate to designate Q and *Thomas* as sayings gospels,[2] he recognizes that the designation "gospel" cannot be made without careful qualification. After all, no apparent title for Q has survived, and any incipit that may have prefaced the sayings collection has been lost or obscured in the process of editing Q. John S. Kloppenborg[3] highlights three possibilities for an incipit: (1) *houtoi hoi logoi hous elalēsen Iēsous (kai Iōannēs)*, "These are the sayings that Jesus (and John) spoke" (cf. the incipit of the *Gospel of Thomas*); (2) *kyriaka logia*, "Oracles of the Lord" (cf. Papias, in Eusebius, *Hist. eccl.* 3.39.1); (3) *logoi (tou kyriou) Iēsou*, "Sayings of (the Lord) Jesus" (cf. Acts 20:35). Robinson gives clear indication of his similar conviction that Q and *Thomas* should be classified among collections of "sayings of the wise" in his essay "LOGOI SOPHON: On the Gattung of Q," where he observes that "one may seek in the term *logoi* the original designation for the gattung";[4] in his recent "Foreword" he also refers to the use of the word *logoi* in such a passage as Q 6:47. Yet in the same "Foreword" Robinson proposes, "The opening line in the original form of Q was probably the first beatitude, which initiates Jesus' inaugural sermon in Q."[5] This blessing upon the poor, Robinson continues, is echoed in Q 7:22, which employs the verb *euangelizontai*, "are given good news (or, the gospel)" (cf. Isa 61:1 LXX), in order to indicate that the poor are given the "gospel" in the teachings of Jesus. (A form of the same verb is used in the Lukan version of Q 16:16.) Robinson observes that Matthew evidently "recognized 'gospel' as an appropriate designation for Q,"[6] since Matthew used the noun *euangelion*, "gospel," in 4:23 and 9:35 to characterize the preaching of Jesus.

The *Gospel of Thomas*, conversely, never employs the term "gospel" within the text, but the titular subscript appended to the Coptic text describes the document as *peuangelion pkata Thōmas*, "The Gospel According to Thomas." The evidence of such Nag Hammadi texts as the *Gospel of Philip* (NHC II,3) and the *Gospel of the Egyptians* (NHC III,2; IV,2) would suggest that the popular title "gospel" could easily be appended to Christian texts in order to indicate their general character as "good news," regardless of the actual gattung of the text. The *Gospel of Truth* (NHC I,3) likewise makes general use of the word "gospel" in its incipit. Robinson's conclusion probably expresses a point of considerable scholarly consensus on this matter: "In general, one may sense that the titles appended as subscriptions at the end of tractates may be logically secondary to the titles implicit in an incipit, even in cases when both were already present when the Nag Hammadi codices were written."[7]

Robinson must add the final disclaimer because of the presence of both an incipit and a titular subscript in the *Gospel of Thomas,* and because the titular subscript itself, though transmitted in Coptic letters, preserves the Greek grammar of the Greek text prior to its translation into Coptic. In this regard we might also point out the nearly identical reference to the (Greek) title of Thomas in Hippolytus, *Ref.* 5.7.20, where the author refers to what is found *en tō kata Thōman epigraphomenō euangeliō,* "in the Gospel entitled 'According to Thomas.'"

Hence, in the balance of the present study we shall examine the internal and the external evidence pertaining to the beginning of the *Gospel of Thomas.* We shall commence our examination by turning to the incipit and the opening two sayings of *Thomas,* and we shall give particular attention to the issue of the gattung of the text. For the incipit specifies, rather precisely, "These are the hidden sayings that the living Jesus spoke," and thus designates the document as a collection of sayings of Jesus — or, more exactly, of "hidden" or "secret sayings."

Internal Evidence:
The Opening of the *Gospel of Thomas*

The beginning of the *Gospel of Thomas* is preserved in two versions: the Greek version of P. Oxy. 654 and the Coptic version (almost certainly translated from a Greek original) found within Codex II of the Nag Hammadi library. The incipit and first two sayings preserved within these two versions are remarkably similar in the Greek and the Coptic, yet the few significant differences indicate that the texts represent two distinct recensions.

Incipit

> *naei ne ᵉnšaje ethēp enta-I(ēsou)s etonh joou auō afshaisou ᵉnči Didumos Ioudas Thōmas*

> These are the hidden sayings that the living Jesus spoke and Judas Thomas the Twin recorded.

The incipit of *Thomas* defines the text as a collection of *ᵉnšaje* or *logoi* (sayings) of Jesus. This designation of gattung is confirmed by the several occurrences of the word *ᵉnšaje* ("sayings" or "words") in the body of the text (cf. sayings 1; 13:6; 13:8; 19:2; 38:1). The *Gospel of Thomas*

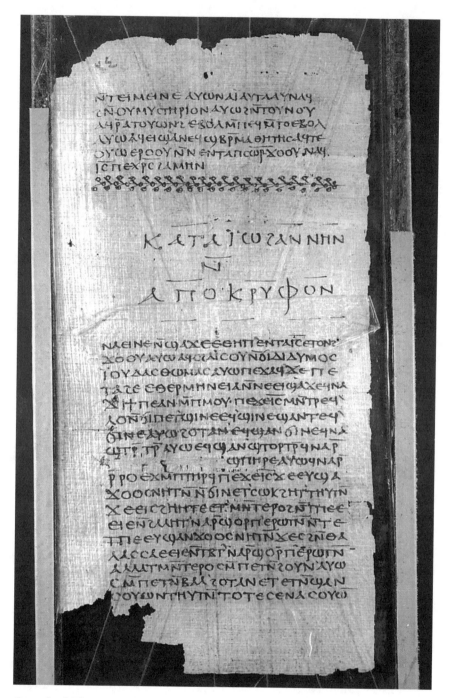

Gospel of Thomas, Nag Hammadi Codex II, page 32: The conclusion of the Apocryphon of John, with the title, and the beginning of the Gospel of Thomas.

thus finds its generic place among the early Christian traditions, oral or written, frequently described as *logoi* (e.g., in the Synoptic Gospels, the Acts of the Apostles, the *Didache, 1 Clement*)[8] or *logia* (so Papias, who also employs the term *logoi*) of Jesus. To cite one example, Acts 20:35 mentions *mnēmoneuein te tōn logōn tou kyriou Iēsou,* "remembering the sayings of the lord Jesus."

In the *Gospel of Thomas* the incipit employs a series of descriptive terms to bring further specification to the sayings of Jesus. To begin, the sayings of the *Gospel of Thomas* are identified as "hidden" or "secret" sayings. This identification of the esoteric quality of the sayings corresponds to statements emphasizing the revelation of what is hidden throughout the text. In saying 6:3–4 Jesus says, "For there is nothing hidden that will not be revealed, and there is nothing covered that will remain undisclosed" (cf. also sayings 5, 17, 108). Such an identification of hiddenness or secrecy can also be made in other texts that claim that sayings of Jesus have a hidden or secret dimension. Thus Luke 9:44 has Jesus exhort his disciples or followers to listen to *tous logous toutous* (these sayings), though according to 9:45 *to rhēma touto* (this saying) was *parakekalymmenon ap' autōn* (hidden from them). Further, Luke 24:44 has the risen Christ declare, "These are my sayings (*logoi*) that I spoke to you while I was still with you." The risen Christ then "opened their minds" (24:45) to understand the Scriptures. As is well known in scholarly discussions, Robinson sees a similar concern for riddles or obscure sayings in the Gospel of Mark, where Jesus speaks to outsiders enigmatically, *en parabolais,* "in parables" (Mark 4:11) that are resolved for the disciples by means of deeper and often allegorical interpretations. When Jesus is alone (*kata monas,* Mark 4:10) with them, *to mystērion tēs basileias tou theou,* "the mystery of the kingdom of God" (Mark 4:11) is disclosed to the disciples. This process of disclosure may compare well, hermeneutically, with the interpretation of the riddle-like "hidden" or "secret" sayings of the *Gospel of Thomas.*

The incipit of *Thomas* continues its specification by indicating that the secret sayings are those not simply of Jesus, but rather of "the living Jesus" (*I(ēsou)s etonh, Iē(sou)s ho zōn*). The use of this phrase in early Christian literature suggests that "the living Jesus" typically refers to the spiritual, divine Christ, who is to be associated with life and truth and whose sayings thus take on the character of revealed wisdom. It seems highly unlikely that the phrase means to refer to anything like the resurrected Christ (in, say, the Lukan sense). Hence, in the *Apocalypse of Peter* (NHC VII,3) the savior says to Peter, "That one whom you see upon the cross, glad and laughing, is the living Jesus (*peton^{e}h I(ēsou)s*). But that one into whose hands and feet they hammer the nails is the fleshly part, which is the substitute that is being put to shame, the one who came into being in his likeness. But look at him and me" (81,15–24). In the *Gospel of the Egyptians* (NHC III,2) the career of the great Seth and the saints is said to be established "through the incorruptible one, begotten by the word, even the living Jesus (*Iē(sou)s petonh*), even the one whom the great Seth has put on" (63,25–64,3). In the First Book of Ieou there are additional references to *I(ēsou)s petonh*, "the living Jesus," as in the prologue, which reads, "I have loved you. I have wished life for you — the living Jesus, who knows the truth." And even in the *Gospel of Thomas* itself mention is also made elsewhere of such related terms as *petonh*, "the living one" (*Thomas* 59; 111:2), and *peiōt etonh*, "the living father" (*Thomas* 3:4; 50:2).

The apostolic guarantor or recorder of these "hidden sayings" of "the living Jesus," according to the incipit of *Thomas*, is Didymos Judas Thomas, that is, Judas called (twice) the Twin (in Greek and Aramaic [cf. also the Syriac]). Among the several individuals named Judas in the New Testament is Judas the brother of Jesus (cf. Matt 13:55; Mark 6:3; Jude 1). An apostle named Thomas (or Thomas Didymos, "Thomas the Twin," in John) is also mentioned in the New Testament (cf. Matt 10:2–4; Mark 3:16–19; Luke 6:14–16; Acts 1:13 [lists of the twelve]; John 11:16; 14:5, 22 [?]; 20:24–29; 21:1–2). Thomas is acclaimed as the compiler not only of the *Gospel of Thomas* but also of the *Book of Thomas* (NHC II,7), the *Infancy Gospel of Thomas*, and apparently the *Apocalypse of Thomas*,[9] and he is the protagonist in the *Acts of Thomas*. Among Syrian Christians he is called Judas Thomas and is presented as the twin brother of Jesus. In the *Book of Thomas* Jesus calls Thomas *pasoeiš auō pašb^{e}r^{e}mmēe* "my twin and my true friend" (138,7–8), and in the *Acts of Thomas* the apostle is addressed by the donkey as "twin of Christ (*ho didymos tou Christou*), apostle of the most high and fellow initiate into the secret word of Christ (*symmystēs tou logou tou Christou tou apokryphou*), who receives his secret sayings (*ho dechomenos autou ta apokrypha logia*)" (39; cf. also the Syriac translation of John 14:22, as well as the legend of Abgar of Edessa in Eusebius, *Hist. eccl.* 1.13.1–22; 2.1.6–7). This evidence all indicates a particular devotion to the figure of Judas Thomas in Syria, particularly eastern Syria (Osrhoëne, and its capital city Edessa), and suggests that the *Gospel of Thomas* may well have originated in this region.

But is there any other way to understand this peculiar figure of Thomas in the *Gospel of Thomas*? In the *Gospel of Thomas* the only other mention of the person of Thomas (apart from the presumably secondary titular subscript) is to be found in saying 13, a saying that communicates, by means of a brief dialogue, this gospel's version of the story familiar from the New Testament as the story of Peter's confession on the road near Caesarea Philippi (Matt 16:13–23; Mark 8:27–33; Luke 9:18–22). According to the *Gospel of Thomas* it is Thomas who becomes spiritually intoxicated (13:5) and who hears from Jesus "three sayings" (or, "three words," 13:6) that elucidate a oneness with Jesus. (Compare also saying 108, which incorporates similar motifs to those of saying 13, and clearly articulates the salvific possibility of a mystical union between the divine Christ—i.e., "the living Jesus"—and the believer: "I myself shall become that person, and the hidden things will be revealed to that one.") That it is the Twin, the recorder of the sayings of Jesus, who is spiritually one with the divine according to saying 13, may provide another way of understanding the role of Judas the Twin in the *Gospel of Thomas*. This way would be especially pleasing to gnostic readers, who commonly emphasized the need for one to identify with one's spiritual, enlightened double, one's "better half," that is, one's twin. As the *Gospel of Thomas* says repeatedly, salvation is achieved when the two become one (sayings 22:4; 106:1), when people become a single one (*oua ouōt*, sayings 4:3; 22:5; 23:2; cf. also 48) and are alone (*monakhos*, or "solitary," sayings 16:4; 49; 75).

The Greek version of the incipit (P. Oxy. 654.1–3) closely parallels the Coptic (we may ignore the one clear instance of dittography) except for the name assigned to the apostolic recorder of the sayings. In the Greek he is merely named [*Iouda ho*] *kai Thōma*, "[Judas, who is] also (called) Thomas."

Saying 1

auō pejaf je petahe ethermēneia ⁿnneeišaje fnaji tipe an ⁿmpmou

And he said, "Whoever discovers the interpretation of these sayings will not taste death."

Saying 1 explicates the means by which one can appropriate the "hidden sayings" of Jesus. One must discover the *hermēneia*, the interpretation of the hidden sayings. As Kloppenborg puts it very aptly, "[T]he reader is to penetrate the opacity of the written word by means of a hermeneutical key which would unlock the secret of life."[10] The goal of this quest is salvation itself, for when one attains interpretive insight one "will not taste death." This figure of speech ("will not taste death," *fnaji tipe an ᵉmpmou, [thanatou] ou mē geusētai*) is attested several times in the *Gospel of Thomas* (cf. 18:3; 19:4; 85:2; also 111:2 ["will not see death"]) and in the literature of the period (cf. Matt 16:28; Mark 9:1; Luke 9:27; 2 Esd 6:26). Indeed, saying 1 in general is so reminiscent of John 8:52 ("...and you say, 'If anyone keeps my word [*ton logon mou*], that person will never taste death [*ou mē geusētai thanatou eis ton aiōna*]'") that Robinson observes, probably somewhat too strongly, "It is this original concept which is apparently presupposed in Saying 1,"[11] and Stephen J. Patterson concludes, more modestly, "For both Thomas and John, hearing and understanding ("keeping") the words of Jesus is the key to salvation."[12] For in spite of these close parallels, there is no compelling evidence to suggest that *Thomas* saying 1 is literarily dependent upon the Gospel of John.

Who the speaker actually is in saying 1 of the *Gospel of Thomas* remains textually ambiguous. The antecedent of *pejaf*, "he said," could be either Jesus or Thomas, and since Thomas is the closer antecedent, one might conclude that Thomas is to be understood as the speaker with an editorial comment on the sayings of Jesus.[13] Furthermore, the aorist verbal form *eipen* (he said) used in the quotation formula for saying 1 in P. Oxy. 654 is also unusual, since ordinarily the Oxyrhynchus papyrus fragments use the historical present form *legei* (he says) in the quotation formulas. The fact remains, however, that the incipit proposes Jesus to be the speaker of sayings and Thomas the recorder of sayings, so that saying 1, in spite of its ambiguities and peculiarities, may be attributed most safely to Jesus.

The Greek version of saying 1 (P. Oxy. 654.3–5) parallels the Coptic to a considerable extent (including the uncertain character of the quotation formula), but note should be taken of the word [*heurē*], "[finds]," restored in line 4. Admittedly the verbal form is in a lacuna, and evidence derived from a restoration is seldom the most convincing. Yet Harold W. Attridge's restoration follows Henri-Charles Puech and employs a form of the same verb favored by Joseph A. Fitzmyer, Otfried Hofius, and M. Marcovich.[14] The matter of the Greek verb becomes significant on account of the possibility of a *Stichwort* connection between sayings 1 and 2.

Saying 2

peje I(ēsou)s m^entreflo ^enči petšine efšine šantefčine auō hotan efšančine fnašt^ert^er auō efšanštort^er fna^er špēre auō fna^er ^erro ej^em ptērf

Jesus said, "Let one who seeks not stop seeking until one finds. When one finds, one will be troubled. When one is troubled, one will marvel and will rule over all."

Gospel of Thomas saying 2 follows naturally after saying 1, and explains the process of the interpretation of the secret sayings of Jesus. Here again Kloppenborg offers sagacious observations: "The second saying further elucidates the soteriological and hermeneutical program of Thomas.... Given the context, which calls for the interpretation of Jesus' words, what seems to be described here is a process of 'sapiential research' wherein the student passes through the perplexity of gnomic formulation to a state of 'rest' and 'rule.' "[15] The numerous parallels in the Greco-Roman, Jewish, and Christian literature of the period indicate the extent to which the sapiential quest was a matter of concern to religious folk of Mediterranean antiquity. Thus Epicurus, in his Epistle to Menoeceus (cf. Diogenes Laertius 10.135), observes that the study of wise teachings leads ultimately to immortality; Sir 6:27–31 and especially Wis 6:12, 17–20 urge the reader to seek wisdom so that one may progress through a series of developmental stages and eventually find rest (so Sirach) or a kingdom (so Wisdom); according to Matt 7:7–8 and Luke 11:9–10 (= Q 11:9–10) Jesus enjoins his followers to seek and find; and such Christian documents as the *Gospel of the Hebrews* (fragments 4a and 4b), the *Dialogue of the Savior* (NHC III,5:9–12; 20), the *Book of Thomas* (140,40–141,2; 145,8–16), and the *Acts of Thomas* (136) cite sayings similar to *Thomas* 2. The Greek version of the saying in P. Oxy. 654.5–9 differs from the Coptic version in that it adds rest (as do several of the parallel texts listed above) to the progressive stages of enlightenment: *ka[i basileusas epanapa]ēsetai,* "and [having ruled], one will [rest]."

The connection between sayings 1 and 2 of the *Gospel of Thomas* may possibly be established, formally, by means of the *Stichwort heurē*, "finds," that is most likely to be restored in the Greek version of saying 1 (P. Oxy. 654.4) and that is found twice in the Greek version of saying 2 (P. Oxy. 654.7). (The Coptic text, however, employs a form of the verb *he*, "discovers," in saying 1 and forms of the verb *čine*, "finds," in saying 2.) For years scholars have attempted to identify a guiding principle of organization to account for the sequence of the sayings in the *Gospel of Thomas*. To date none of the suggestions[16] concerning the overall structure of *Thomas* has proved convincing. Instead, the sequence of the sayings may be due, occasionally, to similarities of form (cf. the parables of sayings 8–9, 63–65, 96–98) or, fairly often, to catchword connections of the sort that we may be able to notice in the Greek version of sayings 1–2.

More significant differences among Coptic *Thomas* sayings and the three Greek Oxyrhynchus papyrus fragments may also be documented, and these differences may have an impact upon our evaluation of the structure of the *Gospel of Thomas*. For instance, P. Oxy. 654.27–31 adds a statement, not found in Coptic *Thomas* saying 5, about what is buried being raised; P. Oxy. 1.23–30 combines sayings that in Coptic *Thomas* are designated as 30 (different version) and 77:2–3 (different order for the clauses); and P. Oxy. 655.i.1–17 incorporates several statements that are not found in Coptic *Thomas* saying 36 but are reminiscent of portions of Q 12:22–31. These observations illustrate how readily modifications could be made in an ancient collection of sayings, and encourage us to be modest in our conclusions regarding sequence and order in a text, like the *Gospel of Thomas,* that is representative of what we might call a loose-leaf gattung.

In sum: The internal evidence of the beginning of the *Gospel of Thomas* places the text in the gattung of collections of sayings, here of Jesus. By means of a series of specifications in the incipit ("…hidden sayings…the living Jesus spoke…Judas Thomas the Twin recorded") the text calls attention to the enigmatic character of the sayings and the authoritative character of the speaker, whose insights are established by the "Twin." The first two sayings then explicate the way in which the reader will penetrate and assimilate the hidden wisdom of the sayings and thus attain life.

The External Evidence:
The *Gospel of Thomas* and Ancient Sayings Collections

Two studies on Q have shed a goodly amount of light on the gattung of Q and the *Gospel of Thomas* by examining a wide variety of sayings collections. Such external evidence for the sayings collection as a literary genre helps us test our observations based upon the internal evidence of the beginning of *Thomas,* and allows us to place *Thomas* in the broader world of sayings sources in the ancient world.

Robinson's painstaking study, "LOGOI SOPHON: On the Gattung of Q," discusses Q and *Thomas* as collections of *logoi* to be understood as wisdom sayings within the context of ancient Near Eastern and particularly Jewish wisdom. Robinson terms this gattung *logoi sophōn,* "sayings of the wise" (cf. Prov 22:17, given at the opening of this essay), and suggests that the literary genre exhibits a trajectory "from Jewish wisdom literature through Gnosticism, where the esoteric nature of such collections can lead to the supplementary designation of them as 'secret sayings.' "[17] While still an example of the gattung of "sayings of the wise," the *Gospel of Thomas* provides hints, Robinson proposes, of the more speculative interests of Gnosticism, whose divine revealer functioned as the more radical heir of personified Wisdom. Hence within Christian Gnosticism the "sayings of the wise" eventually gave way to the gattung of the dialogue of the risen Christ with his disciples.

Robinson's brief comment on the need to explore Greek literature[18] and passing references to Egyptian and Mesopotamian Wisdom literature[19] have been heeded by Kloppenborg, whose revised dissertation, *The Formation of Q,* provides a marvelous survey of the international world of ancient wisdom and the place of Q and *Thomas* within that world. Kloppenborg identifies several "modalities" of ancient wisdom collections — the Near Eastern instruction, the Hellenistic gnomologium, the chriae collection — all of which are of interest for the study of the *Gospel of Thomas.* According to Greek rhetoricians, wisdom sayings could take the form of gnomai or chreiai/chriae, and for a rhetorician like Theon, the determining characteristic of a chreia was that it was attributed to a particular speaker. According to this definition the *Gospel of Thomas,* with its *logoi* attributed (by means of quotation formulas) to Jesus, is a collection of chreiai. (Kloppenborg employs the categories of Theon to term *Thomas* "a collection of 'declaratory' (*apophantikai*) chriae.")[20]

While the opening of the *Gospel of Thomas* makes use of both a title (cf. the incipit) and an exordium (cf. saying 1), after the manner of the Egyptian instructions of Ptahhotep and Amenemhat I,[21] the emphasis at the beginning of *Thomas* upon interpreting obscure and hidden sayings is more reminiscent of Pythagorean sayings. Thus Iamblichus, *De vita pythagorica* 161, observes concerning Pythagoras, "He was also accustomed to reveal a boundless and complex meaning to his pupils in a symbolic manner (*symbolikō tropō*) through very short utterances, just as Pythian (Apollo) and nature itself indicate an infinite and abstruse mass of ideas and results through handy sayings or seeds small in size." Kloppenborg concludes that the *Gospel of Thomas* developed, within the gattung of ancient sayings collections, an esoteric hermeneutic by placing more emphasis upon the authoritative and divine character of the speaker ("the living Jesus") and "by employing a hermeneutic of 'penetration' when describing the intended response to the wise sayings" (i.e., the interpreter "will not taste death," "will marvel," "will rule over all," "will [rest]").[22] Q, on the other hand, developed the historicizing possibilities implicit in chreiai (sayings attributed to historical characters) and added a narrative preface, and thus began to move toward biography, as Kloppenborg also demonstrates in his discussion of the "narrative space" defined at the beginning of Q.[23]

The studies of Robinson and Kloppenborg confirm and enrich several of the observations made in our study of the opening of the *Gospel of Thomas*. Two questions remain, and while they cannot be considered in detail here, they deserve to be posed. (1) If Q incorporates biographical or proto-biographical characteristics, as Kloppenborg notes, does not *Thomas* do the same, only to a less developed extent? After all, *Thomas*, like Q, makes use of chreiai, and these attributed sayings often are provided the context of a statement or query to which Jesus responds (cf. sayings 6, 12, 18, 20, 21, 22, 24, 37, 43, 51, 52, 53, 72, 79, 91, 99, 100, 104, 113, 114), a dialogue in which Jesus is a participant (cf. sayings 13, 60, 61, 72[?], 73–75[?]), or even a limited amount of narrative description (cf. sayings 13, 22, 60, 100). That the traditions within those chreiai could be expanded further into narrative accounts is clear from the *Inf. Gos. Thom.* 7:1–4, which describes old Zacchaeus reflecting upon being overcome by the child Jesus in a manner that recalls *Gospel of Thomas* saying 4, and from the *Inf. Gos. Thom.* 12:1–2, which tells the story of a miracle of eight-year-old Jesus with elements from the parable of the sower (*Gospel of Thomas* saying 9). (2) If the tendency within Christian Gnosticism is to make increasing use of the gattung of the dialogue of the risen Christ with his disciples, as Robinson proposes, do we not see more than a few hints of this tendency internally within the *Gospel of Thomas?* To be sure, the incorporation of leading motifs and perhaps even sayings from the *Gospel of Thomas* in such documents as the *Book of Thomas* (with an incipit that is very similar to that of the *Gospel of Thomas*)[24] and the *Dialogue of the Savior*[25] confirms the tendency Robinson is suggesting. But even within the *Gospel of Thomas* are there not indications of movement toward the form of the dialogue or the discourse? (Robinson himself, more recently, seems to acknowledge as much when he speaks of the presence of "a kind of fused cluster or compressed discourse" in the *Gospel of Thomas.*)[26] There are numerous examples either of short dialogues or of questions and answers in the *Gospel of Thomas*, as we have seen. Almost certainly sayings 73–75 should be understood as a short dialogue, with the ambiguous *pejaf* (He said) of saying 74 translated as "Someone said" (cf. the vocative *pjoeis*, "Master," in saying 74, apparently addressed to Jesus). Furthermore, the juxtaposition of sayings with statements or queries from disciples of Jesus (e.g., sayings 20–22) may anticipate the literary form of the dialogue or the question and answer (*erōtapokrisis*).[27] Lastly, although there may often be a nearly mechanical use of the quotation formula in the *Gospel of Thomas* (so Robinson), at times multiple *logoi* of varying form and content may be lumped together into a cluster and introduced by means of a single *pejaf* (e.g., saying 21). At other times (cf. saying 27) the Greek fragment (P. Oxy. 1) employs a quotation formula but the Coptic version does not.

All of this suggests that the subtler issues regarding the gattung of the *Gospel of Thomas* may well be more perplexing and slippery than the beginning of the text would allow us to imagine.

Notes

1. λόγοις σοφῶν παράβαλλε σὸν οὖς
καὶ ἄκουε ἐμὸν λόγον,
τὴν δὲ σὴν καρδίαν ἐπίστησον,
ἵνα γνῷς ὅτι καλοί εἰσιν.
2. James M. Robinson, "Foreword," in *Q — Thomas Reader* (ed. John S. Kloppenborg, Marvin W. Meyer, Stephen J. Patterson, and Michael G. Steinhauser; Sonoma, Calif.: Polebridge, 1990), viii.

3. John S. Kloppenborg, *Q Parallels: Synopsis, Critical Notes, and Concordance* (Foundations and Facets; Sonoma, Calif.: Polebridge, 1988), 2.

4. James M. Robinson, "LOGOI SOPHON: On the Gattung of Q," in *Trajectories Through Early Christianity* (ed. James M. Robinson and Helmut Koester; Philadelphia: Fortress, 1971), 79.

5. Robinson, "Foreword," viii.

6. Ibid., vii.

7. Robinson, "LOGOI SOPHON," 78.

8. See Ibid., 85–95.

9. Cf. Montague Rhodes James, *The Apocryphal New Testament* (Oxford: Clarendon, 1953), 555–62.

10. John S. Kloppenborg, *The Formation of Q: Trajectories in Ancient Wisdom Collections* (Studies in Antiquity and Christianity; Philadelphia: Fortress, 1987), 305.

11. Robinson, "LOGOI SOPHON," 80.

12. Stephen J. Patterson, "The Gospel of Thomas: Introduction," in *Q — Thomas Reader* (ed. John S. Kloppenborg, Marvin W. Meyer, Stephen J. Patterson, and Michael F. Steinhauser; Sonoma, Calif.: Polebridge, 1990), 107.

13. Cf. Marvin Meyer, *The Gospel of Thomas: The Hidden Sayings of Jesus* (San Francisco: HarperSanFrancisco, 1992), 68.

14. Joseph A. Fitzmyer, "The Oxyrhynchus Logoi of Jesus and the Coptic Gospel According to Thomas," in *Essays on the Semitic Background of the New Testament* (ed. Joseph A. Fitzmyer; London: Chapman, 1971), 355–433; Otfried Hofius, "Das koptische Thomasevangelium und die Oxyrhynchus-Papyri Nr. 1, 654 und 655," *EvT* 20 (1960): 21–42, 182–92; M. Marcovich, "Textual Criticism on the *Gospel of Thomas*," *JTS*, New Series 20 (1969): 53–74.

15. Kloppenborg, *The Formation of Q*, 305.

16. Cf. R. Schippers, "Het evangelie van Thomas een onafhankelijke traditie? Antwoord aan professor Quispel," *GTT* 61 (1961): 46–54; Yvonne Janssens, "L'Évangile selon Thomas et son caractère gnostique," *Mus* 75 (1962): 301–25; David H. Tripp, "The Aim of the 'Gospel of Thomas,'" *ExpTim* 92 (1980/81): 41–44; Stevan L. Davies, *The Gospel of Thomas and Christian Wisdom* (New York: Seabury, 1983); John Dart, *The Jesus of Heresy and History: The Discovery and Meaning of the Nag Hammadi Gnostic Library* (San Francisco: Harper & Row, 1988); and Francis T. Fallon and Ron Cameron, "The Gospel of Thomas: A Forschungsbericht and Analysis," *ANRW* 2.25.6 (1988): 4195–4251.

17. Robinson, "LOGOI SOPHON," 71.

18. Ibid., 74.

19. Ibid., 110.

20. Kloppenborg, *The Formation of Q*, 291; cf. Ronald F. Hock and Edward N. O'Neil, *The Chreia in Ancient Rhetoric*, vol. 1: *Progymnasmata* (SBLTT 27, Graeco-Roman Religion 9; Atlanta: Scholars, 1985).

21. Kloppenborg, *The Formation of Q*, 296, 329, 333.

22. Ibid., 327.

23. John S. Kloppenborg, "City and Wasteland: Narrative World and the Beginning of the Sayings Gospel (Q)," in *Semeia 52: How Gospels Begin* (ed. Dennis E. Smith; Atlanta: Scholars, 1990), 145–60.

24. Cf. John D. Turner, *The Book of Thomas the Contender from Codex II of the Cairo Gnostic Library from Nag Hammadi (CG II,7)* (SBLDS 23; Missoula, Mont.: Scholars, 1975).

25. Cf. Helmut Koester and Elaine Pagels, "Introduction," in *Nag Hammadi Codex III,5: The Dialogue of the Savior* (ed. Stephen Emmel; NHS 26; Leiden: E. J. Brill, 1984), 1–17.

26. Robinson, "Foreword," ix.

27. Cf. Kurt Rudolph, "Der gnostische 'Dialog' als literarisches Genus," in *Probleme der koptischen Literatur* (ed. Peter Nagel; Wissenschaftliche Beitrage, K2; Halle-Wittenberg: Martin-Luther-Universität), 85–107.

3

Seeing or Coming to the Child of the Living One?

More on *Gospel of Thomas* Saying 37

In a note published in *Harvard Theological Review* in 1995,[1] Gregory J. Riley suggests a new reading for a damaged portion of *Gospel of Thomas* saying 37. Previously, the saying was translated in this fashion:

> His followers said, "When will you appear to us and when shall we see you?" Jesus said, "When you strip without being ashamed and you take your clothes and put them under your feet like little children and trample them, then [you] will see the child of the living one and you will not be afraid."[2]

Riley questions the translation of the portion of the saying in Nag Hammadi Codex II, p. 39, at the end of line 34 (the last line), where the papyrus is damaged, and proposes that the reading "the[n yo]u [w]ill come" is preferable to "then [you] will see." The proposed reading, if adopted, would significantly change the traditional interpretation of this saying, which has been understood to refer to enlightenment that comes from ritual participation in baptism or unction.[3]

Riley's suggestion emerges from his examination of photographs of the Coptic manuscript of the *Gospel of Thomas* saying 37, particularly plate 49 published in *The Facsimile Edition of the Nag Hammadi Codices: Codex II*.[4] On the basis of this examination, he proposes the reading *tot[e tet]n̄[n]ēu* rather than *totē [tet]nanau* as Bentley Layton and I read it.[5] (The key issue is whether *ē* or *a* is more probable as the penultimate Coptic letter on the line.) Riley defends his reading by claiming that his reconstruction makes more sense of the apparent ink traces and the space available on the manuscript.

Gospel of Thomas, Nag Hammadi Codex II, page 39: The reading of a portion of saying 37, at the end of the last line on this page, is discussed in the present essay.

Here I argue that Riley is mistaken in his interpretation of the evidence of the Coptic text, and that the reading that refers to seeing the child of the living one remains the more likely one. I base my argument on my own examination of the relevant photographs and the Coptic manuscript, as well as my assessment of the ink traces and the space available on the manuscript.

A quick glance at the Coptic text of *Gospel of Thomas* saying 37 on plate 49 of the *Facsimile Edition* makes it obvious how Riley could think *ē* more probable than *a* near the end of line 34. In the *Facsimile Edition*, a black horizontal line seems to link the vertical ink strokes that are visible. Yet, conversely, in the other photographs, the negatives, and the microfilm in the Nag Hammadi Archive housed in the Institute for Antiquity and Christianity at Claremont Graduate University, there is no real evidence whatsoever for such a horizontal ink stroke near the end of line 34.

Furthermore, during a careful examination of the papyrus itself in October 1997, in the Coptic Museum in Old Cairo,[6] I was unable to see any evidence of such a horizontal ink stroke. I undertook this examination of the papyrus in natural, artificial, and ultraviolet light, with the aid of a magnifying glass. I was able to ascertain that the profile of the papyrus at the bottom right of manuscript p. 39 corresponds very well to the profile of the papyrus in the *Facsimile Edition* plate, with the possible exception of the black line seen only in that plate. In my examination of the papyrus, however, I was also able to see a tiny vertical papyrus fiber extending into the space (seen as a black line in the *Facsimile Edition*) between the vertical ink strokes in line 34. While this is not clearly visible in the published *Facsimile Edition*, this tiny fiber is clear as a white fleck in the original photograph reproduced as plate 49 in the *Facsimile Edition*. Hence, the space appearing as a black line in the *Facsimile Edition* must be simply the empty space, still seen today, where a bit of papyrus once broke off the page.

The discrepancy between Riley's observation and mine can be explained without great difficulty. The photograph used in the *Facsimile Edition* as plate 49, representing Nag Hammadi Codex II, p. 39, derives from the series of photographs made by the Center of Documentation in Cairo and provided to UNESCO in 1965–66.[7] The photographs in this series were taken against a black background, so that the color of the ink and the color of the background are indistinguishable on the photographs. In a conversation in February 1997, James Brashler, who worked in Stuttgart preparing the photographs for publication in the *Facsimile Edition,* explained to me how the black backgrounds of such photographs had to be painted out, and how readily mistakes could have been made. (Brashler admitted that the work often was done without an adequate Coptic transcription of the texts.)[8] In his review of the *Facsimile Edition: Codex II,* Bentley Layton has also called attention to these sorts of problems with plates in the published edition, and he concludes, "L'examen du ms., ou à tout le moins de bonnes épreuves photographiques exemptes de retouches, demeure essentiel ("Examining the manuscript, or at the very least good photographic prints that have not been retouched, remains essential.")."[9]

The black horizontal line Riley saw on plate 49 of the *Facsimile Edition,* then, is not ink at all but rather an unretouched portion of the black background of the photograph. There is thus no manuscript evidence for the horizontal ink stroke that would have made the reading of an *ē* probable.

Without clear manuscript evidence for the horizontal stroke of an *ē,* the ink traces and the available space on the manuscript support the Coptic transcription of Layton and myself. The second vertical stroke (of the two specified strokes) corresponds to the style of the scribal hand for writing the letter *a.* The relative crowding of the letters at the end of line 34 (which prompted Riley to prefer eight Coptic letters instead of the nine of Layton's and my transcription) reflects the scribal propensity to squeeze letters onto the ends of lines rather than opt for an awkward line break.[10] A perusal of the ends of lines on this Coptic page and adjacent pages in Codex II gives a number of good examples of this scribal tendency.

In conclusion, the reading *naụ* in *Gospel of Thomas* saying 37 remains the probable reading, much more likely than Riley's proposed rending, and the saying is best understood to present Jesus recommending enlightenment and clarity of vision. As this scholarly note itself may suggest, the advice recommending clarity of vision may apply not only to "the child of the living one," as the *Gospel of Thomas* would have it, but also to the very ink traces to be examined by scholars studying the *Gospel of Thomas.*

Notes

1. Gregory J. Riley, "A Note on the Text of the *Gospel of Thomas* 37," *HTR* 88 (1995): 179–81.

2. Meyer, *The Gospel of Thomas*, 39. Compare similar translations in Antoine Guillaumont et al., *The Gospel According to Thomas: Coptic Text Established and Translated* (New York: Harper & Row, 1959), 23; and Bentley Layton, ed., *Nag Hammadi Codex II,2–7, Together with XIII, 2*, Brit. Lib. Or. 4926(1) and P. Oxy. 1,654, 655* (NHS 20–21; Leiden: E. J. Brill, 1989), 1.69.

3. Jonathan Z. Smith, "The Garments of Shame," *HR* 5 (1966): 217–38; Wayne A. Meeks, "The Image of the Androgyne: Some Uses of a Symbol in Earliest Christianity," *HR* 13 (1973–74): 165–208; Dennis R. Macdonald, *There Is No Male and Female: The Fate of a Dominical Saying in Paul and Gnosticism* (HDR 20; Philadelphia: Fortress, 1987); and April D. DeConick and Jarl Fossum, "Stripped Before God: A New Interpretation of Logion 37 in the *Gospel of Thomas*," *VC* 45 (1991): 123–50.

4. *The Facsimile Edition of the Nag Hammadi Codices: Codex II* (Leiden: E. J. Brill [Department of Antiquities of the Arab Republic of Egypt, with UNESCO], 1974) pl. 49. In a footnote, Riley also states that he examined microfilm at the Institute for Antiquity and Christianity, Claremont Graduate University, but it should be noted that the microfilm in question is of poor quality, and hence not particularly helpful. The Greek fragments of the *Gospel of Thomas* preserved in the Oxyrhynchus papyri cannot help with regard to saying 37, since P. Oxy. 655 breaks off before the line in question.

5. Layton, *Nag Hammadi Codex II*, 1.68; Meyer, *The Gospel of Thomas*, 38.

6. I thank Madame Samiha Abd El-Shaheed and the staff of the Coptic Museum for allowing me access to the Coptic manuscript of the *Gospel of Thomas*.

7. *The Facsimile Edition of the Nag Hammadi Codices: Codex II*, xvii.

8. I have not yet been able to find out whether the collotype plates on which Brashler worked are still in existence and are available for examination.

9. Bentley Layton, "Bulletin: Gnosticisme," *RB* 83 (1976): 459.

10. Compare also the discussion in Marvin Meyer, *The Letter of Peter to Philip: Text, Translation, and Commentary* (SBLDS 53; Atlanta: Scholars, 1981), 79.

4

"Be Passersby"

Gospel of Thomas Saying 42, Jesus Traditions,
and Islamic Literature

Pound for pound and word for word, *Gos. Thom.* saying 42 is the most
beguiling saying in the *Gospel of Thomas.* Composed of a quotation
formula plus two Coptic words, this saying has prompted scholars to
scramble in an effort to provide satisfactory interpretations of the saying.
In this essay I seek to join the scholarly scramble by examining the Coptic
of *Gos. Thom.* 42 and reconstructions of the saying in other languages,
evaluating attempts to translate and interpret the saying, and exploring
similar themes in literature useful for our study of sayings of Jesus in the
Gospel of Thomas, particularly Islamic literature. At the end of all this
I shall venture to propose a trajectory of transmission and development
of the saying and themes connected to the saying.[1]

Coptic and Other Languages

Gos. Thom. 42 occupies the entirety of line 19 on page 40 of Nag
Hammadi Codex II: *peje I(ēsou)s je šōpe etet^en^erparage.* The Coptic
grammatical forms in the line are not difficult to identify. After a con-
ventional quotation formula, the saying itself consists of the imperative
šōpe followed by the second person plural circumstantial *etet^en^erparage.*
The circumstantial (*e-*) employs the auxiliary *^er-* (from *eire*) with the
pronominal *tet^en-,* as is common with a verb of Greek derivation (here,
parage, from *paragō*).

The Coptic grammatical forms of *Gos. Thom.* 42 are clear enough,
but the translation and interpretation are not. Part of the difficulty of
translation stems from disagreement about the understanding of the

syntactical construction of the saying. The most straightforward understanding of the syntax seems to me to be that it is to be identified as a
periphrastic imperative, in this case *šōpe* with the circumstantial. Bentley Layton gives several examples of this construction, for example 1 Pet
1:16: *šōpe etet^enouaab,* "be holy" (Greek, *hagioi esesthe,* with variant
readings for the imperative, *ginesthe* and *genesthe*). Such an understanding of the syntax suggests the following sort of translation of *Gos. Thom.*
42: "Be passersby," "Become passersby," or simply "Pass by."[2]

Conversely, a few translators of *Gos. Thom.* 42 have understood the
syntactical construction as the imperative *šōpe* with a circumstantial
indicating simultaneity of action. This understanding of the syntax is
certainly possible, but it may be a more difficult grammatical analysis in
a text like the *Gospel of Thomas* that often uses *šōpe* (or the equivalent)
with an element of specification to indicate transformation: a person will
become a single one, the lion will become human, the female will become
male, Jesus will become the person who drinks from Jesus' mouth, and
so on.[3] Nonetheless, this understanding of the syntax, if accepted, suggests a translation of *Gos. Thom.* 42 like the following: "Come into
being as you pass away," "Come to be as you pass by," or "Come to be
and pass by."[4]

Some scholars have gone further in attempting to understand the lan-
guage of *Gos. Thom.* 42 and have tried to recover an earlier Greek or
Semitic version of the saying. Inspired either by the verb of Greek derivation in *Gos. Thom.* 42 or by the likelihood of a Greek *Vorlage* to the
Coptic *Gospel of Thomas,* a number of scholars have reconstructed a
Greek version of saying 42. Most obvious may be *ginesthe paragontes.*[5]
We might observe that variations on the Greek imperative are possible
(*genesthe* or *esesthe,* as with 1 Pet 1:16, above), and perhaps we might
even consider a simple Greek imperative for the clause (*paragete*). Other
suggestions have included *este parerchomenoi*[6] and *ginesthe peratai;*[7] in
an aside Tjitze Baarda also mentions *ginesthe paroditai* (compare the
Acts of John) or *ginesthe pariontes* or *ginesthe diodeuontes* (compare
Epictetus).[8] According to the evidence of Greek sources and Coptic translations of Greek sources, all these versions are possible reconstructions
of a Greek version of *Gos. Thom.* 42.

Baarda goes beyond this point of reconstruction of a Greek version of
saying 42, as do Joachim Jeremias and Gilles Quispel, and all three have
attempted to reconstruct what they assume to be a Semitic — Aramaic

or Hebrew — original version of *Gos. Thom.* 42. For the second word, after the imperative, Jeremias and Quispel have suggested a form derived from *'br,* understood as "wanderer" or "wandering teacher," and Baarda has suggested *'ibrî,* "Hebrew."[9]

We shall discuss these proposed Semitic versions more fully later, but here we consider the possible implications of an assumed Semitic original version for the organization of the sayings in the *Gospel of Thomas,* particularly in the thinking of Baarda. The question of the sequence of sayings in the *Gospel of Thomas* has proved to be a vexing one to scholars for a long time, and to date no overall organizational scheme has proved convincing. While there may be clusters of sayings — parables, for instance — most helpful for understanding the sequence of the *Gospel of Thomas* have been proposals regarding *Stichwörter,* catchwords that may connect one *Thomas* saying to another in a series. Ordinarily the possible catchword connections in the *Gospel of Thomas* have been discussed on the level of Coptic and Greek words.[10]

Baarda uses his supposition of a Semitic original and his reconstruction of a Semitic word for "Hebrews" to suggest an organized sequence of two (or more) sayings in the middle of the *Gospel of Thomas.* Baarda first recollects a comment by Rodolphe Kasser concerning a possible relationship between *Gos. Thom.* 42 and 43, and then he refers to a scholarly attempt to identify *Gos. Thom.* sayings 37–42 and 43–50 as clusters of sayings. On the basis of the Semitic original he believes he has recovered, Baarda can provide the connection that Kasser sought and — voilá — a sequence of sayings emerges in the *Gospel of Thomas.* According to Baarda, sayings 42 and 43 are very closely related: "[T]ogether these two sayings comprise a dialogue between Jesus and his disciples. On this view, the dialogue runs as follows:

> Jesus said: 'Be (*šōpe*) *Hebrews.*'
> His disciples said to Him: 'Who are you,
> that you say *that* to us?'
> (Jesus said:) 'Through what I say to you,
> do you not recognise who I am?
> But you have become (*-šōpe*) *as the Jews,*
> for they love the tree and hate its fruit,
> and they love the fruit and hate the tree.' "[11]

Baarda's bold solution to questions raised by Gos. Thom. 42, fascinating as that solution is, is as strong — or as precarious — as his assumption of a Semitic original for saying 42 and his understanding of passersby as "Hebrews."

Multiple Translations and Interpretations

There are three basic translations and interpretations of Gos. Thom. 42, and they are based on understandings of the Coptic and other texts associated with the Coptic. We shall consider these three seriatim.

First, "Come into being as you pass away," with variations. This interpretation is based upon a feasible but somewhat difficult understanding of the Coptic of the Gospel of Thomas. It has been advocated largely by earlier interpreters of the Gospel of Thomas, such as Bertil Gärtner, Robert M. Grant, and David Noel Freedman with William R. Schoedel, Johannes Leipoldt, and others.[12] Baarda accepts the grammatical legitimacy and defensibility of this translation and interpretation, though he himself ends up taking a different approach.[13] According to this translation and interpretation, the saying communicates a powerful, paradoxical message: embrace existence and also nonexistence, being and also nonbeing, life and also death. And the imperative is simply but emphatically put: šōpe, "become," "be."

There are plenty of other texts from antiquity and late antiquity that communicate a similar message, and in similar words. In the New Testament, 1 Cor 7:31 and other texts use the same Greek verb with the meaning "pass away," and 2 Cor 4:16 offers what may be taken to be a similar message in different words ("Though our outer person is wasting away, our inner one is being renewed day by day"). Acts John 76 contains the same sort of message with nearly as dramatic a delivery as the Gospel of Thomas: apothane hina zēsēs, "die that you may live." The Mithras Liturgy likewise includes paradoxical lines in its words to be uttered by the initiate: "Lord, having been born again, I am passing away (apogignomai); growing and having grown, I am dying; having been born from a life-producing birth, I am passing on (poreuomai), released to death" (PGM IV,718–22). And, Gärtner emphasizes, Gos. Thom. 11 also has the verb parage (twice), with the same meaning proposed by Gärtner and friends for saying 42.[14]

Thus understood, *Gos. Thom.* 42 may be poignant and potent, but, Stephen Patterson objects, it does not cohere with the overall message of the *Gospel of Thomas.* He points out that Thomas Christians do not come into being because they already exist (saying 19), and they do not pass away because they are immortal (sayings 1, 11, 18, 19, 85, 111).[15] Quispel critiques Grant in a similar vein, only more sharply, for being enamored of the gnostic hypothesis and a gnosticizing translation. He states that Grant, "épris de l'hypothèse gnostique, découvre dans ces mots les profondeurs de la gnose naassénienne" ("enamored of the gnostic hypothesis, discovers in these words the profundities of Naassene gnosis"), and so Grant (or Schoedel) translates saying 42 as he does — to which Quispel adds, "C'est d'autant plus profond que c'est incompréhensible. Mais il faut se souvenir que ὁ παράγων est un substantif grec qui veut dire 'le passant.' " ("This is all the more profound because it is incomprehensible. But it must be remembered that *ho paragōn* is a Greek substantive that means 'the passerby.' ")[16]

These are powerful critiques of *Gos. Thom.* 42 interpreted as "Come into being as you pass away," but the book should not be closed on this interpretation just yet. For what if some interpreter from antiquity or late antiquity is in fact a gnostic or mystic who reads the saying in this way?

Second, "Be Hebrews." In his quest for an original Semitic version of *Gos. Thom.* 42, Baarda proposes that the Coptic may derive from the Greek *ginesthe peratai,* where a *peratēs* is a traveler or wanderer like Abraham, and that *peratai* may reflect "Hebrews."[17] He observes that the Septuagint of Gen 14:13 translates "the Hebrew"[18] (as in Abram the Hebrew) with *tō peratē* (Symmachus later translates with *tō Hebraiō*). Baarda goes on to show how Philo allegorizes the word "Hebrew" to indicate a *peratēs* in *De migratione Abrahami,* how Origen understands the meaning of "Hebrews" to be *peratikoi,* and how Hippolytus calls a second-century gnostic group Peratae.[19] This evidence leads Baarda to understand *Gos. Thom.* 42 originally to employ the Semitic for "Hebrews."

So Baarda seeks and finds a Semitic original lurking behind a Greek version of a Coptic saying. The original, which might reflect "the earliest periods of (Palestinian?) transmission," may then be appropriately reconstructed.[20]

At the conclusion of his article Baarda raises questions to help explain what is at stake in his translation and interpretation of *Gos. Thom.* 42:

Is it possible that here Thomas is taking us back to a phase in history when the church, or a particular community or group within it, set itself up against the Jews as the new Israel, in which the shibboleth was no longer the law but being a child of Abraham? Was there a time when the followers of Jesus distanced themselves as the true *Hebrews* from their fellow countrymen, who to them were only *Jews*, who to their mind were only playing off the law against Jesus? It is tempting to reflect on this possibility but, ultimately, one should not dwell too long on the saying in the Coptic Gospel of Thomas, "Be passers-by."[21]

Indeed, is it possible? And indeed, one should not reflect too long on such anti-Jewish sentiments. Baarda's interpretation is learned and brilliant. It is an ingenious and subtle reading of *Gos. Thom.* 42, but it may be too ingenious and subtle for its own good. It is founded upon an uncertain assumption of a Semitic original supported with a tenuous understanding of obscure texts in several languages. At the end of the day this understanding does not fully persuade. Still, the general point that Baarda substantiates — and that Jeremias and Quispel substantiated before him, with their similar concern for a Semitic original — namely, that themes reminiscent of *Gos. Thom.* 42 are at home in a Semitic context, may prove quite helpful.

Third, "Be passersby," with variations that massage the meaning and interpret the precise nuance of the saying. This translation or one very much like it is usually used these days by scholars, yet the disarmingly simple wording leaves ample room for speculation about what exactly is meant. Just what is one to pass or pass by?

In *The Gnostic Scriptures* Bentley Layton opts for this translation and refers to epitaphs on tombstones: "Epitaphs on Greek tombstones of the period often salute the 'stranger' or 'passerby' (usually called *xenos* or *parodités*), as though in the words of the corpse buried in the tomb."[22] Layton then mentions *Gos. Thom.* saying 56, with the world described as a carcass or corpse.[23]

A couple examples of such epitaphs on tombstones may be given. One tombstone has an epitaph that directly addresses one passing by: "Hello, passerby (*parodeita*).... Then hear, stranger (*xeina*), my country and name...."[24] Another has an epitaph that quotes what the tombstone, or the one buried by the tombstone, says: "[T]he tombstone calls to all passing by (*parerchomenois*): here lies the body of Makaria, always remembered...."[25]

For Layton and others, *Gos. Thom.* 42 may call upon one to pass by the world, in fairly general terms (as, for Layton, one passes by a tombstone and a corpse). Passing by or overcoming the world is a theme well attested in the *Gospel of Thomas*, and not only in saying 56 (and saying 80). Saying 27, for example, makes use of the image of fasting from the world (and perhaps observing a sabbath from the world) to proclaim the importance of abstaining from the world: "If you do not fast from the world, you will not find the kingdom. If you do not observe the sabbath as a sabbath, you will not see the father."

In his brief discussion of *Gos. Thom.* 42 Layton alludes to another way of understanding what it means to pass by. When he states that saying 42 may also be understood as recommending the wandering life of one like Thomas himself as presented in the *Acts of Thomas*,[26] he introduces the theme of itinerancy, particularly within the context of Syrian Christianity. Others have followed the same basic approach, including Jeremias and Quispel, who also see the life of the wanderer in the Hebrew Scriptures and the Talmud (*b. Sanh.* 70a; 103b).[27] Quispel translates saying 42, "Werdet Wanderer!" and he goes on to observe, "Wahrscheinlich bezieht sich das Wort auf die judenchristlichen Wanderlehrer und Wanderpropheten, welche das Wort Gottes verkündeten. Allerdings betrachten die pseudo-klementinischen *Recognitiones* alle Christen als Reisende auf dem Wege zur Gottesstadt" ("Probably the word refers to the Jewish-Christian wandering teachers and prophets who preached the word of God. Indeed, the Pseudo-Clementine *Recognitions* considered all Christians as travelers on the road to the city of God.").[28] Quispel then traces the theme of itinerancy within Syrian Christian sources, including, in addition to the *Acts of Thomas*, Addai, Ephrem Syrus, Macarius, and the *Liber Graduum*. He concludes, "So enthüllt das *Thomasevangelium* die Zusammenhänge zwischen den palästinensischen Wanderlehrern und den Wandermönchen der gesamten syrischen Christenheit." ("Thus the *Gospel of Thomas* reveals the connections between the Palestinian wandering teachers and the wandering monks of the whole of Syrian Christendom.")[29]

Recently Stephen Patterson has suggested the translation "Become itinerants" for *Gos. Thom.* 42,[30] and Arthur Dewey, in a somewhat similar vein, has brought forward "Be (or become) transient (or transients)";

Dewey also allows for more fluid translations: "Get going," "Be on the way."[31] Patterson's interpretation follows rather closely the contributions of Jeremias and Quispel. According to Patterson, Thomas Christians are social radicals who pass by the world literally and concretely, wandering from place to place and living the radical life of the homeless itinerant. *Gos. Thom.* 42 then is consonant with saying 14: "When you go into any region and walk through the countryside (*etet^enšanbōk ehoun ekah nim auō ^entet^emmooše h^en ^enkhōra*), when people receive you, eat what they serve you and heal the sick among them. For what goes into your mouth will not defile you; rather, it is what comes out of your mouth that will defile you." Like Quispel in the passage quoted above, Patterson places the *Gospel of Thomas* within the broader world of Palestinian and Syrian itinerancy, with Q, the *Didache,* the *Pseudo-Clementines,* and additional Syrian Christian sources, and he sees a saying like *Gos. Thom.* 42 as showing a continuation of the itinerant lifestyle of the Jesus movement.[32]

Dewey presses *Gos. Thom.* 42 even more vigorously, not so much to explore the meaning of Palestinian and Syrian itinerancy, but rather to argue that the saying may go back to the historical Jesus with a more aphoristic and ambiguous meaning. Initially Dewey wonders whether the saying might simply reflect the mission instructions in Q (Q 10:2–16), where Jesus is presented explaining how the disciples are to go forth as wandering missionaries. Discreetly, in a footnote, Dewey asks whether *hypagete,* "Be on the way," of Luke 10:3, may be from Q and not from Luke, and then he speculates about whether *hypagete* could be the Greek *Vorlage* for *Gos. Thom.* 42. There is nothing inherently profound about this Greek word, however, since *hypagete* is a common expression in ancient literature, and *hypagete* and other forms of *hypagō* are used extensively in early Christian literature. He also argues that Matt 10:16b, Matthew's addition to the Q mission instructions, makes use of the imperative of *ginomai* with an adjective, in a manner that is somewhat like the form of *Gos. Thom.* 42: "So be shrewd (*ginesthe oun phronimoi*) as snakes and innocent as doves."[33] We may compare this Greek version with the Coptic of *Gos. Thom.* 39, which uses the Coptic imperative: *šōpe ^emphronimos....*

The appearance of the edition of Q from the International Q Project confirms that *hypagete* most likely is from Q. In *The Critical Edition of Q,* the text of Q 10:3 is given as follows: *[hypagete;] idou apostellō hymas hōs (probata) en mesō lykōn,* where the sigla (square brackets) around *hypagete* indicate that only the Lukan text is represented here.[34]

Dewey admits that he is tempted by *hypagete,* but he does not yield to the temptation. He admits that the saying of *Gos. Thom.* 42 might come from some common, everyday utterance, but he believes it may be a common, everyday utterance of Jesus and not simply a saying like that found in the mission instructions in Q.

Thus, in general Dewey joins his voice to the chorus of scholars who maintain that the historical Jesus preached and practiced a life of passing by for God and God's kingdom. After all, in one, itinerant sense of passing by, Jesus says in *Thomas,* "[Foxes have] their dens and birds have their nests, but the child of humankind has no place to lay his head and rest." Jesus says essentially the same thing in Q, the Synoptic Gospels, and, we shall see, Islamic sources.[35]

But Dewey's real contribution to the discussion of *Gos. Thom.* 42 may lie in the interpretation he gives to the saying as an aphorism of the historical Jesus with, as he puts it, "an ambiguous edge."[36] He states, "I submit that the saying may well be invitational — in an aphoristic sense, that is, without full scale plans or institutionalized context. This saying would reflect the open drive of Jesus' experiment, expressing an invitation to enter into this unfinished revisioning of life style and society."[37] To the voting fellows of the Jesus Seminar, to whom his article is addressed, Dewey recommends a red vote for *Gos. Thom.* 42. He can recommend attribution of a saying to the historical Jesus with no greater conviction than that.

Dewey admits that as a saying of Jesus *Gos. Thom.* 42 is ambiguous, and I believe he is right — perhaps more so than he himself realizes. For that ambiguity, I suggest, may extend both to the hermeneutic of the *Gospel of Thomas* and to the rhetoric of the historical Jesus. I have argued elsewhere that a hermeneutical ambiguity characterizes the sayings — *ᵉnšaje ethēp,* "hidden sayings," "secret sayings" — in the *Gospel of Thomas,* and that these sayings are presented as obscure sayings that need the interpretive engagement of the readers.[38] The hermeneutical principle articulated at the opening of the *Gospel of Thomas* implies an interactive hermeneutic and a way of salvation through wisdom and understanding: "Whoever discovers the interpretation (*hermēneia*) of these sayings will not taste death." Readers and interpreters are encouraged to find a hermeneutical key to unlock the meaning of the sayings, and, depending on the approaches of the readers and interpreters, a variety of interpretations may emerge from their creative encounter with the sayings. I agree with the approach of Richard Valantasis, who calls the theology of the *Gospel of Thomas* a performative theology. This theology, Valantasis affirms, emerges from the active response of readers and interpreters to the sayings of Jesus in the *Gospel of Thomas*, as these readers "construct their own narrative and theology linking the individual sayings into a cohesive text."[39] Hence, there may be no single authoritative interpretation of *Gos. Thom.* 42. Readers of the *Gospel of Thomas* are to discover for themselves what it means to be passersby. As *Thomas* says, *šine auō tetnačine.*

But a deliberate and even playful ambiguity may also characterize the rhetorical approach of the historical Jesus.[40] To state it succinctly: I suggest Jesus was an itinerant Jewish preacher of wisdom who proclaimed the kingdom or reign of God in terms that left much to the creative imagination, who told open-ended kingdom stories and parables and expected listeners to draw their own conclusions, who asked interlocutors to look at a coin and decide for themselves to whom it belongs, who practiced an alternative lifestyle, called the hungry, the thirsty, and the disenfranchised fortunate, and encouraged love for all, even enemies. That sort of historical Jesus could have said "Be passersby" in a way that might make people pause, think, and respond. Dewey states he prefers the translation "Be transients" (or the like) for *Gos. Thom.* 42, "because it catches the ambiguity of the Coptic and quite likely that of the original. A double sense of finitude and movement/mission is present in both."[41] Whatever we think of Dewey's exact formulation, we may appreciate his concerns. The historical Jesus, too, may have said, "Seek and you will find," and when the *Gospel of Thomas* presented these words as words of Jesus, it may have understood Jesus quite well. The *Gospel of Thomas* took the rhetoric of a preacher of wisdom and made it into a salvific hermeneutic: "Let one who seeks not stop seeking until one finds. When one finds, one will be troubled. When one is troubled, one will marvel and will rule over all."[42] This, for *Thomas,* is the kingdom or rule of God.

Islamic Texts and *Thomas*

In his discussion of *Gos. Thom.* 42, Jeremias compared it to a saying known from Islamic tradition, and thus he addressed an issue that is potentially of great value for the study of sayings of Jesus and the *Gospel of Thomas*. That issue is the use of Islamic literature, particularly Islamic texts with sayings of Jesus, in the study of such documents as the *Gospel of Thomas* — and in the present essay, *Gos. Thom.* 42.

In the Qur'an and other Islamic texts, Jesus (in Arabic, *'Isa*) appears in a large number of passages, especially as a speaker of wise sayings. Although previously some scholars have published studies of these sayings,[43] the appearance of Tarif Khalidi's book, *The Muslim Jesus,* has made many sayings and stories of Jesus in Islamic literature readily available.[44]

In his introduction Khalidi surveys the impact of eastern Christianity and the biblical and extracanonical texts of eastern Christianity upon the formation of Islam and the image of prophet Jesus within Islam. He describes the process by which this impact occurred as one of encounter and emanation:

> [T]he overall process by which the Muslim gospel came into being must be thought of not as a birth but more as an emanation, a seepage of one religious tradition into another by means textual and nontextual alike. The overwhelming Christian presence in central Islamic regions such as Syria, Iraq, and Egypt in the first three centuries of Islam meant intimate encounters with a living Christianity suffused with rich and diverse images of Jesus. Doubtless the slow but steady increase in the number of converts from Christianity played an important intermediary role, as witnessed in the *isnad* ["transmission"] of some sayings and stories as well as in the putative Christian origin of several transmitters, which is revealed in their personal names. But the Qur'anic fascination with Jesus must also have been a powerful stimulus in the assembly and diffusion of the gospel in the Muslim environment.[45]

One of the texts of eastern Christianity, especially Syrian (and perhaps Egyptian) Christianity, that may have had an impact on Islam is the *Gospel of Thomas,* and so it comes as no surprise that there are parallels between sayings of Jesus in the *Gospel of Thomas* and sayings of Jesus in Islamic literature. These parallels deserve careful attention, but here we can only cite examples.

Abu Hamid Muhammad al-Ghazali was an eleventh- to twelfth-century Muslim professor, theologian, and mystic who collected sayings of Jesus and had them published in the greatest of his literary works, *Ihya'* *'ulum al-din, The Revival of the Religious Sciences.* In this work he includes a partially familiar story and saying of Jesus. Seeking shelter, Jesus finds a tent occupied by a woman and a cave inhabited by a lion, and he says, "My God, you have given everything a resting place, but to me have you given none." God replies, "Your resting place is in the house of my mercy. . . ."[46] While this saying resembles Q 9:58 (Matt 8:20; Luke 9:58), it also recalls the version in *Gos. Thom.* saying 86 (cited above), with its modest allusion to rest.[47] Furthermore, if the versions of the saying in Q (Matthew and Luke) and *Thomas* make use of "child of humankind" ("son of man," using the Semitic idiom) as a general reference to a person, and probably in this case to Jesus himself, the version in al-Ghazali has Jesus simply speak of himself directly in the first person singular.

Again, al-Ghazali also has this saying of Jesus: "Jesus said, 'Evil scholars are like a rock that has fallen at the mouth of a brook: it does not drink the water, nor does it let the water flow to the plants. And evil scholars are like the drainpipe of a latrine that is plastered outside but filthy inside; or like graves that are decorated outside but contain dead people's bones inside.' "[48] Here the reference to the drainpipe and the graves recalls Q 11:44 (Matt 23:27–28; Luke 11:44). The image of the rock at the mouth of the brook is similar in sentiment to Q 11:52 (Matt 23:13; Luke 11:52) and *Gos. Thom.* saying 39, but a more vivid parallel is to be located in folk stories about grouchy dogs in mangers full of hay, as in Aesop and Lucian — and *Gos. Thom.* saying 102.[49]

In Islamic texts there are also passages that shed light on *Gos. Thom.* 42. In some Islamic texts Jesus describes himself as a homeless wanderer, an itinerant in the service of wisdom. In al-Ghazali (above), Jesus says he has no resting place; he also says, "My seasoning is hunger, my undergarment is fear of God, my outer garment is wool, my fire in winter is the sun's rays, my lamp is the moon, my riding beast is my feet, and my food and fruit are what the earth produces. At night I have nothing and in the morning I have nothing, yet there is no one on earth richer than I."[50] Other sayings place Jesus on the road, walking about and commenting on what he passes on the way. Again in al-Ghazali, Jesus passes by a pig and gives greetings, and he passes by the stinking carcass of a dog. In the latter instance it is said, "One day Jesus was walking with his disciples, and they passed by the carcass of a dog. The disciples said, 'How this dog stinks!' But Jesus said, 'How white are its teeth!' "[51]

A goodly number of sayings of Jesus in Islamic texts have him assume a critical stance toward the world and the pleasures of the world. In Abu Talib al-Makki, Jesus renounces the world and calls it a pig, without the friendliness of the previous porcine greeting.[52] In Abu Bakr ibn Abi al-Dunya, Jesus tells his disciples to renounce the world and its pleasures, as ascetics, and then they will pass through the world and they will not be anxious.[53]

The language of passing by the world and passing through the world is also reflected in a famous Islamic saying of Jesus, the very saying that attracted the attention of Jeremias. This is an inscription from a mosque in Fatehpur Sikri, India, dating from the time of the Grand Mogul Akbar: "Jesus said, 'This world is a bridge. Pass over it, but do not build your dwelling there.' "[54] This saying has been commented on by scholars, recently by Khalidi, who mentions several attestations and versions of the saying. A few scholars, such as Asin, Baarda, and Jeremias, have traced the saying back to the very beginnings of Islam. Some have compared the structure of the saying to another Semitic saying, *Pirke Avot* 4:21, about this world as a vestibule for the world to come. Jeremias suggests that the saying about the bridge may be pre-Islamic, and Baarda agrees.[55]

This saying is also to be found in the *Disciplina clericalis* of Petrus Alphonsi, in Latin: *seculum est quasi pons, transi ergo, ne hospiteris*. Petrus Alphonsi is known to have gathered much of his wisdom from sources to the east, and he attributes this saying to a philosopher. Baarda observes, "It is very likely that Petrus Alphonsi borrowed the metaphor from Arabic literature."[56]

It is conceivable, then, as some scholars have intimated, that the motif of passing by in the *Gospel of Thomas* may be connected to motifs of passing, particularly passing over the bridge of the world, in Islamic literature.[57]

Conclusion: A Passing Trajectory

I trust this essay indicates, at least in a small way, the significance of Islamic literature and sayings of Jesus preserved in Islamic texts for the study of Jesus traditions. With regard to *Gos. Thom.* 42, it may be possible to suggest, here at the end of the essay, a trajectory of transmission and development for themes linked to *Gos. Thom.* 42. Such a suggestion must be tentative. Yet, on the basis of the observations in the previous pages, I propose a reasonable case can be made for the identification of five historical moments in the development of themes of passing by.

First, I suggest, like Dewey, that the historical Jesus spoke of passing by in aphorism, though the precise form of the aphorism has proved to be elusive. He not only spoke of passing by, he also lived in those terms, as a Jewish preacher of wisdom with an itinerant lifestyle and a challenging rhetorical style. He spoke and lived in this way within a Jewish heritage that offered reflections, we have seen, on passing by. Jesus encouraged listeners to encounter his words creatively, so that a call to passing by could entail a fundamental challenge to various aspects of everyday life.

Second, Q people assumed an itinerant lifestyle, and they incorporated a mandate for itinerancy into the mission instructions of Q. Their interest in itinerancy was expressed in continuity with the lifestyle of Jesus. The opening of the mission instructions has Jesus commissioning the disciples in a manner that almost anticipates *Gos. Thom.* 42, in one way of understanding it: "Be on the way. Look, I am sending you like sheep in the middle of wolves. Take no money, no bag, no sandals, no staff. Do not greet anyone on the road" (Q 12:3–4).

Third, a cryptic saying attributed to Jesus, "Be passersby," was incorporated into the *Gospel of Thomas,* most likely in Syria, as a saying to be interpreted by those who would seek and find and live. The *Gospel of Thomas* presents an interactive hermeneutic that is in some respects reminiscent of the rhetorical style of Jesus, but in the *Gospel of Thomas* it is presented as a means of salvation. While such a hermeneutic allows for a number of different interpretations of *Gos. Thom.* 42, even "Come into being as you pass away," one interpretation may well have understood Jesus to be proclaiming that readers of *Thomas* should pass by the world and renounce the world.

Fourth, as early as the time of Muhammad, or even before, themes of passing by, as in the *Gospel of Thomas,* passed from Christian sources in Syria or Egypt into the world of prophet Muhammad and Islam. These themes were incorporated into the traditions of Islam, and Jesus became a prophet preaching about renouncing, passing by, and passing over the world.

Fifth, in his research for his book of quotable quotes and sermon illustrations, Petrus Alphonsi learned about the Islamic saying that the world is a bridge to be passed over, and he added this saying to his collection as the wisdom not of Jesus but of a philosopher.

That was Spain, in the twelfth century, and that was the first time that we know of that the saying, variously at home in the world of the Middle East, made its way to Europe. Finally it has made its way to the desks of scholars — hopefully not the evil scholars exposed in the *Gospel of Thomas* and Islamic texts — and now it is up to us to interpret what it means to be passersby.

Notes

1. In this essay the English translations of ancient and late antique sources are my own, unless otherwise indicated. Translations of the sayings in the *Gospel of Thomas* are taken from Meyer, *The Gospel of Thomas*.

2. See Bentley Layton, *A Coptic Grammar, with Chrestomathy and Glossary, Sahidic Dialect* (Porta Linguarum Orientalium, Neue Serie 20; Wiesbaden: Harrassowitz, 2000), 294.

3. On transformation in the *Gospel of Thomas*, see Meyer, "Albert Schweitzer and the Image of Jesus," 82–83.

4. See the discussion in Tjitze Baarda, "Jesus Said: Be Passers-By; On the Meaning and Origin of Logion 42 of the Gospel of Thomas," in *Early Transmission of Words of Jesus: Thomas, Tatian, and the Text of the New Testament* (ed. J. Helderman and S. J. Noorda; Amsterdam: VU Boekhandel/Uitgeverij, 1983), 180–81.

5. So, among others, Joachim Jeremias, *Unbekannte Jesusworte* (3d ed.; Gütersloh: Gerd Mohn, 1963), 107.

6. Rodolphe Kasser, *L'Évangile selon Thomas: Présentation et commentaire théologique* (Bibliothèque théologique; Neuchâtel: Delachaux & Niestlé, 1961), 71.

7. Baarda, "Jesus Said: Be Passers-By," 193–94.

8. Ibid., 192.

9. Discussion in Baarda, "Jesus Said: Be Passers-By," 194–95.

10. See Patterson, *The Gospel of Thomas and Jesus*, 94–110.

11. Baarda, "Jesus Said: Be Passers-By," 196.

12. Gärtner, *The Theology of the Gospel*; Robert M. Grant and David Noel Freedman, *The Secret Sayings of Jesus, with an English Translation of the Gospel of Thomas by William R. Schoedel* (Garden City, N.Y.: Doubleday/London: Collins, 1960); Johannes Leipoldt, *Das Evangelium nach Thomas: Koptisch und Deutsch* (TU 101; Berlin: Akademie-Verlag, 1967).

13. Baarda, "Jesus Said: Be Passers-By," 180–81.

14. Gärtner, *The Theology of the Gospel*, 244.

15. Patterson, *The Gospel of Thomas and Jesus*, 129.

16. Gilles Quispel, "L'Évangile selon Thomas et les origines de l'ascèse chrétienne," in *Gnostic Studies*, vol. 2 (Leiden: Nederlands Historisch-Archaeologisch Instituut te Istanbul, 1975), 104.

17. In Hebrew, עבריים.

18. In Hebrew, העברי.

19. Baarda, "Jesus Said: Be Passers-By," 193–95.

20. Ibid., 195: הוו עברין (Aramaic) or היו עברים (Hebrew).

21. Ibid., 197.

22. Layton, *The Gnostic Scriptures*, 387.

23. Compare also *Gos. Thom.* 80, with reference to the body (ⲡⲥⲱⲙⲁ) rather than a corpse (ⲡⲧⲱⲙⲁ); see Meyer, *The Gospel of Thomas*, 91, note to saying 56, on the Aramaic word פגרא as either "body" or "corpse." Perhaps compare the Greek Platonic (and Orphic) identification of σῶμα and σῆμα.

24. G. H. R. Horsley, *New Documents Illustrating Early Christianity: A Review of Greek Inscriptions and Papyri Published in 1977* (North Ryde, N.S.W., Australia: Ancient History Documentary Research Centre, Macquarie University, 1982), 55.

25. G. H. R. Horsley, *New Documents Illustrating Early Christianity: A Review of Greek Inscriptions and Papyri Published in 1978* (North Ryde, N.S.W., Australia: Ancient History Documentary Research Centre, Macquarie University, 1983), 107.

26. Compare the *Acts of Thomas* in general, and *Acts Thom.* 4 and 109 on being a stranger in a foreign land.

27. Jeremias, *Unbekannte Jesusworte*, 110; Quispel, *Makarius*, 20–21. The Hebrew word in question is עבר.

28. Quispel, *Makarius*, 21.

29. Ibid., 22.

30. Patterson, *The Gospel of Thomas and Jesus*, 131.

31. Arthur J. Dewey, "A Passing Remark: Thomas 42," *FF Forum* 10 (1994): 83–84.

32. Patterson, *The Gospel of Thomas and Jesus*, 158–70. On the possibility of a common tradition or common sayings tradition behind Q and the *Gospel of Thomas*, see Stephen J. Patterson, "Wisdom in Q and Thomas," in *In Search of Wisdom: Essays in Memory of John G. Gammie* (ed. Leo G. Perdue, Bernard Brandon Scott, and William Johnston Wiseman; Louisville: Westminster/John Knox, 1993), 187–221; and Crossan, *The Birth of Christianity*.

33. Dewey, "A Passing Remark," 81.

34. James M. Robinson, Paul Hoffmann, and John S. Kloppenborg, *The Critical Edition of Q* (Hermeneia; Philadelphia: Fortress; Leuven: Peeters, 2000), 162–63.

35. *Gos. Thom.* 86; compare Matt 8:20 (Q); Luke 9:58 (Q); more discussion below and in Meyer, *The Gospel of Thomas*, 101, with a reference to Plutarch's *Life of Tiberius Gracchus* 9.4–5.

36. Dewey, "A Passing Remark," 84.

37. Ibid., 81–82. Dewey adds that such an ambiguous aphoristic saying of Jesus fits well within the world of Jewish wisdom and the world of Cynic traditions, and thus he relates his interpretation in part to the controversial theories regarding Jesus, Q, and the Cynics as expounded in Burton L. Mack, *A Myth of Innocence: Mark and Christian Origins* (Philadelphia: Fortress, 1988); Leif E. Vaage, *Galilean Upstarts: Jesus' First Followers According to Q* (Harrisburg, Pa.: Trinity Press International, 1994); and others.

38. See Meyer, "Albert Schweitzer and the Image of Jesus," 77–78; Meyer, "*Gospel of Thomas* Logion 114 Revisited," 104–6.

39. Valantasis, *The Gospel of Thomas*, 196.

40. For discussion about the *Gospel of Thomas* and the historical Jesus, and references, see Dewey, "A Passing Remark"; Meyer, "Albert Schweitzer and the Image of Jesus"; Patterson, *The Gospel of Thomas and Jesus.*

41. Dewey, "A Passing Remark," 83.

42. *Gos. Thom.* 2; P. Oxy. 654.5–9 adds the stage of rest to the process of seeking and finding: "and [having ruled], one will [rest] (κα[ὶ βασιλεύσας ἐπαναπα]ήσεται)." Compare the *Gospel of the Hebrews* and the *Book of Thomas,* and also see below on rest.

43. See Michael Asin y Palacios, *Logia et Agrapha Domini Jesu apud Moslemicos Scriptores* (PO 13.3, 335–431; 19.4, 531–624; Paris: Firmin-Didot, 1919, 1926; Turnhout, Belgium: Brepols, 1974); Roderic Dunkerley, *Beyond the Gospels* (Harmondsworth, Eng.: Penguin, 1957); Jeremias, *Unbekannte Jesusworte;* D. S. Margoliouth, "Christ in Islam: Sayings Attributed to Christ by Mohammedan Writers," *ExpTim* 5 (1893–94): 59, 107, 177–78, 503–4, 561; Meyer, "Did Jesus Drink from a Cup?," 143–56; Meyer, *The Unknown Sayings of Jesus;* William G. Morrice, *Hidden Sayings of Jesus: Words Attributed to Jesus Outside the Four Gospels* (Peabody, Mass.: Hendrickson, 1997); Muhammad 'Ata ur-Rahim, *Jesus, Prophet of Islam* (Elmhurst, N.Y.: Tahrike Tarsile Qur'an, 1991); James Robson, *Christ in Islam* (New York: E. P. Dutton, 1930); James Hardy Ropes, "Agrapha," in *A Dictionary of the Bible* (ed. James Hastings; New York: Scribner's; Edinburgh: T. & T. Clark, 1904), extra vol., 343–52.

44. Tarif Khalidi, *The Muslim Jesus: Sayings and Stories in Islamic Literature* (Convergences: Inventories of the Present; Cambridge, Mass., and London: Harvard University Press, 2001).

45. Ibid., 29–30.

46. For the translations of Islamic texts, I have consulted the Arabic and Latin of Asin y Palacios, *Logia et Agrapha Domini Jesu,* along with other translations, and I have been assisted by Ra'id Faraj. For the present passage in al-Ghazali, see Meyer, *The Unknown Sayings of Jesus,* 153.

47. On rest compare also the addition to *Gos. Thom.* 2 in P. Oxy. 654.5–9 (cited above), and *Gos. Thom.* 50, 51, 60, 61, and 90.

48. Meyer, *The Unknown Sayings of Jesus,* 148.

49. Compare the note on Aesop, Lucian, and *Thomas* 102 in Meyer, *The Gospel of Thomas,* 105.

50. Meyer, *The Unknown Sayings of Jesus,* 154.

51. Ibid., 152.

52. Khalidi, *The Muslim Jesus,* 138–39.

53. Ibid., 117.

54. See Meyer, *The Unknown Sayings of Jesus,* 156, with the note on p. 178, for discussion and additional parallels to this saying in Islamic texts.

55. See Baarda, "Jesus Said: Be Passers-By," 188.

56. Ibid., 189.

57. Ibid., 190, with references.

5

Making Mary Male

The Categories "Male" and "Female"
in the *Gospel of Thomas*

The Coptic *Gospel of Thomas* is one of the most spectacular of the
more than fifty tractates filling the thirteen codices of the Nag Hammadi library. Discovered in December 1945 by several Egyptian *fellahin,*
the Nag Hammadi tractates were subjected to a variety of political and
scholarly ploys, and were not made available in their entirety until the
very end of 1977, when the last of the volumes of manuscript pages in
the *Facsimile Edition* and the one-volume edition of *The Nag Hammadi
Library in English* finally appeared.[1] One of the very first of the documents to be published was the *Gospel of Thomas*, and its appearance has
already stimulated the production of numerous articles and monographs
by the scholars who have recognized its significance for our knowledge
of Christian origins and early church history. Since the time of its initial
publication scholars have suggested a variety of interpretations of the
Gospel, and to date no consensus has been reached. Yet, in my estima-
tion, a reasonably strong case can be made that the *Gospel of Thomas,*
in its present form, belongs at least on the periphery of Christian Gnosticism, and to that extent the Coptic text may be termed a gnosticizing
gospel.[2]
    One of the distinctive features of the *Gospel of Thomas* is its use of
sexual imagery and the categories "male" and "female." Before turning
to a discussion of such themes as these, we first should observe that they
find their place within the generally ascetic, world-renouncing message
of the *Gospel of Thomas.*[3] According to this tractate, spiritual persons
come from the light, go to the light, and belong to the light of God; they
can hardly identify with the darkness of this present world. Logion or
saying 29 maintains that the world of flesh is a world of poverty; Jesus

states, "Yet I marvel at how this great wealth" — the human spirit — "has come to dwell in this poverty." A later logion (56) puts it even more graphically: "Jesus said, 'Whoever has come to know the world has discovered a carcass, and whoever has discovered a carcass, of that person the world is not worthy" — that is to say, the one who seeks after the world finds it to be mortal, full of decay and death; but this discovery, troubling as it is, leads to the realization that the spiritual person is superior to this world of death. The insightful person, then, should renounce the world and the values of the world. Saying 110 has Jesus say, "Let someone who has found the world and has become wealthy renounce the world"; in the next logion the justification is given: "Whoever has found oneself, of that person the world is not worthy." Traditional Jewish and Jewish Christian formulations can be used and transcended in the *Gospel of Thomas* (logion 27) as the ascetic message is delivered with power: Jesus claims, "If you do not fast *from the world,* you will not find the kingdom. If you do not observe the sabbath as *a sabbath,* you will not see the father" (emphases mine). These lines, with their parallel structures, proclaim fasting and sabbath-observance, but on a more comprehensive level, far beyond the limits of Torah-piety: the true fast is abstinence from the world, the true sabbath is rest from the cosmos.[4]

On the other hand, those who choose to ignore the true fast and the true Sabbath, and show loyalty to the values of the world, are roundly condemned in the *Gospel of Thomas.* Your finely dressed kings and great men, Jesus warns, will not find truth, and your tradesmen and merchants will not enter the kingdom (cf. logia 64 and 78). For the true kingship is spiritual, and the true kingdom is of the father. As logion 81 states, "Let one who has become wealthy rule, and let one who has power renounce (it)." Thus are spiritual wealth and kingship embraced, and worldly power renounced.

It is within such a context that several statements are made concerning sexuality and sexual values. In this study we shall isolate and discuss five themes having to do with sexual imagery in the *Gospel of Thomas.*

Sexual Imagery in the *Gospel of Thomas*

First of all, the *Gospel of Thomas* emphasizes the central place of the family, but the family properly understood. As in the Synoptic Gospels

(Matt 10:34–36 = Luke 12:49–53), so also in the *Gospel of Thomas* (logion 16) Jesus claims to throw division upon family life: "For there will be five in a house: There will be three against two and two against three, father against son and son against father, and they will stand alone." While the first part of this saying parallels the New Testament gospels to a considerable extent — although, unlike the New Testament versions, no mothers and daughters are mentioned in the enumeration of the dissenting parties in the *Gospel of Thomas* — the conclusion illustrates more of a gnosticizing, ascetic tendency. The reference in the present logion to the family members *standing* may very well reflect the tradition of the divine or liberated person as one who is standing, a tradition to be noted with clarity in such gnostic systems as that of the first-century C.E. teacher Simon Magus.[5] The Coptic word translated "alone" in the translation given above is *monakhos,* a Greek loan word that functions as a *terminus technicus* with definite ascetic overtones. The implication is that the *monakhos* is a lonely or solitary one who is not one of the masses, but rather is free from distracting social and sexual ties. Hence it is appropriate that later this Greek term can be used to designate *monks* per se.

If the previous saying, like several others in the *Gospel of Thomas* (cf. 55, 79, 99), recommends the rejection of the physical family for the sake of higher values, two additional logia near the end of the collection speak even more clearly about the nature of the family. Logion 105 is brief but enigmatic: "Jesus said, 'Whoever knows the father and the mother will be called the child of a whore.' " It might be suggested that this saying means to refer, albeit in an oblique fashion, to polemical statements about the birth of Jesus. According to certain Jewish traditions surrounding Yeshu ben Pantera, Jesus was born of fornication as the son of Mary and a Roman soldier named Pantera (or Panther).[6] Another interpretation of this logion takes a different approach. According to this alternate understanding, the saying intends to urge the reader to resist the temptation to identify with one's earthly family. Indeed, the saying points out, the person who values physical familial ties, who acknowledges the role of physical parents, knowingly succumbs to the lure of the lower values and unseemly sexuality of this world.

An additional logion or two can provide clarification of the position of the *Gospel of Thomas* on the family. If a saying such as number 99 can hint, like the New Testament (cf. Mark 3:32–35 = Matt 12:45–50

= Luke 8:20–21), at the existence of a spiritual family by having Jesus assert, "Those here who do the will of my father are my brothers and my mother," then saying 101 makes the character of the family even clearer. Although the papyrus of this section is damaged, the present saying may be partially restored as follows: Jesus states, "Whoever does not hate [father] and mother as I do cannot be a [follower] of me, and whoever does [not] love [father and] mother as I do cannot be a [follower of] me. For my mother [. . .], but my true [mother] gave me life."[7] The conundrum of the first two statements is resolved by the third, which posits the existence of two mothers, of two orders of family. The physical family is established through sexual ties, and is involved in the dark uncertainties and false dealings characteristic of this world, and hence is to be hated and repudiated. But the true family, the spiritual family, is to be maintained in love, for it mediates life. Here the *Gospel of Thomas* has Jesus speak of his "true mother," presumably his spiritual mother. Such a statement is reminiscent of other references to the spiritual mother of Jesus in gnostic documents and other ancient literature. In the Jewish-Christian *Gospel of the Hebrews,* for example, Jesus describes his relationship to his mother the holy spirit (fragment 3); likewise, the *Apocryphon of James* from Nag Hammadi recommends that one become like "the child of the holy spirit" (I 6, 20–21); and the *Gospel of Philip* polemicizes against the doctrine of Mary the mother of Jesus conceiving by the holy spirit (cf. Matt 1:18 ff.) by raising the rhetorical question, "When did a woman ever conceive by a woman?" (II 55, 25–26). These references all contribute to the familiar position of the spirit as female, especially in Semitic contexts, and the Trinity as a heavenly nuclear family, not unlike classical Egyptian divine families or triads (e.g., father Osiris, mother Isis, son Horus; or father Amun, mother Mut, son Khonsu).[8]

In this regard it is helpful to add a note concerning gnostic christology. Numerous Christian gnostics wished to pay particular homage to the divine nature of Christ, and to derive the whole being of Christ from the pleroma of God, so that they easily could move in the direction of Docetism. It can be said by such gnostic believers that when Jesus walked on the sand he left no footprints, and that when the crucifixion took place the true Christ, the spiritual being, stood apart laughing at the ignorant powers of the world who mistakenly thought they were executing him.[9] Obviously this sort of christological perspective could have implications for gnostic evaluations of the family of Jesus, and such is in fact the case. Sometimes the gnostic sources de-emphasize or even depreciate the human parentage of Jesus, so that greater value is placed upon his divine parentage. To cite an example of such a tendency: the gnostics mentioned by Irenaeus and Epiphanius describe the heavenly Christ passing through mother Mary as water passes through a pipe.[10] It is this sort of depreciation of Jesus' human parentage and exaltation of his divine family that seems to be observed in the Gospel of Thomas.

The second theme to be isolated in the Gospel of Thomas is that of the wedding chamber. This motif occurs explicitly only twice in the Gospel, in logia 75 and 104, and only the former occurrence is really significant for our purposes. According to that saying Jesus speaks as follows: "There are many standing by the door, but those who are alone (monakhos) will enter the wedding chamber." This concept of believers entering the wedding chamber is a familiar concept in gnostic texts.[11] To be sure, the wedding chamber and the sacred marriage figure prominently in a wide variety of religious traditions, from early antiquity and on. Mention may be made of ruler and fertility cults in the ancient Near East, Greek and Hellenistic mystery religions, and also certain Jewish and Christian texts; in each of these settings the concept of the sacred marriage comes to expression in one way or another. But in gnostic sources the image of the wedding chamber is especially prominent as a way of depicting the primal unity and heavenly wholeness that is possible when the soul is conjoined with its divine mate, its *alter ego*. As this salvific marriage is described in the *Exegesis on the Soul*, it is perfectly and permanently fulfilling and satisfying. The soul, described in the usual fashion as a woman, is joined to her heavenly bridegroom, her brother, and "[once] they unite [with one another] they become a single life" (II 132, 34–35), thus re-establishing the primordial oneness that existed before the fall of the soul from God, and repairing the torn and broken character of human existence.

This imagery did not go unnoticed by the opponents of the Christian gnostics, the heresiologists. They were quick to snatch up the vivid descriptions and nasty rumors, and circulated the libel that some of the gnostics were wild libertines, freely practicing all sorts of shameful and forbidden things, secretly seducing women, and fleshing out the mystery of the syzygy and the wedding chamber in a most corporeal fashion.[12]

That some of the gnostics may have been libertines remains a real possibility, but the evidence of the texts from the Nag Hammadi library indicates that many gnostics had a very different understanding of the mystery of the wedding chamber from that attributed to them by the heresiologists. Both the *Exegesis on the Soul* and the *Gospel of Philip* are emphatic in declaring that the true wedding chamber is to be distinguished from fleshly marriage and sexual intercourse. In the *Gospel of Philip* the wedding chamber functions, alongside baptism, chrism, Eucharist, and redemption, as one of the mysteries or sacraments. It is in the wedding chamber that the restoration of the original integrated existence is achieved. The *Gospel of Philip* proclaims that "Christ came to repair the separation which was from the beginning and again unite the two, and to give life to those who died as a result of the separation and unite them" (II 70, 13–17). The wedding chamber, the tractate continues, is for the sake of "undefiled marriage," and undefiled marriage is by no means to be equated with "the marriage of defilement" (II 82, 2 ff.). In the words of this *Gospel*, the undefiled marriage "is not fleshly but pure. It belongs not to desire but to the will. It belongs not to the darkness or the night but to the day and the light" (II 82, 6–10). So pure, so spiritual is the wedding chamber that it can even be compared to "the holy of holies" (cf. II 69, 24–25).

To conclude, then, on the wedding chamber: a similar conception of the pure, asexual wedding chamber seems operative in the *Gospel of Thomas*. Such is intimated in logion 75 by the linking of the terms *monakhos* and "wedding chamber": it is precisely the solitary ones, with their association with purity and chastity, who are worthy of the sacred marriage.

A third sexual motif in the *Gospel of Thomas* concerns children and their attributes.[13] The *Gospel of Thomas* and gnostic sources are not unique in their emphasis upon children. Throughout antiquity, in Hellenistic, Jewish, and Christian sources, children are commonly alluded to as representative of innocence, sinlessness, and sexual naiveté and purity. The gnostic sources, too, wish to provide such a positive evaluation of children, and thus can describe gnostic believers and even gnostic saviors as children. In the *Gospel of Thomas* it is claimed, in general, that babies at the breast resemble those who will enter the kingdom (logion 22), and that those who become children will know the kingdom and will be great (logion 46). Furthermore, in logion 4, a saying about reversals of fortune and value, it is observed that a young child only seven days old is the one who will communicate life to an old man. The specific reference to the one-week-old baby seems intended to highlight the unspoiled, un-worldly character of the child; he has not yet been circumcised![14] Logion 21 likens the followers of Jesus to children living in an alien field, the world of flesh and corporeality. Jesus says, "When the owners of the field come" — that is, the harsh rulers of this world — "they will say, 'Give our field back to us.' They take off their clothes in front of them in order to give it back to them, and they return their field to them." Here the removal of one's clothing seems to be linked, in a symbolic way, to the release of one's claim upon a piece of property. Thus the true children of the light are to let go of this world, take off the bodies that are cloth-ing them, and be liberated from mortal existence to immortal life. The reference to stripping recalls the shameless and innocent nakedness of children in general, to say nothing of the "naked but not ashamed" first parents in Eden (Gen 2:25); but this stripping motif refers even more easily to the ancient concept of naked souls wearing clothing put on in incarnation and taken off in ecstasy or death. Logion 37 communicates similar ideas with several of the same images: salvation will take place, Jesus declares, "When you strip without being ashamed and you take your clothes and put them under your feet like little children and tram-ple them" — that is to say, when you, as children, or newly initiated believers, show utter disdain for your sinful, worldly garments.

The fourth theme to be isolated is that of wholeness, specifically as described in logion 22. Throughout the *Gospel of Thomas* one of the most terse and significant terms to be used is the Coptic phrase *Oua ouōt*, a phrase that is translated in the *Nag Hammadi Library in English* as "one and the same." *oua ouōt* seems to be an intensive form of the number one, so that I prefer "single one" as the most pleasing rendition of the phrase in English. In any case, *oua ouōt* functions importantly to designate the wholeness, beyond the division and fragmentation of human existence, that the gnostics judged characteristic of salvation.

This concept of wholeness comes to a focus in logion 22. This saying indicates that nothing less than a totally new being is required if one is to enter the kingdom: what is needed is unification, integration, as-similation, transformation, *oua ouōt*. The *Gospel of Thomas* puts it as follows: "Jesus said to them (i.e., his disciples), 'When you make the two into one, and when you make the inner like the outer and the outer like the inner, and the upper like the lower, and when you make male and female into a single one (*oua ouōt*), so that the male will not be male nor the female be female, when you make eyes in place of an eye, a hand in place of a hand, a foot in place of a foot, an image in place of an image, then you will enter [the kingdom].' "

This saying might provoke us to provide parallels, which are many and varied; or survey interpretations, which are equally numerous and diverse; or discuss Jung and the *coincidentia oppositorum*. These things will not be attempted here.[15] For the purposes of this study the statements about "male" and "female" in the saying are of the most interest. At first glance we might conclude, as many commentators have concluded, that logion 22 advocates androgyny, the restitution of the original unified sexual condition. Such a conclusion would certainly be in full harmony with much of what is characteristic of late antiquity in general and the Nag Hammadi tractates in particular. Not only do these tractates describe countless gods, demigods, aeons, powers, and human souls as androgynous, "according to the immortal pattern" (II 102, 3), as the tract *On the Origin of the World* states. Tractates like the *Gospel of Philip* also suggest that salvation entails the restoration of original androgynous unity: "When Eve was still in Adam death did not exist. When she was separated from him, death came into being. If he again becomes complete and attains his former self, death will be no more" (II 68, 22–26). Hence, as we have seen, the place of the wedding chamber.

Yet a careful reading of the text of the *Gospel of Thomas* prompts us to take a slightly different approach with regard to logion 22. To be sure, male and female are to become *oua ouōt;* but the saying goes on to specify that this transformation is to take place by means of the mutual elimination of sexual characteristics rather than the hermaphroditic manifestation of complete sexual features. In the carefully chosen words of the *Gospel*, "the male will not be male nor the female be female." This sort of transformation is similar to that mentioned by Paul in Gal 3:27–28, where he transmits a baptismal formula pronounced over an initiate to show that the initiatory sacrament effects a oneness that overcomes the social, ethnic, and sexual categories of human existence: "[F]or all of you who were baptized into Christ have put on Christ. There is neither Jew nor Greek, there is neither slave nor free, *ouk eni arsen kai thēly* ("there is not male and female"); for you all are one in Christ Jesus."[16] Even closer to the approach of the *Gospel of Thomas* is the Hellenistic Jewish thinker Philo of Alexandria, whose writings in general resemble features of the *Gospel of Thomas* to a remarkable extent.[17] In terms of the present issue Philo insists that God, the logos, the heavenly human, and the rational soul are not associated with the sphere of male and female; rather, the male-female polarity is a feature of the lower, mortal, created world. Furthermore, this contrast also reflects the cosmic difference between "oneness" and "twoness." Clearly Philo values "oneness" over "twoness"; not only is God an unmixed oneness, but the human stamped with God's image is also an asexual unity. In his tract *De opificio mundi* Philo observes that, with regard to the heavenly human, "[T]he one that was after the (divine) image was an idea or type or seal, an object of thought (*noētos*), incorporeal, neither male nor female, by nature incorruptible" (134). Similarly, for a world lost in duality, salvation entails the movement from multiplicity to asexual unity once again.

To return to the *Gospel of Thomas:* like Philo, the *Gospel of Thomas* logion 22 also proclaims a salvific oneness and unity. Furthermore, in both sources the character of this unified state is not seen as androgynous, or supersexual, but instead as asexual.

The Female Becoming Male

If we may assess the evidence of the first four themes related to sexual imagery in the *Gospel of Thomas*, we conclude that they are unanimous in recommending asexuality. Whether through the adoption of appropriate motifs such as the nature of children and the essence of unification, or the adaptation of ideas like the family and the wedding chamber, the *Gospel of Thomas* announces that the properly spiritual person is one who transcends sexuality and renounces the enslaving life and divisive categories of sexuality, as a part of his or her renunciation of this world of darkness and acceptance of the world of freedom and light.

If this assessment is correct, then the fifth and final theme to be discussed presents us with an initial jolt: the concluding logion in the *Gospel of Thomas*, saying 114, states that if Mary is to realize salvation, she must become male. Indeed, one German commentator, Johannes Leipoldt, sadly concludes, "es ist bedauerlich, daß das Buch mit einem Mißklang endet." ("It is regrettable that the book ends with a dissonance.")[18] Although the *Gospel* elsewhere advocates a life exalted above the disjointed life of maleness over against femaleness, here the final saying appears to fall back into a crass chauvinism: "Simon Peter said to them (i.e., the other disciples), 'Mary should leave us, for females are not worthy of life.' Jesus said, 'Look, I shall guide her to make her male, so that she too may become a living spirit resembling you males. For every female who makes herself male will enter heaven's kingdom.' "

The German commentator just mentioned is representative of many modern readers, for whom the conclusion of the *Gospel of Thomas* is a considerable embarrassment. Many might wish that the final logion of the text could be removed from a document that otherwise is so consistent in its liberating message. Indeed, from a critical point of view, we could feel a certain amount of justification were we to judge saying 114 to be an alien intrusion into the gospel. After all, the *Gospel of Thomas* is a collection of sayings, and the addition of a new saying appended to the end of the collection would be a simple matter for a scribe copying out a new edition of the text. Furthermore, we know from the Oxyrhynchus papyri that there were in fact different versions or editions of the *Gospel of Thomas,* so that the suggestion that logion 114 might represent a later addition is not impossible. Finally, current scholarly opinion proposes some sort of a link between the Nag Hammadi library and Christian monks in the area, particularly the Pachomian brothers living at Pabau (modern Faw Qibli) — and monks might be especially tempted to add a saying like logion 114.[19]

On the basis of the evidence, however, I judge that it is unnecessary to hear a dissonant chord reverberating from the last saying of the *Gospel of Thomas.* Hence, in the following pages I shall suggest the conclusion that the message of logion 114 may be seen as harmonious with the rest of the *Gospel.*

If saying 114 in general makes modern readers feel uneasy, Peter in particular emerges as especially hostile toward Mary. While Jesus insists that Mary can be saved, Peter doubts even that! Peter's place in gnostic literature is prominent, which comes as no surprise considering the universal testimony in early Christian literature that Peter is not only an apostle but often the first of the apostles. Hence gnostic literature, too, has to come to terms with Peter. Sometimes, as in the *Apocalypse of Peter* and the *Letter of Peter to Philip,* Peter is made to function as an enlightened gnostic teacher. Adopted as a forthright guarantor of the gnostic Christian cause, Peter in such gnostic texts transcends the authority of the Great Church and the claims of the Great Church concerning him. At other times, as in the *Gospel of Thomas,* Peter is presented as an ignorant sexist, and may be portrayed in such a way as to reflect contemporary sexist attitudes in the Hellenistic environment and the Great Church, as perceived by the gnostics. Thus also in the *Gospel of Mary* Peter is pictured as hot-tempered, "contending against the woman (Mary) like the adversaries," even though, as Levi states, "the savior made her worthy" and "loved her more than us" (BG 18, 9–15). Similarly in *Pistis Sophia* Peter rails against Mary and the verbosity of her speeches; Mary in turn responds, "I am afraid of Peter, for he threatens me and hates our sex (*genos*)" (72).[20]

In the *Gospel of Thomas*, too, it is Mary against whom Peter speaks. A definite identification of this Mary is impossible; the possibilities include (in descending order of likelihood) Mary Magdalene, certainly the best single choice, Mary the mother of Jesus, Mary Salome, or some other Mary.[21] Perhaps the safest conclusion is that a "universal Mary" is in mind, and that specific historical Marys are no longer clearly distinguished, just as other historical personages may be blended into a "universal James" or a "universal Philip" in later Christian literature. On the other hand, Mary Magdalene does play a leading and specific role in such gnostic documents as the *Gospel of Philip*, where Mary Magdalene assumes the part of the true gnostic, and she and Jesus are described as having an intimate relationship with each other. In this *Gospel* it is said that Jesus loved Mary most of all the disciples and "[used to] kiss her [often] on her [mouth]" (II 63, 35–36). In the *Dialogue of the Savior*, too, a certain Mary — probably Magdalene — is addressed as "sister," is acclaimed as "a woman who knew all" (III 139, 12–13), and is taken in rapture with Judas and Matthew to the boundary of heaven and earth.

According to *Gospel of Thomas* logion 114 Mary will be saved when she becomes a male, a living spirit. Such a statement of sexual transformation is by no means rare in the ancient world, but may be found, with varying implications, in a number of sources. I cite a few examples of such statements by way of illustration. In his *Metamorphoses* books 9 and 12 Ovid speaks of women being changed into men in answer to prayer; thus do the gods answer prayer and deliver women from painful and difficult circumstances. In the *Timaeus* 90–91 Plato discusses similar matters in connection with reincarnation, and considers the possibilities of wicked men being punished with reincarnation as women (90E): in his hierarchy of beings women are considered to be situated below men and just above beasts (pity, then, the fate of wicked women!). In Egyptian mythology Isis can be said to make herself into a man (by being joined to Osiris? by bearing Horus?), and women can likewise be transformed, joined at death to the god Osiris. Within Christianity the Jewish Christians of the *Pseudo-Clementines* recommend that believers leave behind this inferior world, this lustful body — all that can be characterized as female — and embrace the higher world, the world of eternal life and spirit — which can be characterized as male. In this context we may also call to mind transvestite and other practices, whereby pious Christian women can be described as rejecting femininity and sexuality by dressing like men or looking like men: such is the case with the personified virtue Continence daughter of Faith in the Shepherd of Hermas, Thecla and Charitine in the apocryphal acts of the apostles, and so on. We may complete this quick survey by recalling the evidence, even down to the medieval inquisition records, that some Christians have suggested that women are changed into men in order to enter paradise.[22]

Of special importance for our discussion of sexual transformation in the *Gospel of Thomas* is Philo of Alexandria. Philo waxes perversely eloquent in the choice of colorful and descriptive phrases he uses to deride the imperfect status of femaleness. A partial list of such phrases includes the following: "weak, easily deceived, cause of sin, lifeless, diseased, enslaved, unmanly, nerveless, mean, slavish, sluggish."[23] As he explains in his *Quaestiones et solutiones in Exodum,* where he seems to allude to the absence of a penis on the female body, "the male is more perfect than the female. Wherefore it is said by the naturalists that the female is nothing else than an imperfect male" (book 1, 7).[24] For Philo the masculine principle is preferable to the feminine: after commenting on the feminine name and the masculine nature of wisdom, Philo continues by observing, in his tract *De fuga et inventione,* "As indeed all the virtues have women's titles, but powers and activities of consummate men (*andrōn teleiotatōn*). For that which comes after God, even though it may be the highest of all other things, occupies a second place, and therefore was termed feminine to express its contrast with the maker of the universe, who is masculine, and its affinity to everything else. For preeminence always pertains to the masculine, and the feminine always comes short of and is lesser than it" (51). Here Philo can symbolize as masculine what elsewhere, as we have seen, he describes as asexual. And here he establishes, in a fashion typical of several philosophical schools, a hierarchy of being, and claims that femaleness is on the side of passivity, corporeality, and *aisthēsis*, while maleness is on the side of activity, incorporeality, and *nous*. So progress, he concludes, "is indeed nothing else than the giving up of the female gender (*genos*) by changing into the male" (*Quaestiones et solutiones in Exodum*, book 1, 8). In my analysis Philo's brand of Hellenistic Judaism brings us very close to Gnosticism and especially the *Gospel of Thomas* in the use of terminology and theme.

Like Philo, and the *Gospel of Thomas*, other gnosticizing texts likewise can castigate femaleness and praise maleness, and recommend the transformation to maleness. In certain of these texts the female is portrayed like the fertility goddess, the earth mother, characterized, according to the gnostics, by passion, lust, and flesh. Indeed, like the fertility goddess, the female in gnostic interpretation can represent the human cycle of life, from birth to death. With regard to one typical manifestation of fertility piety, namely the piety expressed in the Eleusinian mysteries, the Christian heresiologist Hippolytus, in his discussion of the Naassene gnostics (*Refutatio omnium haeresium* 5.7.34), tells us that one of the most sacred of the utterances of the initiates is *hye kye*, "Give rain, give produce." This utterance is composed of two imperatives, one apparently directed to the sky father and the other to the earth mother. The situation evoked by these commands entails a cosmic act of intercourse between heaven and earth, with the semen of the sky entering the womb of the earth, thus producing a state of fertility and life in the world. To be sure, the Eleusinian mysteries, centering as they do on the careers of the two grain-goddesses of the earth, Demeter and Kore (or Persephone), admit that decrease and death are also part of the rhythm of the life cycle in the cosmos. Yet the mysteries celebrate the triumph of life over death, both in the realm of crops and in the life of humans, who may also transcend death through their initiation experiences.[25]

With a radicalization of these sorts of concerns, the gnostics have overturned the values of such fertility piety, and emphatically have shown the cycle of life to be a cycle of death. The focus is upon the earth, the arena of sexuality, procreation, and death, according to the gnostics. In the words of the tractate *On the Origin of the World*, "[T]he first sensual pleasure sprouted upon the earth. The woman followed the earth, and marriage followed the woman, and reproduction followed marriage, and death followed reproduction" (II 109, 21–25).[26] The source of all the manifestations of life and death, the female as depicted by the gnostics shows the ambiguities and possibilities of the fertility goddess: she can be mother, lover, revealer, bestower of life, and bringer of death. As mother Sophia, she can fall from grace in the divine realm, and through her blunder this world of passion and darkness comes into being, in a manner reminiscent of the fall of Eve as recounted in the Hebrew Bible. Yet even in her product, her "abortion of darkness" (*Apocryphon of John* BG 46, 10–11), there is a spark of light and life, for she is, after all, the divine mother. Hence, while the heavenly light is dimmed (the gnostics refer to this as the "deficiency," in contrast to the fullness) on account of "the disobedience and the foolishness of the mother" (*Ep. Pet. Phil.* VIII 135, 11–12), the light may be restored and the mother may be transformed, as the whole cosmic order is returned to heavenly bliss once again.

The fallen mother, and indeed all who participate in the "deficiency," may be transformed: this is the message of hope in many gnostic documents. But such a transformation frequently is depicted as overcoming all that is associated with the female in this world. According to the *Tripartite Tractate* from Nag Hammadi, when deprived of the male the female is weak (I 78, 8–13). In the *First Apocalypse of James* James apparently can call women "powerless vessels" (V 38, 21–22); in this case, however, these "powerless vessels" too have been transformed, and made potent. The female in this world, the *Dialogue of the Savior* insists, gives birth to mortality and death: in this text Christ is made to say, "The one who is from the truth does not die; the one who is from the woman dies" (III 140, 12–14). At times two cosmic realms may even be distinguished, as in the *Testimony of Truth,* where it seems that the male is put on the side of the day, the light, and the incorruptible, but the female is relegated to the night, the darkness, and the corruptible (IX 40, 23–29).

With such an image of the role of the female in this world, it is no wonder that some ascetic gnostic texts are clear in their denunciation of and opposition to the deeds of femaleness. If the *Book of Thomas* pronounces a woe upon those "who love intimacy with womankind and polluted intercourse with it" (II 144, 9–10), the *Dialogue of the Savior* is even more explicit in citing the command, "Destroy the works of femaleness" (III 144, 19–20).[27] Furthermore, the *Second Treatise of the Great Seth* warns the reader against becoming female, "that you may not give birth to evil and what is related to it: jealousy and division, anger and wrath, fear and a divided heart, and empty, non-existent desire" (VII 65, 24–31). Finally, a similar warning is issued by the Nag Hammadi text *Silvanus,* which counsels the readers against separating from the life of the *nous,* since then "you have cut off the male and turned yourself to the female alone," and have thus become *psychikos,* only a person of *psychē* (VII 93, 11–13).

Since for gnostics femaleness can encompass passion, earthliness, and mortality, it is reasonable to see how they can propose that all humans are involved in femaleness. Such universal participation in femaleness is made even more obvious by virtue of the Hellenistic theory on the soul. As has already been mentioned in passing, *psychē,* the feminine term for "soul," is presented throughout the Greek-speaking world as a female, and the subsequent myths of the soul show the career of the female *psychē* of all human beings. The Nag Hammadi library, too, includes a gnosticizing document recounting the myth of the soul. Entitled *Exegesis on the Soul,* this tractate gives a dramatic account of the fall, prostitution, and eventual salvation of the soul: she — indeed, every gnostic — finally is saved and transformed by being reunited with her heavenly brother in the spiritual wedding chamber.

If such is femaleness, gnostic texts are also clear in their praise of maleness. Often the male is portrayed, like the familiar sky father, as linked to that which is divine and heavenly; and maleness increasingly is removed from that which is sensual and mundane. Numerous divine beings — even female beings! — can be described with honorific epithets suggesting the supremacy of the category "male": the male virgin, the thrice-male child, the great male Barbelo, the thrice-male father, and so on. Sometimes tractates become so enamored of these honorific epithets and symbolic attributions that they stumble over their syntax, as in the *Three Steles of Seth,* which refers to "the malenesses that really are to become male three times" (VII 120, 17–19). Furthermore, as in Philo, gnostic texts specify that the *nous,* the mind and the link with the divine, is male. The tractate *Silvanus,* just quoted to illustrate a similar point, asserts that "reason and mind are male names" (VII 102, 15–16), and the *Testimony of Truth* commends the insight of the one who "is a disciple of the mind which is male" (IX 44, 2–3). Thus, in contrast to femaleness, the male in gnostic sources represents that which is on the side of mind, heavenliness, and perfection.

Several gnostic texts besides the *Gospel of Thomas* allude to the possibility that the female can be transformed, and depict this as the transformation of the female into the male. For our purposes four citations should suffice.[28] First of all, the fragmentary teachings of the

Valentinian teacher Theodotus, preserved in Clement of Alexandria's *Excerpta ex Theodoto*, state that the followers of Theodotus designate the male as angels, and the female as "themselves, the superior seed" (21.1). The excerpt goes on to describe how the female, that is to say, the Valentinian gnostics themselves, must become male and unite with the angels in order that she — or they — may enter into the fullness of the divine. "Therefore," the fragment summarizes in a parallel fashion, "it is said that the woman is changed into a man and the church here below into angels" (21.3). A later excerpt of Theodotus amplifies upon this idea, and indicates that when a female seed (i.e., the spark of light here below) becomes male it is liberated, for "no longer is it weak and subjected to the cosmic (powers)" (79). In a word, it has become heavenly. Secondly, the Naassenes as described by Hippolytus confess that only pure, transformed, spiritual people can approach "the gate of heaven," "the house of .God." Combining several of the sorts of motifs we have noted throughout this study, the Naassenes assert that "when people come there they must lay down their clothing and all become bridegrooms, being rendered wholly male through the virgin spirit" (*Refutatio* 5.8.44). Thirdly, the Nag Hammadi tractate that goes by the title *First Apocalypse of James* uses poetic parallelism to connect the female with perishability and the male with imperishability: "The perishable has [gone up] to the imperishable, and the female element has attained to this male element" (V 41, 15–18). And lastly, another Nag Hammadi tractate, *Zostrianos*, concludes with a dynamic sermon preached to awaken "an erring multitude" (VIII 130, 14), and part of the sermon is delivered as follows: "Flee from the madness and the bondage of femaleness, and choose for yourselves the salvation of maleness" (VIII 131, 5–8). Here again, as in the previous passages, the female is linked to the enslavement of earthly existence, and maleness promises true freedom.

In the wake of the preceding discussion, *Gospel of Thomas* logion 114 can be understood as quite compatible with the perspective of the rest of the *Gospel*. Although the categories "male" and "female" have a different symbolic value in the final logion from the rest of the tractate, these categories as employed in the *Gospel of Thomas* reflect the varieties of contemporary Hellenistic and gnostic usage. Indeed, they can do no other; and it is precisely here, on the symbolic values of "male" and "female," where more critical research is needed. Yet the message intended by saying 114 is appropriate within a world-renouncing, liberating document like the *Gospel of Thomas*. What is true for Mary as a woman is equally true for all those who participate in femaleness. Sensuality and sexuality are overcome, the dying cosmos of the mother goddess is transcended, and she — and all human beings — who are physical and earthly can be transformed to the spiritual and heavenly.

Notes

1. This study was first presented, in an earlier draft, as a paper for the symposium "In Her Image" held at the University of California at Santa Barbara in April 1980, and for the Hutchins Center for the Study of Democratic Institutions, Santa Barbara, in June 1980. Since then it has been discussed at a meeting of the New Testament Seminar at Claremont Graduate School in April 1983. I am indebted to various colleagues for their formal reactions to the paper at these meetings and their informal suggestions since then. Photographic reproductions of the Nag Hammadi texts may found in *The Facsimile Edition of the Nag Hammadi Codices* and English translations in *The Nag Hammadi Library in English* (Leiden: E. J. Brill; San Francisco: Harper & Row, 1977; paperback edition, 1981). Most of the translations of Nag Hammadi texts used in this essay are based on the latter volume, though at times I have modified the translation in consultation with the Coptic text. The translations of the sayings from the *Gospel of Thomas* are from Meyer, *The Gospel of Thomas*. The references to Nag Hammadi texts (except the *Gospel of Thomas*, where sayings numbers are employed) include codex numerals, and page and line numbers; the abbreviation BG refers to the Berlin Gnostic Codex 8502, which is similar to the Nag Hammadi texts and is published along with them.

2. On the interpretation of the *Gospel of Thomas* cf. the entries listed in David M. Scholer, *Nag Hammadi Bibliography 1948–1969* (NHS 1; Leiden: E. J. Brill, 1971), updated annually in the autumn issue of *Novum Testamentum*. For a fine article reviewing the various approaches see Gilles Quispel, "The *Gospel of Thomas* Revisited," in *Colloque internationale sur les Textes de Nag Hammadi* (ed. B. Barc; Quebec: L'Université Laval, 1981), 218–66. A brief, balanced discussion has also appeared in John Dominic Crossan, *Four Other Gospels: Shadows on the Contours of Canon* (Minneapolis: Winston [Seabury], 1985), 23–37.

3. Cf. the excellent study by Ernst Haenchen, "Die Anthropologie des Thomas-Evangeliums," in *Neues Testament und christliche Existenz: Festschrift für Herbert Braun* (ed. H. D. Betz and L. Schottroff; Tübingen: J. C. B. Mohr [Paul Siebeck], 1973), 207–27.

4. On Jewish Christianity, Gnosticism, and the *Gospel of Thomas*, cf. Alexander Böhlig, "Der jüdische und judenchristliche Hintergrund in gnostischen Texten von Nag Hammadi," in *Le Origini dello gnosticismo* (ed. U. Bianchi; Leiden: E. J. Brill, 1967), 109–40; Henri-Charles Puech, "The Gospel of Thomas," in *New Testament Apocrypha*, vol. 1 (ed. E. Hennecke and W. Schneemelcher; Philadelphia: Westminster, 1963), 278–307; Gilles Quispel, "Gnosticism and the New Testament," *VC*

19 (1965): 65–85; R. McL. Wilson, "Jewish Christianity and Gnosticism," *RSR* 60 (1972): 261–72.

5. See Werner Foerster, *Gnosis* (vol. 1; Oxford: Clarendon, 1972), 27–32.

6. Discussion and references may be found in Joseph Klausner, *Jesus of Nazareth* (New York: Macmillan, 1925), 17–54.

7. On the restoration see Layton, *Nag Hammadi Codex II,2–7*, 1.88–89; *The Nag Hammadi Library in English*, 129; Meyer, *The Secret Teachings of Jesus* (New York: Random House, 1984), 107 ("For my mother [brought me forth]"?).

8. Further discussion in Elaine H. Pagels, "What Became of God the Mother? Conflicting Images of God in Early Christianity," *Signs* 2 (1976): 293–303; Elaine H. Pagels, *The Gnostic Gospels* (New York: Random House, 1979), 48–69.

9. Note, for example, *Acts John* 93; *Treat. Seth* VII 55,9–56,19; Coptic *Apocalypse of Peter* VII 81,3–24; Irenaeus, *Adversus haereses* 1.24.4.

10. *Adversus haereses* 1.7.2; *Panarion* 31.7.4; see the brief discussion, with additional bibliography, in Marvin Meyer, *The Letter of Peter to Philip*, 154–57, 186–87.

11. Cf. Robert M. Grant, "The Mystery of Marriage in the Gospel of Philip," *VC* 15 (1961): 129–40.

12. The question of whether or not a flagrantly libertine Gnosticism existed in the ancient world remains controversial. For two approaches cf. Hans Jonas, *The Gnostic Religion* (Boston: Beacon, 1963), 270–81, and Frederik Wisse, "Die Sextus-Sprüche und das Problem der gnostischen Ethik," in *Zum Hellenismus in den Schriften von Nag Hammadi* (ed. A. Böhlig and F. Wisse; Wiesbaden: Otto Harrassowitz, 1975), 55–86.

13. On the place of children in the *Gospel of Thomas*, and antiquity in general, see J. Z. Smith, "The Garments of Shame," 217–38; Gärtner, *The Theology of the Gospel*, 217–29.

14. A Jewish boy was usually circumcised on the eighth day; cf. Gen 17:12, Phil 3:5.

15. Note may be taken, however, of several items relevant for logion 22: 2 *Clem.* 12; Clement of Alexandria, *Stromateis* 3.13 §92; Marie Delcourt, *Hermaphrodite* (London: Studio Books, 1961); Mircea Eliade, *Mephistopheles and the Androgyne* (New York: Sheed & Ward, 1965); Klijn, "The 'Single One,'" 271–78; especially Meeks, "The Image of the Androgyne," 165–208.

16. Note that Paul's style involves "neither...nor" constructions except for the description of "male and female," which may hark back to Gen 1:27 and the distinguishing of the two sexes. See the discussion in Hans Dieter Betz, *Galatians* (Hermeneia; Philadelphia: Fortress, 1979), 195–200.

17. Cf. Klijn, "The 'Single One,'" esp. pp. 276–78. Particularly helpful for the present discussion has been Richard A. Baer, *Philo's Use of the Categories Male and Female* (Leiden: E. J. Brill, 1970). Here the text consulted and translations employed (with occasional modification) for Philo are taken from the Loeb Classical Library edition.

18. Leipoldt, *Das Evangelium nach Thomas*, 77. James LaGrand has echoed these sentiments by charging that logion 114 contains "the most outrageous sayings in *Thomas*.... Peter's request... seems cruel and misogynist, and Jesus' response seems

to do nothing more than temper the inhumane spirit of the request with casuistry" ("How Was the Virgin Mary 'Like a Man'?" *NovT* 22 [1980] 106–7). Similarly, John Dominic Crossan finds "ineffable chauvinism" in logion 114 (*Four Other Gospels*, 34).

19. Cf. Davies, *The Gospel of Thomas and Christian Wisdom*, 152–53. For a discussion on the possible Pachomian provenance of the Nag Hammadi library, see James M. Robinson, "Introduction," in *The Nag Hammadi Library in English* (Leiden: E. J. Brill; San Francisco: Harper & Row, 1977; paperback edition, 1981); Frederik Wisse, "Gnosticism and Early Monasticism in Egypt," in *Gnosis: Festschrift für Hans Jonas* (ed. B. Aland; Göttingen: Vandenhoeck & Ruprecht, 1978), 431–40. On the Greek fragments cf. Marcovich, "Textual Criticism on the *Gospel of Thomas*," 53–74.

20. On Peter in gnostic literature cf. Pheme Perkins, "Peter in Gnostic Revelation," *Society of Biblical Literature: 1974 Seminar Papers*, vol. 2 (ed. G. W. MacRae; Cambridge, Mass.: Society of Biblical Literature, 1974), 1–13; Pheme Perkins, *The Gnostic Dialogue* (New York: Paulist, 1980), 113–56. For a Coptic text and English translation of the *Pistis Sophia* see Carl Schmidt and Violet MacDermot, *Pistis Sophia* (NHS 9; Leiden: E. J. Brill, 1978).

21. Cf. *The Interpreter's Dictionary of the Bible*, vol. 3 (Nashville: Abingdon, 1962), 288–93, for descriptions of the several women named Mary in the early Christian movement.

22. Cf. Ovid, *Metamorphoses* 9.666 ff.; 12.171 ff. (see also Plutarch, *Quomodo quis suos in virtute sentiat profectus* 75EF; Phlegon of Tralles, *Mirabilia* 6 [a young girl sprouts male genitals, καὶ ἡ κόρη ἀνὴρ ἐγένετο], etc.; Delcourt, *Hermaphrodite*, 33–43); Plato, *Timaeus* 42A-D; Hermann Kees, *Aegypten* (*Religionsgeschichtliches Lesebuch;* ed. A. Bertholet; Tübingen: J. C. B. Mohr [Paul Siebeck], 1928), 18, 30 (also K. H. Rengstorf, "Urchristliches Kerygma und 'gnostische' Interpretation in einigen Sprüchen des Thomasevangeliums," *Le Origini dello Gnosticismo,* 569–72); *Pseudo-Clementine Homilies* 2.15, 3.27, 19.23, 20.2; Herm.*Vis.* 3.8.4; *Acts of Paul and Thecla* 40; *Acts of Philip* 44 (Delcourt, *Hermaphrodite*, 84–102); Puech, "The Gospel of Thomas," 303 (references to medieval inquisition records; cf. F. P. Badham and F. C. Conybeare, "Fragments of an Ancient (? Egyptian) Gospel Used by the Cathars of Albi," *HibJ* 11 [1913]: 805–18, along with Grant and Freedman, *The Secret Sayings of Jesus,* 81–82, 197–98); also Clement of Alexandria, *Stromateis* 6.12 §100; Methodius of Olympus, *Symposium* 8.7–8.

23. Compiled by Meeks, "The Image of the Androgyne," 176, from Baer, *Philo's Use of the Categories Male and Female,* 42.

24. Note may also be taken of the male devotees of the Great Mother Cybele and Attis. In moments of religious frenzy and ecstasy, such worshipers could achieve the ultimate identification with Attis through an act of self-castration. Thereafter such a man can be described by Augustine as *effeminatus* and *semivir;* in poem 63 of Catullus such an emasculated person is said to have become a woman! Cf. Maarten J. Vermaseren, *Cybele and Attis* (London: Thames & Hudson, 1977), esp. 181–82. On the Naassene gnostics participating in these mysteries, but drawing spiritual or ethical conclusions, see Hippolytus, *Refutatio omnium haeresium* 5.6.3–11.1, esp. 5.7.13–15 and 5.9.10–11.

25. On this utterance in the Eleusinian mysteries cf. also Proclus, *In Timaeum* 293C; K. Kerényi, *Eleusis* (New York: Schocken, 1977), 141–42. In general see Ugo Bianchi, *Le Origini dello Gnosticismo* (Leiden: E. J. Brill, 1967), 9–13, 724–27, 740–44. Here it may be recalled that while numerous religious traditions within the Indo-European sphere posit a sky father and an earth mother, other Mediterranean traditions can suggest a sky mother and an earth father; cf. Egypt, with Nut the heavenly mother, her star-studded body arching over the earth and supported by the four pillars, that is, her arms and legs, and Geb the earth father, whose bodily undulations can represent the topographical features on the face of the earth.

26. This passage in the tract *On the Origin of the World* has been emended by Hans-Gebhard Bethge; see the resultant translation in *The Nag Hammadi Library in English*, 168. For a parallel to this passage cf. the *Authoritative Teaching* VI 23, 7–26.

27. The conclusion to the text *Dialogue of the Savior*, still fragmentary, has been improved considerably through the identification of a fragment now at Yale University; cf. Stephen Emmel, "A Fragment of Nag Hammadi Codex III in the Beinecke Library: Yale Inv. 1784," *BASP* 17 (1980): 53–60 (see the paperback edition of *The Nag Hammadi Library in English*, 237–38). On the particular statement in question cf. also Clement of Alexandria, *Stromateis* 3.9 §63.

28. The translations of Clement of Alexandria and Hippolytus are taken from Foerster, *Gnosis*. Additional references to the female becoming male may be found in the Valentinian gnostic Heracleon's comments (fragment 5) on John 1:23 (in Foerster, *Gnosis*, vol. 1, 163), and in the Nag Hammadi text *Marsanes* X 9, 1–3 (see Birger A. Pearson, *Nag Hammadi Codices IX and X* [NHS 15; Leiden: E. J. Brill, 1981], 274–75). Here I am concerned only with statements recommending sexual transformation, where the female is specifically said to become male (Coptic ϩοογⲧ). Mary's statement in the *Gospel of Mary* (BG 9, 18–20) that the savior has "made us into men" employs the more neutral ⲣⲱⲙⲉ, and thus is a statement describing humanization (against Pagels, *The Gnostic Gospels*, 67; and Perkins, *The Gnostic Dialogue*, 134, 140–41; cf. also the *Gospel of Mary* 18, 16 (ⲣⲱⲙⲉ) par. P. Ryl. 463 (ἄνθρωπον), Ignatius's *Romans* 6.2 (ἄνθρωπος ἔσομαι), and probably Eph 4:13 (εἰς ἄνδρα τέλειον). Further, it should be noted that the possibility of the transformation as described in logion 114 may be paralleled by the suggestion of the transformation of the lion in the enigmatic saying 7 (this leonine logion is the subject of the Ph.D. dissertation of Howard M. Jackson, Claremont Graduate School, 1983, published as *The Lion Becomes Man: The Gnostic Leontomorphic Creator and the Platonic Tradition* [SBLDS 81; Atlanta: Scholars, 1985]). As there is hope for the woman, claims the *Gospel of Thomas*, so also is there hope for the lion.

6

Gospel of Thomas
Saying 114 Revisited

Simon Peter said to them, "Mary should leave us, for females are not worthy of life." Jesus said, "Look, I shall guide her to make her male, so that she too may become a living spirit resembling you males. For every female who makes herself male will enter heaven's kingdom" (*Gos. Thom.* 114).[1]

With these words that seem to flaunt blatantly patriarchal values, the Nag Hammadi edition of the *Gospel of Thomas* comes to a close. Many students of Nag Hammadi texts have mused on these words, and not a few have offered interpretations to help explain them. Hence, it seems entirely appropriate that we revisit that last, perplexing saying in the *Gospel of Thomas*.

A number of years ago I too entered the Thomasite hermeneutical arena by addressing *Gos. Thom.* 114. I attempted to interpret saying 114 within the larger context of the use of the categories "male" and "female" in the *Gospel of Thomas*.[2] I tried to identify some of the ways in which gender and gender transformation were evaluated in the Greco-Roman world, and on the basis of this I concluded that *Thomas* 114 employed the categories "male" and "female" symbolically to proclaim a message of liberation:

[T]he message intended by saying 114 is appropriate within a world-renouncing, liberating document like the *Gospel of Thomas*. What is true for Mary as a woman is equally true for all those who participate in femaleness. Sensuality and sexuality are overcome, the dying cosmos of the mother goddess is transcended, and she — and all human beings — who are physical and earthly can be transformed to the spiritual and heavenly.[3]

Other scholars have also traversed the intellectual landscape of antiquity and late antiquity in search of themes and parallels to help explain *Thomas* 114.[4] The search has proved to be an intellectual adventure yielding interesting and oftentimes curious results. Some scholars have recognized a similar sort of misogyny in other ancient and late antique sources, such as the *Gospel of Mary* and *Pistis Sophia*, while others have been more optimistic in sensing that the saying in *Thomas* advocates androgyny or even the elevation of Mary. Some scholars have pointed to parallels in the *Pseudo-Clementines*, in gnostic texts, in sources recommending transvestite practices, or elsewhere. One scholar has singled out the lament of Isis, "I made myself into a man," to explain *Thomas* 114. Jorunn Jacobsen Buckley has understood *Thomas* 114 to reflect an initiation ritual with two stages of transformation, female into male and male into living spirit. This recalls Gen 2, she has suggested, and the transformation is something like a "backward" or reversed creation, back to the future, if you will. Stevan Davies and others have despaired of understanding *Thomas* 114 in a way that might be compatible with the rest of the gospel, for example saying 22, and so Davies has proposed in *The Gospel of Thomas and Christian Wisdom* that saying 114 is a later addition to the *Gospel of Thomas*. He has done so on the basis of four considerations: (1) the literary device of Peter addressing the other followers occurs nowhere else in the gospel; (2) the theme of Jesus "guiding" someone occurs nowhere else in the gospel; (3) the theme of becoming a living spirit occurs nowhere else in the gospel; and (4) saying 114 is in direct contradiction to saying 22.

I here return to *Gos. Thom.* saying 114 and advance four suggestions for the ongoing discussion of this elusive saying. My suggestions are meant to guide and limit the interpretation of *Thomas* 114. If it seems that some of these suggestions run counter to my own earlier interpretation of *Thomas* 114, then kindly accept this essay as a statement of partial repentance.

Gospel of Thomas

First, to be fair to the complexity and vigor of the Thomas tradition and the collections within the tradition, we do well to consider not simply the Coptic translation of the *Gospel of Thomas* but also the Greek versions, and to be cautious about drawing conclusions regarding the overall theology and message of the gospel.

The manuscript evidence for the *Gospel of Thomas* includes the Coptic translation (almost certainly from a Greek original) in the fourth-century Nag Hammadi collection of codices housed at the Coptic Museum in Cairo, and three Greek Oxyrhynchus papyrus fragments (1, 654, 655), housed in the Bodleian Library at Oxford, the British Library, and Houghton Library at Harvard. The similarities among these manuscripts suggest that all represent versions of what we now call the *Gospel of Thomas,* but the differences extend to matters of wording and order of sayings. This fluidity in the textual tradition of the Gospel — or Gospels — of Thomas is underscored by the evidence of the testimonies. In his discussion of the Naassenes, Hippolytus of Rome cites a saying, only partially parallel to *Thomas* 4, that he claims comes from a *Gospel of Thomas.*[5] Later he cites another saying of the Naassenes, and although he does not assert that it derives from *Thomas,* it parallels, again only in part, *Thomas* 11.[6] Further, among other testimonia are several statements declaring that a *Gospel of Thomas* was in use among the Manichaeans; Cyril of Jerusalem (*Catechesis* 6.31) charges that this Thomas was no follower of Jesus, but rather was one of the wicked followers of Mani. Within the Manichaean Psalm Book there are also a goodly number of themes and phrases reminiscent of the *Gospel of Thomas.*

As a collection of sayings, the *Gospel of Thomas* is open to easy modification. In the *Gospel of Thomas,* sayings could theoretically be added, deleted, and rearranged with little difficulty, particularly since no large organizational scheme, such as that proposed by Stevan Davies, seems operative in the *Gospel of Thomas,* but only limited points of linkage supplied by *Stichwörter* and small subcollections of parables and similar sayings. The limited evidence of the Coptic manuscript and the Oxyrhynchus papyrus fragments seems to support such possibilities of modification.

If, then, sayings in the Thomas tradition may have gone through significant changes and modification, we may well speak of Gospels of Thomas rather than a *Gospel of Thomas.* We may follow what Helmut Koester has done with the Markan tradition where he has isolated gospel texts (including *Secret Mark,* canonical Mark, Matthew, Luke, and Carpocratian Mark) as representing a continuously developing Markan tradition.[7] And as a result, if we speak of Gospels of Thomas, we shall need to reflect upon the likelihood of a multiplicity of perspectives, points of view, and literary styles in the production of the Gospels of Thomas.

All of this, of course, will have obvious implications for our interpretation of *Thomas* 114. We may acknowledge saying 114 in the Coptic *Gospel of Thomas* within the Nag Hammadi library, but we may be open to a number of options in the textual history of the saying, even the suggestion (with which I still disagree; see below) that *Thomas* 114 is a late and idiosyncratic addition. And we may exercise more modesty about the theology or message of the *Gospel of Thomas* as a whole and the place of saying 114 within the gospel.

Interactive Interpretations

Second, to be fair to the hermeneutical principle articulated at the opening of the *Gospel of Thomas,* we do well to approach the sayings of *Thomas* as hidden sayings that invite and even require interpretation, so that a given saying, such as *Thomas* 114, may be sufficiently and deliberately vague to allow for different interpretations. In other words, there may be no single, authoritative interpretation of saying 114 at all, or at least none we can ever recover.

The *Gospel of Thomas* is said to be composed of *ᵉnšaje ethēp* — hidden sayings, secret sayings, or with Bentley Layton, obscure sayings.[8] The riddle-like quality of the sayings is established at the opening of the gospel: "Whoever discovers the interpretation of these sayings will not taste death" (saying 1). The sayings by themselves are inconclusive and of little value, unless they are interpreted. Layton puts it well: "Without recognition of their hidden meaning, Jesus' sayings are merely 'obscure.' "[9] But then Layton goes on to say that the interpretive clue of the hidden meaning of the sayings is hinted at in *Thomas* 18, 29, and 50, sayings that Layton claims reflect the Hellenistic myth of the soul. I am not as confident as Layton about this identification of the interpretive clue, though it is attractive to connect the supposedly key sayings in the *Gospel of Thomas* to a tradition like that of the "Hymn of the Pearl." Nor am I confident that we are able to locate a single hermeneutical key to unlock the entirety of the Gospel — or Gospels — of Thomas.

"These are the hidden sayings" — what characterizes all these sayings is that they are all hidden, that is to say, they are all capable of interpretation and in fact require interpretation. Such is self-evident in some cases, for example, the four riddles of saying 11, or perhaps the parables. Yet all the sayings in the *Gospel of Thomas,* including saying 114, are hidden and demand interpretation. It seems that it is in and through this quest for meaning, the meaning of hidden sayings, that one is to find oneself and God, according to the *Gospel of Thomas.* In short, the *Gospel of Thomas*'s sayings require interaction.

Richard Valantasis has taken an approach rather like this in his recent study of the *Gospel of Thomas.*[10] He calls the theology of the *Gospel of Thomas* a performative theology, and he describes the interpretation of the hidden sayings in this manner:

> The readers and the interpreters of sayings . . . construct their own narrative and theology linking the individual sayings into a cohesive text. In that strategy, the readers mirror the activity of the recorder [here I would say recorders] of the sayings who has already constructed a meaningful meta-text [here I would say texts] of collected individual sayings. The recorder has also constructed a voice for the meta-text and described that voice as the "living Jesus" whose speaking conveys life, meaning, knowledge, immortality, and all the riches of the kingdom.[11]

Again, "the theology emerges from the readers' and the hearers' responses to the sayings and their sequence and their variety."[12] Valantasis is, I believe, on the right track.

Gos. Thom. saying 114 is a saying that remains in a number of respects hidden and obscure. We do not know what sort of editor incorporated the saying into the collection, when, nor why it was incorporated; we do not know how early readers interpreted the saying — readers who were seekers of the wisdom of Jesus, the Thomasite Christians who belonged to this tradition, gnostics, Manichaeans, mystics of one sort or another, or Pachomian monks who perused the Nag Hammadi texts. All such readers may have sought to discover the interpretation of this saying, but the saying is open to a wide variety of interpretations.

Patriarchal Values

Third, however early readers — or we, for that matter — decide to interpret *Thomas* 114, they — and we — do well to seek an interpretation among the options offered by the patriarchal world of antiquity and late antiquity, which exalted the phallus, literally and symbolically, in several different ways.

In her book *The Reign of the Phallus* Eva Keuls describes the power of men and the repression of women in classical Athens by interpreting the literature and the art of the period, and she concludes that Athens was a phallocracy, which championed males and male power with images and themes of the triumph of the phallus and the suppression of women.[13] These images can be seen in the art of the period and the perspectives of many an ancient author. In Plato and others, for instance, a hierarchy of beings is established, and in the *Timaeus* Plato suggests that women are situated below men and just above beasts. Reincarnation, then, entails moving up and down the ladder of beings: a punishment may involve becoming female in the next life, a reward may involve becoming male. Karen Torjesen has added that many of these statements exalting maleness and devaluing femaleness may reflect classical and post-classical biological and philosophical theories supporting a single sex, the male with his phallus being more perfect and complete, and the female being less perfect and incomplete, and even stunted or inverted.[14]

As we noted in passing earlier in this essay, other ancient texts and traditions besides *Thomas* 114 exalt maleness and recommend that the female become male. Further, within gnostic texts this theme of gender transformation, with the female becoming male, occurs quite frequently. I have discussed these texts elsewhere and I need not rehearse them here again. This theme continues on down through medieval inquisition records concerning the Cathari.[15] We may wish to admit that this theme actually continues in subtle and not so subtle ways to the present day. In these texts the female is typically depreciated — a better word may be demonized — and comes to symbolize perishability, corporeality, and all that characterizes this mortal world, while the male typically is glorified and comes to symbolize imperishability, incorporeality, and all that characterizes God and God's world. Being male and becoming male is lauded, but being female and becoming female is deplored, as in the *Second Treatise of the Great Seth,* where Jesus commands, "Do not become female, that you may not give birth to evil and what is related to it: jealousy and division, anger and wrath, fear and a divided heart, and empty, nonexistent desire" (NHC VII,2:65,24–31).

Rarely does a religious text from antiquity and late antiquity recommend that one become female. However, occasionally a more positive assessment can be given to the male becoming female. Here we might also recall the more feminine appearance of Dionysos in the *Bacchae,* where he appears with fair skin and long curls, and he is questioned about this appearance by the macho-man Pentheus, who himself later cross-dresses as a woman, only to be torn to pieces when exposed as a peeping Pentheus. One rather positive assessment of the male becoming female is given within the context of the mysteries of the Great Mother Cybele and Attis, mysteries that at times feature flamboyant male followers of the Great Mother emulating the mythical act of Attis and, in a state of ecstasy, castrating themselves, thus becoming Galli. Thereafter, they could go about dressed in women's clothing, as drag queens of the Great Mother, for they had become female. The Latin poet Catullus reflects upon the deed done by an initiate — *notha mulier,* "a counterfeit woman" — and has the initiate say, when he (or she) awakens from his (or her) stupor,

A woman now, I have been man, youth, and boy;
I was athlete, the wrestler.
There were crowds round my door, my fans slept on the doorstep;
There were flowers all over the house
When I left my bed at sunrise.
Shall I be a waiting maid to the gods, a slave of Cybele?
I a maenad, I a part of myself, I impotent?

The more positive aspect of this confession about the male becoming female is given a more realistic twist, however, when the initiate goes on to say, "I regret now, now, what I have done, I repent of it, now!" Catullus agrees, and prays at the end of his poem to the Great Mother Cybele,

May all your fury be far from my house.
Incite the others, go. Drive other men mad.[16]

Also in agreement are Christian authors, like Arnobius and Augustine, who were fascinated and horrified by the wild spectacles of the Galli.

Arnobius calls them *semiviri,* Augustine terms them *effeminati.* Nonetheless, these savage acts of self-castration may have made an impact upon Christianity, especially among the Montanists and ascetics who chose to attain greater spirituality through castration, and thus become God's eunuchs.[17]

Whether the language of gender transformation in the *Gos. Thom.* saying 114 is completely consonant with saying 22 may remain somewhat uncertain. *Thomas* 22 affirms that you will enter the kingdom when, among other things, "you make male and female into a single one (*oua ouōt*), so that the male will not be male nor the female be female." This smacks of androgyny, though the repudiation of both maleness and femaleness may give us reason to pause. Richard Valantasis labels this the third gender (compare males, females, and androgynes in, for example, Plato's *Symposium*). In her recent doctoral dissertation Donna Wallace studies such sources as Ovid's *Metamorphoses* and concludes that bisexuality or androgyny may sometimes be equated with asexuality.[18] Further, Philo of Alexandria gives ample evidence that it was possible for a single author to articulate both the transformation of the female into male (in *Quaestiones et solutiones in Exodum*) and the sexual or asexual oneness of the divine and the human stamped with God's image (in *De opificio mundi*).[19] Indeed, in a particular way of considering androgyny, is not the female becoming male a transformation into androgyny, a sexual completeness and perfection, as the single sex theories maintain, for the imperfect female sprouts a phallus and therein attains androgynous wholeness? Donna Wallace struggles to understand sayings 22 and 114, and she concludes by affirming that both sayings advocate a kind of androgyny, in the first case (saying 22) what she calls "pure androgyny," in the second case (saying 114) what she calls "male androgyny."[20] While I am not altogether pleased with this nomenclature, I certainly agree, against Stevan Davies, that sayings 22 and 114 do not necessarily contradict each other, and that becoming male may be understood in an androgynous fashion. Such also seems implied by Phlegon of Tralles, who, writing in his *Mirabilia,* describes the young woman Philotis growing a penis and becoming a man, as an androgyne.[21]

I remain convinced, as I suggested some years ago, that the most compelling interpretation of *Gos. Thom.* saying 114 is a symbolic interpretation. On this point I remain unrepentant. Mary becomes male, the female becomes male, we all become male symbolically when what is physical and earthly is transformed into what is spiritual and heavenly. This use of gender categories may be offensive to our modern sensitivities, but what is intended in the *Gospel of Thomas,* in my interpretation, is a message of liberation.

Transformations

Fourth, and briefly, we do well to keep in mind that *Gos. Thom.* 114, like many other sayings in the *Gos. Thom.,* advocates transformation.[22] The language of transformation in Coptic often uses a form of the verb *šōpe* (become) or its equivalent. In the Coptic *Gospel of Thomas* salvific transformation occurs when the first will be last and will become a single one (saying 4), when the lion will become human (saying 7), when the two will become one — "But," Jesus goes on to warn, "when you become two, what will you do?" (saying 11). Again, transformation occurs when the inner is like the outer, and the outer is like the inner, and the upper like the lower, and eyes replace an eye, and a hand replaces a hand, and a foot replaces a foot, and an image replaces an image (saying 22). Once again, transformation occurs, Jesus says, when one drinks from his mouth and becomes like him, and Jesus himself "shall become that person" (saying 108). So when the Coptic text concludes with the stark assertion that the female needs to become male, it does so in the interests of the transformation of the person, whoever he or she might be, who is trying to discover the interpretation of these hidden sayings.

Notes

1. Unless otherwise indicated, the translations employed in this essay are my own. See Meyer, *The Gospel of Thomas.* A version of this essay was presented at the annual meeting of the Society of Biblical Literature in Boston, November 1999. My thanks to colleagues for their comments at that time and since. This essay was originally published in a volume dedicated to Hans-Martin Schenke, a colleague who did a great deal to advance the study of Nag Hammadi texts and to propose creative and bold solutions to interpretive dilemmas within those texts.

2. Meyer, "Making Mary Male," 554–70.

3. Ibid., 567.

4. Compare the sources listed in Meyer, "Making Mary Male." To the studies mentioned there the following, among others, may be added: Peter Brown, *The Body and Society: Men, Women, and Sexual Renunciation in Early Christianity* (New

York: Columbia University Press, 1988); Jorunn Jacobsen Buckley, "An Interpretation of Logion 114 in *The Gospel of Thomas*," *NovT* 27 (1985): 245–72; Jorunn Jacobsen Buckley, *Female Fault and Fulfillment in Gnosticism* (Chapel Hill and London: University of North Carolina Press, 1986); Elizabeth Castelli, " 'I Will Make Mary Male': Pieties of the Body and Gender Transformation of Christian Women in Late Antiquity," in *Body Guards: The Cultural Politics of Gender Ambiguity* (ed. Julia Epstein and Kristina Straub; London and New York: Routledge, 1991), 29–49; Davies, *The Gospel of Thomas and Christian Wisdom;* Ismo Dunderberg, "Thomas' I-sayings and the Gospel of John," in *Thomas at the Crossroads* (ed. Risto Uro; Edinburgh: T. & T. Clark, 1998), 33–64; Anne McGuire, "Women, Gender, and Gnosis in Gnostic Texts and Traditions," in *Women and Christian Origins* (ed. Ross S. Kraemer and Mary R. D'Angelo; New York and Oxford: Oxford University Press, 1999), 257–99; Elaine H. Pagels, "Exegesis of Genesis 1 in the Gospels of Thomas and John," *JBL* 118 (1999): 477–96.

5. Hippolytus, *Refutatio omnium haeresium* 5.7.20: " . . . concerning which they explicitly teach in the Gospel entitled 'According to Thomas,' saying thus, 'One who seeks will find me in children from seven years, for there, hidden in the fourteenth age, I am revealed.' "

6. Hippolytus, *Refutatio omnium haeresium* 5.8.32: "So they say, 'If you ate dead things and made them living, what will you do if you eat living things?' "

7. Helmut Koester, "History and Development of Mark's Gospel," 35–57. Compare also Hans-Martin Schenke, "The Mystery of the Gospel of Mark," *SecCent* 4 (1984): 65–82.

8. Layton, *The Gnostic Scriptures*, 376–99.

9. Ibid., 376.

10. Valantasis, *The Gospel of Thomas*.

11. Ibid., 196.

12. Ibid., 7.

13. Eva C. Keuls, *The Reign of the Phallus: Sexual Politics in Ancient Athens* (Berkeley: University of California Press, 1993).

14. Karen Torjesen, "Wisdom, Christology, and Women Prophets," pp. 186–200 in *Jesus Then and Now: Images of Jesus in History and Christology*, ed. Marvin Meyer and Charles Hughes (Harrisburg, Pa.: Trinity Press International, 2001), especially p. 196; Thomas Laqueur, *Making Sex: Body and Gender from the Greeks to Freud* (Cambridge, Mass.: Harvard University Press, 1990).

15. Compare I. Döllinger, *Beiträge zur Sektengeschichte des Mittelalters*, vol. 2 (Darmstadt: Wissenschaftliche Buchgesellschaft, 1968), 191; Badham and Conybeare, "Fragments of an Ancient (? Egyptian) Gospel," 805–18.

16. Catullus, *Poem 63;* the translation is that of C. H. Sisson, as given in Meyer, *The Ancient Mysteries*, 127–28.

17. Compare Vermaseren, *Cybele and Attis*, 181–82.

18. Donna Kennon Wallace, "Androgyny as Salvation in Early Christianity" (Ph.D. diss., Claremont Graduate University, 2000). In this connection Wallace makes special mention of the work of Marie Delcourt and Georgia Nugent. The literature on androgyny is immense. Compare, among other studies, Delcourt, *Hermaphrodite;* Eliade, *Mephistopheles and the Androgyne;* Klijn, "The 'Single One' in

the Gospel of Thomas," 271–78; MacDonald, *There Is No Male and Female*; Meeks, "The Image of the Androgyne," 165–208; Georgia Nugent, "The Sex Which Is Not One: Deconstructing Ovid's Hermaphrodite," *Differences* 2 (1990): 160–85; June Singer, *Androgyny: Toward a New Theory of Sexuality* (Garden City, N.Y.: Anchor Press/Doubleday, 1976); Elémire Zolla, *The Androgyne: Reconciliation of Male and Female* (New York: Crossroad, 1981).

19. Compare Baer, *Philo's Use of the Categories Male and Female*.

20. Wallace, "Androgyny as Salvation in Early Christianity," 103–41, 241–43.

21. Phlegon of Tralles, *Mirabilia* 7. Here (compare elsewhere in Phlegon) Philotis is described as an ἀνδρόγυνος, and in the tale that is told Phlegon writes, μορίων αὐτῇ προφανέντων ἀρρενικῶν ἀνὴρ ἐγένετο. Hence Philotis became a man — and an androgyne. See also Ovid's *Metamorphoses*.

22. On the theme of transformation in the *Gospel of Thomas*, see also Meyer, "Albert Schweitzer and the Image of Jesus," 72–90.

Part Two

SECRET GOSPEL
OF MARK

After Mark 10:34

And they come to Bethany. This woman whose brother had died was there. She came and knelt before Jesus and says to him, "Son of David, have mercy on me." But the followers rebuked her.

Then Jesus became angry and went with her into the garden where the tomb was. At once a loud voice was heard from the tomb, and Jesus went up and rolled the stone away from the door of the tomb. At once he went in where the youth was. He reached out his hand, took him by the hand, and raised him up. The youth looked at Jesus and loved him, and he began to beg him to be with him. Then they left the tomb and went into the youth's house, for he was rich.

Six days later Jesus told him what to do, and in the evening the youth comes to him wearing a linen shroud over his naked body. He stayed with him that night, for Jesus was teaching him the mystery of the kingdom of God.

And from there he got up and returned to the other side of the Jordan.

After Mark 10:46a

The sister of the youth whom Jesus loved was there, along with his mother and Salome, but Jesus did not receive them.

7

The Youth in
the *Secret Gospel of Mark*

In the summer of 1958, as Morton Smith tells the story, there occurred a remarkable manuscript discovery in the Judean desert. Some seventeen years after he had first visited the Greek Orthodox Monastery of Mar Saba during the winter of 1941, Smith returned to the monastery, with the permission of the Patriarch Benedict, in order to study and catalogue the manuscripts in the monastery library.[1] Then, Smith reports in the popular publication of his findings, on a certain afternoon he deciphered a text that began, "From the letters of the most holy Clement, the author of the *Stromateis*. To Theodore."[2] This text attributed to Clement of Alexandria was written in cursive Greek on two and one-half pages at the back of a printed edition of the letters of Ignatius of Antioch.[3] Smith quickly photographed the manuscript; for years those photographs remained the only published facsimiles of the text.[4] A number of scholars examined the photographs of the manuscript in order to attempt to date the scribal hand. "The consensus," Smith concludes, "would date the hand about 1750, plus or minus about fifty years."[5]

In 1973, fifteen years after the manuscript discovery itself, the scholarly and popular editions of the text appeared, and almost at once controversy began to swirl around the text. Such controversy has focused upon questions concerning the authenticity, the contents, and the interpretation of the text. As John Dominic Crossan has said briefly and well, "The authenticity of a text can only be established by the consensus of experts who have studied the original document under scientifically appropriate circumstances."[6] In the case of the Mar Saba manuscript, Morton Smith was the only scholar who actually saw the original text, and his photographs were the only other verification of the text. This

Clement of Alexandria, Letter to Theodore, page 2 (left): The citation of the first fragment of the *Secret Gospel of Mark* begins at line 23, four lines from the bottom of the page; and Clement of Alexandria, Letter to Theodore, page 3 (right): The citation of the first fragment of the *Secret Gospel of Mark* continues through line 11, and the citation of the second fragment is in lines 14–16.

situation led to the famous intimations of possible forgery[7] and the refutations by Smith.[8] Some of these intimations have continued to more recent years, with the publication of Per Beskow's *Strange Tales about Jesus,* corrected in response to Smith's letter in the *Journal of Biblical Literature.*[9] To be sure, there were attempts by at least one other scholar to view the original text. Thomas Talley recalls his efforts: "My own attempts to see the manuscript in January of 1980 were frustrated, but as witnesses to its existence I can cite the Archimandrite Meliton of the Jerusalem Greek Patriarchate who, after the publication of Smith's work, found the volume at Mar Saba and removed it to the patriarchal library, and the patriarchal librarian, Father Kallistos, who told me that the manuscript (two folios) has been removed from the printed volume and is being repaired."[10] I concur with Crossan that the further study of the Mar Saba document should include the independent scholarly verification of the text by means of a careful examination of the original manuscript, and an adequate publication of the text in facsimile edition.

Contents

The Mar Saba manuscript is written in the form of a fragment of a letter from Clement of Alexandria to a certain recipient named Theodore. The fragmentary state of the letter, Smith speculates, may derive from the following circumstances. (1) John of Damascus worked at Mar Saba from 716 to 749 C.E., and cited three passages (in his *Sacra Parallela*) from a collection of letters of Clement of Alexandria. This fact compares well with the *incipit* of the Mar Saba manuscript: *ek tōn epistolōn tou hagiōtatou Klēmentos tou Strōmateōs* (From the letters of the most holy Clement, [author] of the *Stromateis*, 1r, 1).[11] (2) According to J. Phokylides, in the early eighteenth century a great fire burned through a cave used for the storage of manuscripts, and Smith suggests that the collection of Clement's letters may have perished in that disaster. Presumably, however, a number of loose leaves might have been salvaged from the remains of the books and manuscripts. (3) "The fragmentary state of the present letter," Smith hypothesizes, "is best explained by supposing it a copy of such an isolated leaf. Ehrhard (*Kloster* 67) remarks on the large amount of copying of older MSS which went on at Mar Saba in the seventeenth and eighteenth centuries. No doubt someone's attention was attracted by the surprising content of this isolated folio. He studied the text, corrected it to the best of his ability, and copied it into the back of the monastery's edition of the letters of Ignatius, since it resembled them in being a letter from an early father, attacking gnostic heretics."[12]

The letter of Clement is written to commend and support the recipient for his opposition to the gnostic Carpocratians. The Carpocratians were libertine gnostics who allegedly maintained that they were free to do whatever they wished, "sola enim humana opinione negotia mala et bona dicunt" ("for they say that circumstances are evil and good only in human opinion," Irenaeus of Lyons, *Adversus haereses* 1.25.4). The allegation that a studied libertinism is based upon a distinction between *physis* (nature) and *nomos* or *thesis* (convention or opinion) is attested as early as the Greek sophists, and this theory became an important part of philosophical and theological discussion during antiquity (cf., for example, Gal 4:8 and 1 Cor 8:4–6). Irenaeus goes on to declare that in the Carpocratian writings it is stated that "Jesum... in mysterio discipulis suis et apostolis seorsum locutum" ("Jesus spoke in a mystery to his disciples and apostles privately," 1.25.5), a statement that may be compared with the private communication of *to mystērion tēs basileias tou theou* (the mystery of the kingdom of God) in the Mar Saba manuscript (2r, 10). Furthermore, elsewhere in Clement's discussion of the Carpocratians (*Stromateis* 3.2.11) he employs a passage from Jude (vss 8–16) just as in the Mar Saba letter (1r, 3: *houtoi gar hoi prophēteuthentes asteres planētai*, "for these are the wandering stars that have been prophesied").[13]

In its discussion of the Carpocratian gnostics, the letter of Clement uses typical heresiological terminology. They have gone astray as "wandering stars," *hoi apo tēs stenēs tōn entolōn hodou eis aperaton abysson planōmenoi tōn sarkikōn kai ensōmatōn hamartiōn* ("who wander from the narrow way of the commandments into an infinite abyss of carnal and bodily sins," 1r, 3–4). Though they claim to have knowledge *tōn batheōn tou satana* ("of the deep things of Satan," 1r, 5; cf. Rev 2:24), they are falling into falsehood. Though they claim to be free, *douloi gegonasin andrapodōdōn epithymiōn* ("they have become slaves of base desires," 1r, 7). They are, in fact, taught by the *miarōn daimonōn* ("foul demons," 1v, 2–3), and for this reason the Carpocratians accomplish demonic things.

Among their despicable deeds is their use of the Gospel of Mark. According to the Mar Saba letter, a demonically inspired Carpocrates managed to obtain a copy of the Gospel of Mark — *tou mystikou euangeliou* ("the secret gospel," 1v, 6) — from a presbyter in the Alexandrian church. Carpocrates falsified this *Secret Gospel of Mark* in two ways: he interpreted it *kata tēn blasphēmon kai sarkikēn autou doxan* (according to his blasphemous and carnal opinion), and he polluted it by *tais achrantois kai hagiais lexesin anamignys anaidestata pseusmata* ("mixing the most shameless lies with the undefiled and holy words," 1v, 7–9).

In order to distinguish what is holy and true from what is false in the literary tradition of Mark, Clement expands upon the versions of Mark with which he is familiar. Clement grounds Mark in the Petrine apostolic tradition (cf. also *Adumbrationes Clementis Alexandrini in epistolas canonicas;* Eusebius of Caesarea, *Historia ecclesiastica* 2.15; 6.14.5–7; 3.39.15 [Papias]).[14] In doing so Clement isolates three different written versions of the Gospel of Mark. (1) While Peter was still in Rome, Mark composed an account of *tas praxeis tou kyriou* ("the acts of the lord," 1r, 16) for those who were being instructed toward faith and, presumably, baptism. This account constituted a public Gospel of Mark, and in the public version the author presented some of the lord's deeds, *ou mentoi pasas exangellōn, oude mēn tas mystikas hyposēmainōn* ("though not reporting them all, and not even hinting at the secret ones," 1r, 16–17). The public Gospel of Mark seems to be identical, or nearly identical, with the present canonical Gospel of Mark. (2) After the martyrdom of Peter, Mark came to Alexandria, taking with him *kai tatautou (sic)*[15] *kai ta tou Petrou hypomnēmata* ("both his own and Peter's notes," 1r, 19–20). From those *hypomnēmata*, Clement states, Mark added more Petrine materials to the public Gospel of Mark in order to produce a *Secret Gospel (pneumatikōteron euangelion eis tēn tōn teleioumenōn chrēsin*, "a more spiritual gospel for the use of those being perfected" [or, "initiated"]), an amplified version of Mark that also included *ta tois prokoptousi peri tēn gnōsin katallēla* ("the things appropriate for those progressing in knowledge," 1r, 20–22). Clement specifies only two relatively brief sections added to public Mark to produce *Secret Mark*. It may be the case, then, that *Secret Mark* is only slightly longer than public Mark. When Mark died, Clement continues, he left the *Secret Gospel* to the care of the church at Alexandria, *hopou eiseti nyn asphalōs eu mala tēreitai, anaginōskomenon pros autous monous tous myoumenous ta megala mystēria* ("where even now it is very carefully guarded, being read only to those being initiated into the great mysteries," 1v, 1-2). Here, and throughout this section of the Mar Saba letter, Clement utilizes language derived from the world of the Greco-Roman mysteries (e.g., *tēn hierophantikēn didaskalian tou kyriou; logia tina hōn ēpistato tēn exēgēsin mystagōgēsein tous akroatas eis to adyton tēs eptakis [sic] kekalymmenēs alētheias;* "the hierophantic teaching of the lord"; "certain sayings whose interpretation, he knew, would act as a mystagogue to lead the hearers into the inner shrine of the truth hidden seven times," 1r, 23–24, 25–26). Such usage is very much in keeping with other passages in Clement of Alexandria, for instance his *Protreptikos pros Hellenas*, in which he refutes the other mysteries in order to show Christianity to be the true, sacred mystery. (3) Clement claims that the Carpocratians used a falsified version of the *Secret Gospel* that has been amplified and interpreted by means of materials congenial with Carpocratian teachings (cf. *gymnos gymnō*, "naked person with naked person," 2r, 13). Possibly this Carpocratian version was a substantially longer version (cf. *ta de alla ta polla ha egrapsas pseusmata kai phainetai kai estin,* "But the many other matters about which you wrote both appear to be and are lies," 2r, 17). Clement declares that the Carpocratian Gospel of Mark, unlike the public and secret versions, is not authoritative, since the "holy words" of *Secret Mark* have been polluted and falsified. (4) Besides these three written versions of Mark, Clement asserts that unutterable, esoteric truths constituting "the hierophantic teaching of the lord" (1r, 23–24) were not written down by Mark. Rather, this unwritten material was to remain the secret, oral lore of true Christian *gnōsis* (knowledge).

According to the Mar Saba letter, the *Secret Gospel of Mark* contains two sections not included in the public Gospel of Mark: 1v, 23–2r, 11, and 2r, 14–16. The first section, to be located immediately after Mark 10:34, recounts the story of the raising of the *neaniskos* (youth) of Bethany. At the request of the sister of the *neaniskos,* Jesus raised the youth from the tomb. The youth, who loved Jesus, is then taught "the mystery of the kingdom of God." The second section, to be located within Mark 10:46, describes Jesus refusing to accept three women, including the sister and the mother of the *neaniskos.*

For obvious reasons, scholarly research on the Mar Saba manuscript has concentrated on these two fragmentary but fascinating sections, and the perplexing question of the interpretation of the *Secret Gospel of Mark.* To some of the recent research on these two sections we now turn.

Research

While a full discussion of the scholarly literature on the *Secret Gospel of Mark* cannot be attempted here, four contributions deserve brief comment. These four contributions give serious attention to the *Secret Gospel,* and suggest creative approaches to the text. The four studies are: (1) Morton Smith, "Clement of Alexandria and Secret Mark: The Score at the End of the First Decade";[16] (2) Koester, "History and Development of Mark's Gospel"; (3) Schenke, "The Mystery of the Gospel of Mark"; and (4) Crossan, "The Secret Gospel of Mark," in his book *Four Other Gospels.*

Morton Smith

As the subtitle of Smith's review article indicates, his study is an assessment of ten years of comments on the *Secret Gospel of Mark.* Smith

bases his review on some 150 publications, and judges that these publications are representative of scholarly opinion on the *Secret Gospel*.
Smith begins his reflections by addressing himself to the question of the
authenticity of the letter of Clement and the fragments contained within
the letter, and concludes that most scholars now are willing to attribute
the letter itself to Clement of Alexandria. Of the scholars Smith lists
in his bibliography, the vote is as follows: "[T]wenty-five have agreed
in attributing the letter to Clement, six have suspended judgment or
have not discussed the question, and only four have denied the attribution."[17] Regarding the authenticity of the fragments of the *Secret
Gospel*, Smith concludes that "Clement's attribution of the gospel to
'Mark' is universally rejected," and lists three basic positions evident
among scholars: some suggest that the *Secret Gospel* fragments represent
a second-century "apocryphal" gospel, others consider the fragments to
be "a pastiche composed from the canonical gospels," and still others
propose that the *Secret Gospel* is "an expansion of Mark which imitated
Markan style, but used earlier material."[18] Smith also adds that a number of scholars "seemed inclined" to accept at least some of the points
suggested by Smith himself in his outline of the literary history of the
Markan materials.

When Smith turns briefly to his interpretation of *Secret Mark* as
providing evidence for the historical Jesus as a practitioner of secret initiation and an advocate of a libertine and magical life-style, he notes, "Of
course nobody accepted the proposed explanation," though some scholars did leave open the possibility of secret ceremonies in the movement
around Jesus and magical concerns in the early church. One of the chief
sources of disagreement, Smith states, was from scholars who are "the
adherents of current exegetic cliques (form criticism, redaction criticism,
etc.) who were outraged that I had not given their literature of mutu-
ally contradictory conjectures the attention they thought it deserved."[19]
Naturally, Smith's evaluation of the "current exegetic cliques" is deliberately polemical, and reflective of Smith's own exegetical approach. Yet,
in spite of these vehement words, with their rejection of form-critical and
redaction-critical scholarship, Smith's statement still points us toward a
most fruitful way of approaching the *Secret Gospel of Mark*. Instead of
using the fragments to formulate conjectures about the historical Jesus,
after the manner of Smith, we may rather interpret the fragments within
the redactional history of the Markan tradition.

Helmut Koester

Such an interest in the stages of redaction in the Markan trajectory occupies the attention of Helmut Koester in his article on Secret and canonical Mark.[20] Koester ventures to list several proposed stages of redaction as Mark went through several editions. The first stage (1a), says Koester, is the original Gospel of Mark, which was based on a collection of miracle stories and a passion narrative, both with Johannine affinities. A second stage (1b) is an enlarged edition of the original Gospel of Mark, written to include the miracle stories of Mark 6:45–8:26. The next stage (2) is the Gospel of Matthew, a thoroughly revised edition based, in large part, on the enlarged edition of the original Gospel of Mark that constitutes the second redactional stage (1b). A further stage (3) is the Gospel of Luke, another dramatically new edition which is based, in part, on the original Gospel of Mark (1a), but which employs other materials as well. The next stage (4a), Koester continues, is the *Secret Gospel of Mark*, which incorporates the account of, and subsequent reference to, the *neaniskos* who is raised from the dead and initiated into the Jesus movement. A related stage (4b) is the Carpocratian edition of the *Secret Gospel.* The next stage of redaction in the Markan tradition (5a) is the canonical Gospel of Mark, with the *Secret Gospel*'s two reports about the *neaniskos* excised from the text. Finally, Koester concludes, the several endings (the shorter ending, the longer ending, and the Freer logion) added in many later manuscripts after Mark 16:8 illustrate the last redactional stage (5b), and "demonstrate that the history of 'canonical Mark' was still continuing."[21]

The intricacies of this ingenious theory of Helmut Koester need not detain us here. Doubtless the details will receive ample attention in the scholarly debates on Mark. For our purposes it is his statement about the relationship between Secret and canonical Mark that is of paramount concern. For "the conclusion," he writes, "is unavoidable: Canonical Mark is derived from *Secret Mark.*"[22] Koester thus accepts Clement's suggestion of a close link between canonical (or public) Mark and *Secret Mark,* but disagrees with Clement's theory of transmission. Koester supports his contention, first of all, with various pieces of evidence meant to illustrate the close parallels between peculiar features of canonical Mark and the *Secret Gospel.* For example, Mark 4:11 is unique among the Synoptics (contrast Matt 13:11 // Luke 8:10) in using the singular form *mystērion* (mystery) in its reference to the *mystērion* of the kingdom of God; the *Secret Gospel* (2r, 10) also describes Jesus teaching the *neaniskos* the *mystērion* of the kingdom of God (cf. again the citation from Irenaeus, *Adversus haereses* 1.25.5, on the Carpocratians). Likewise, Mark 10:21 is unique among the Synoptics (contrast Matt 19:21 // Luke 18:22) in describing the love of Jesus for the rich interlocutor; both fragments of the *Secret Gospel* also describe the love between Jesus and the *neaniskos*. One final example of Koester's evidence: Mark 14:51–52, the famous pericope about the youth who flees naked at the time of Jesus' arrest, is unique among the Synoptics and has proved to be an interpretive nightmare for a very long time; now the *Secret Gospel* also presents a youth dressed in similar fashion and learning from Jesus about the kingdom of God.

After Koester thus establishes the intimate relationship between leading characteristics of *Secret Mark* and some unusual traits of canonical Mark, and judges that they reflect the same secondary redaction, he can move to his conclusion on the priority of the *Secret Gospel of Mark*. "The basic difference between the two," he offers, "seems to be that the redactor of canonical Mark eliminated the story of the raising of the youth and the reference to this story in Mk 10:46."[23] The rationale for eliminating this story, Koester observes, is clear enough: it was deemed unacceptable for public use in the church, as Clement himself implies. It certainly seems appropriate to assume, along with Koester (and against Clement), that the story of the raising of the youth was eliminated from canonical Mark subsequent to the compilation of *Secret Mark,* particularly since many of the peculiar traits that apparently derive from the Secret Markan redaction linger on the pages of canonical Mark. Further, the Markan account simply reads in an easier and more natural manner when the special materials of the *Secret Gospel* are allowed to function within the story line. Canonical Mark is more abrupt, more opaque at key points, as we should anticipate in a document from which important passages have been removed. Precisely how the text of the *Secret Gospel* allows for a sensible and reasonable reading of the Markan text will be the focus of the next part of this essay.

Hans-Martin Schenke

The third study under discussion here, the 1984 article of Hans-Martin Schenke (originally delivered as a paper during his 1982 tour of the

United States), bases itself very sympathetically upon the prior work of Smith and Koester. Schenke opens his study with a discussion of problems in the Gospel of Mark, including the question of the conclusion of the gospel, the nature of the Markan account of Jesus' baptism, and the enigma of Mark 14:51–52. In this discussion two statements of Schenke hint at his eventual conclusions: first, he suggests that there may be a "possible affinity between the text of Mark and gnostic interpretation";[24] and second, he admits, "I was already more favorably predisposed to Smith's discovery than were a great many of my colleagues."[25] Following a substantial review of scholarly comments and criticisms of Smith's work on the *Secret Gospel,* Schenke turns to Koester approvingly, and acknowledges that he intends to raise additional questions derived from Koester's argument. Schenke's further questions lead him to a provocative proposal, namely that the Carpocratian Gospel of Mark may be taken as the prior form of Mark, from which emerge, consecutively, the "purified and shortened" *Secret Gospel of Mark* and canonical Gospel of Mark.[26] Much more convincing, in my opinion, is his observation, so reminiscent of the study by Robin Scroggs and Kent Groff, that the *neaniskos* of the canonical and Secret Gospels of Mark functions as a "prototype and a symbol of all those who are to be initiated into the higher discipleship of Jesus."[27] The balance of the present essay will enter into the discussion of *Secret Mark* by focusing upon this *neaniskos* as a paradigm of discipleship in Mark.

John Dominic Crossan

The final study to be mentioned is that of Crossan. Crossan analyzes four extracanonical texts, including the *Secret Gospel of Mark,* and shows the light these texts may shed upon the traditions about Jesus and the foundations of Christianity. Crossan employs a "working hypothesis" that is, in part, similar to that of Koester: "I consider that canonical Mark is a very deliberate revision of *Secret Mark.*"[28] Yet his rejection of Koester's "earlier Proto-Mark gospel which was first used in different versions by Luke and Matthew"[29] leaves him without an adequate explanation for the absence of certain redactional traits of *Secret Mark* (dispersed throughout canonical Mark) in the texts of Matthew and Luke.[30] Crossan rightly recognizes, with Koester, parallels between canonical and *Secret Mark,* but copes with these parallels by means of a rather odd theory. Crossan posits that canonical Mark, with anti-Carpocratian intentions, eliminated units of the *Secret Gospel* in this manner: "It is now impossible to tell the full scope of that revision but two features seem certain. First, canonical Mark eliminated both *SGM [Secret Mark]* 2 and 5 [i.e., the quotations peculiar to *Secret Mark*] as discrete literary units. Second, canonical Mark scattered the dismembered elements of these units throughout his gospel."[31] This dismembering and scattering, according to Crossan, account for features of Mark in such passages as 10:17–22 (the story of the rich inquirer), 14:51–52 (the pericope about the naked youth in flight), and 16:1–8 (the *neaniskos* and the women at the tomb).

To sum up on these four recent studies of the *Secret Gospel of Mark*: (1) The studies summarized suggest that a number of scholars seem willing to give the Mar Saba text and the *Secret Gospel of Mark* considerable attention, and to assume thereby the authenticity of the letter of Clement as an ancient text. This assumption is also reflected in the decision to include the Mar Saba text in the second edition of Otto Stählin's *Clemens Alexandrinus*.[32] (2) Few scholars (and none in the studies discussed here) have been convinced by Smith's reconstruction of a libertine Christian tradition grounded in secret teachings of the historical Jesus. Rather, several scholars (e.g., Koester, Schenke, and Crossan) encourage us to evaluate the place of the *Secret Gospel* within early stages of redaction in the Markan tradition. On the other hand, as we have seen, there is still substantial disagreement about specific redactional issues and reconstructions among these scholars. (3) The studies by Koester, Schenke, and Crossan are unanimous in advocating the priority of the text of *Secret Mark* to that of canonical Mark, although they disagree about other matters of transmission within the Markan literary tradition.

Interpretation

My thesis in the balance of the present study builds self-consciously upon the conclusions just drawn. I assume the authenticity of the Mar Saba letter as a copy of an ancient text, and I suggest an interpretation that seeks to understand the text of *Secret Mark* within the Markan redactional tradition. Here we shall undertake a reading of the *Secret Gospel of Mark* that attempts to place the two fragments from Mar Saba within the broader context of the entire *Secret Gospel*. Such an attempt must remain somewhat tentative, on account of uncertainties about the text tradition and textual peculiarities represented by Clement's citations of public and *Secret Mark,* and the relationship of that text tradition to known Markan texts. Further, the precise contours of *Secret Mark* are not known, though the comments of Clement lead us to conclude that *Secret Mark* closely resembled public (or canonical) Mark, except for the inclusion of the two fragments Clement cites. In the surviving portion of his letter Clement himself indicates nothing whatsoever to contradict such a conclusion, and he appears to be turning away from the discussion of peculiarities of *Secret Mark* in the final surviving lines (2r, 17–18).

I propose that a reading of the *Secret Gospel of Mark* exposes a subplot involving the *neaniskos* in the text of *Secret Mark,* a subplot that is presented in only an imperfect and truncated fashion in canonical Mark. This story of the *neaniskos,* I submit, communicates *Secret Mark's* vision of the life and challenge of discipleship, as that is exemplified in the career of the *neaniskos.* This subplot may be elucidated first by means of a word study of the key term *neaniskos,* and then through an exegesis of five pericopae from *Secret Mark,* each of which deals with a *neaniskos,* and each of which is linked to the other pericopae by means of a series of literary connections.

The term *neaniskos* is a widely attested Greek word used to denote a young person or at times a servant. The range in age assumed to be fitting for a *neaniskos* generally includes the twenties and sometimes also the thirties. According to the description of the stages in one's life in Diogenes Laertius, one remains a child (*pais*) for twenty years, then a youth (*neēniskos*) for twenty more years, a mature person (*neēniēs*) for another twenty years, and an older person (*gerōn*) for a final twenty years (8.10). According to Philo of Alexandria, Hippocrates said that there are seven stages of human life, and the fourth is that of the *neaniskos:* one is *neaniskos d' achris auxēsios holou tou sōmatos, es ta tetrakis hepta* — from *ta tris hepta* ("a youth until the growth of the whole body, up to four times seven [years]" — from "three times seven"; *De opificio mundi* 105). In the New Testament and other early Christian literature, too, there are instances of such a general usage of the word *neaniskos* and related terms. In Luke 7:14, where the dead son of the widow of Nain is raised by Jesus in a pericope (7:11–17) without specific parallel in the Synoptics, the youth is addressed as a *neaniskos.* (There are a few parallels between this story and the raising of the *neaniskos* in *Secret Mark:* a *neaniskos* has died, leaving his mother in mourning;

upon arriving, Jesus touches the coffin and addresses the young man with the command *egerthēti* ["arise," 7:14], *kai anekathisen ho nekros kai ērxato lalein* ["and the dead man sat up and began to speak," 7:15]. These parallels may be coincidental, and of no particular importance for our discussion here. Conversely, a case might be made to relate the Lukan pericope more closely to the account in *Secret Mark*.)[33] In the Acts of the Apostles the word *neaniskos* is employed several times: in Acts 2:17 the author uses the poetic parallelism of Joel 2:28 (3:1) to evaluate the Pentecost experience of the *neaniskoi* and the *presbyteroi* (elders); in Acts 5:10 *hoi neaniskoi* of the congregation remove the corpse of Sapphira from the presence of Peter (*hoi neōteroi* [the young men] had accomplished the same task, in 5:6, with Ananias); in Acts 20:12 the most reliable texts recount the story of Paul's raising the *pais* (child) Eutychus, but Codex Bezae (D) refers to him as a *neaniskos;* and in Acts 23:16–22 Paul's nephew is called, in successive statements, a *neanias* (young man) and a *neaniskos*. Again, 1 John 2:13–14, in the context of the author's affectionate references to his believing readers as *teknia* (little children) and *paidia* (children), explains why he is writing to the *neaniskoi: hoti ischyroi este kai ho logos tou theou en hymin menei kai nenikēkate ton ponēron* (because you are strong, and the word of God remains in you, and you have vanquished the evil one). Lastly, it may be noted that *neaniskoi* also appears on the pages of the *Visions* and *Similitudes* of Hermas, and the *Gospel of Peter:* in the former they usually function as visionary or angelic beings; in the latter they play roles within the passion narrative (*Gos. Pet.* 9.37 refers to two young men from heaven, in a manner reminiscent of Luke 24:4 — cf. also Matt 28:2–4; *Gos. Pet.* 13.55 refers to a single *neaniskos* in the otherwise empty tomb, in a manner much like Mark 16:5).

Such references in early Christian literature probably demonstrate only a rather general use of the term *neaniskos*. Scroggs and Groff suggest, "The word *neaniskos* is just possibly a quasi-technical term denoting the class of initiates," but they immediately add, "the evidence is extremely tenuous."[34] Several other passages in the Markan tradition, however, may focus more clearly and specifically upon the *neaniskos* as a paradigmatic disciple, and thus may employ the term *neaniskos* in a more technical sense. Since these passages are all interrelated, in my interpretation, as vignettes that together narrate a significant story about discipleship, I shall offer a brief analysis of five important pericopae that serve to advance the plot of this little story. These passages all are found in the second half of the Gospel of Mark, in Mark 10:13–16:8, and include, of course, the fragments of *Secret Mark*.

Mark 10:17–22

Mark 10:17–22 narrates the story of the so-called rich young ruler. Mark describes this candidate for discipleship only as a rich man (*echōn ktēmata polla,* "having many possessions," 10:22) who claimed to have kept the commandments *ek neotētos* ("from youth," 10:20). Luke adds that he was a ruler (*tis...archōn,* "a certain ruler," 18:18) who was very rich (*ēn gar plousios sphodra,* "for he was very rich," 18:23); Luke's wording is nearly identical to that of *Secret Mark,* which says of the *neaniskos, ēn gar plousios* ("for he was rich," 2r, 6). (Mark also uses *plousios,* "rich," in 10:17 according to several texts, chiefly A, K, and W.) Matthew twice calls the candidate a *neaniskos* (19:20, 22). In his use of this term Matthew arguably may preserve some of the original wording of the pericope: only here, in a synoptic pericope with clear links to the story of the *neaniskos* in *Secret Mark,* does Matthew employ the term. Furthermore, according to Mark 10:21, Jesus *emblepsas autō ēgapēsen auton* (looking upon him, loved him). This reference to the love of Jesus for the youth is made here alone among the Synoptics, although both of the *Secret Gospel* fragments (2r, 4; 2r, 15) employ the same theme of love between Jesus and the *neaniskos;* the first fragment reproduces Mark 10:21 word for word, but attributes the love to the *neaniskos.* (The issue of Lazarus and the Beloved Disciple in the Gospel of John will be addressed below.) The candidate of Mark 10:17–22, however, is scandalized by the cost of discipleship, and he turns away in sadness, unwilling to follow Jesus. This scene in the career of the *neaniskos* ends in vs 22, with the departure of the youth, but the discussion in the following verses of the Gospel of Mark (10:23–31) continues to consider the difficulties of the life of the disciple: it is hard to enter the kingdom of God, and the cost is high.

The account of the rich youth in Mark 10:17–22 follows a related pericope about discipleship, namely the pronouncement story describing the disciples rebuking (*epetimēsan autois,* "they rebuked them") but Jesus blessing the *paidia* ("children," Mark 10:13–16). This familiar scene is common in the world of the Middle East: the children come to see the teacher who is in the village. Yet it is clear from vss 14 and (especially) 15 that in its present form the pericope is not concerned merely with children: the kingdom of God, Mark writes, belongs to such people as the children (so vs 14); and Jesus is made to go on to observe, *amēn legō hymin, hos an mē dexētai tēn basileian tou theou hōs paidion, ou mē eiselthē eis autēn* ("Truly I say to you, whoever does not receive the kingdom of God like a child shall not enter it," vs 15). In other words, in a manner typical of much of early Christian literature, the children are presented as typifying discipleship and the life of discipleship. Such becomes even clearer in vs 24, where Jesus is made to turn to his disciples themselves and address them as children: *tekna, pōs dyskolon estin eis tēn basileian tou theou eiselthein* (Children, how difficult it is to enter the kingdom of God). Although we may not be able to conclude that the author necessarily means to refer to baptism in vss 13–16, certainly the broader context of the pericope raises the issue of baptism (cf. vss 38–40), namely baptism as sacramental participation in the suffering of Jesus on the part of his disciples.

Secret Mark, *Fragment I*

The first fragment of the *Secret Gospel of Mark* (1v, 23–2r, 11), to be placed after Mark 10:34, presents the miracle story of the raising of a *neaniskos*. The parallels noted between the description of the *neaniskos* in this fragment and in Mark 10:17–22 suggest that this youth in *Secret Mark* is the same *neaniskos* as the rich young man who refused to follow Jesus in Mark 10:17–22: in turning from Jesus, it may then be implied, he has turned from life and embraced death. As has been widely discussed in the scholarly literature, the scene described in this fragment is similar to the miracle story of the raising of Lazarus in John 11. A woman in Bethany, in mourning over the death of her brother, approaches Jesus and asks his help. The disciples rebuke her (*epetimēsan autē*, "they rebuked her," 1v, 25; cf. Mark 10:13), but Jesus goes to the tomb and raises the *neaniskos* from the dead. It is then that the *neaniskos* looks upon Jesus and loves him (2r, 4): this verbatim parallel to Mark 10:21 suggests that only after being brought from death to life does the youth return the love with which Jesus loves him in Mark 10:21. Jesus and the *neaniskos* return to the young man's house, and it is added (2r, 6), in a clear reference to Mark 10:22 (cf. also the wording of Luke 18:23), that the *neaniskos* is *plousios* (rich). The final lines of this fragment of *Secret*

Mark depict Jesus initiating the *neaniskos,* now dressed in what several scholars have interpreted to be the ritual garb of early Christian baptism (linen clothing over the naked body),[35] and teaching him the mystery of the kingdom of God. In these lines the language of *Secret Mark* (2r, 8) is precisely the same as Mark 14:51: in both cases the *neaniskos* is described *peribeblēmenos sindona epi gymnou* (wearing linen over his naked body).

The key to understanding the significance of the word *sindōn* (linen) in the *Secret Gospel of Mark* and Mark 14:51 may be found in the only other instance of the usage of this term in the Gospel of Mark: Mark 15:46, where Joseph of Arimathea is said to have wrapped the corpse of Jesus in a *sindōn,* a linen shroud. In the Markan tradition a *sindōn* may represent two items of clothing: the linen garment of initiation of the *neaniskos,* and the linen burial shroud of Jesus. Yet the interplay between the two uses of the term, and the link between baptism and suffering in the Gospel of Mark, lead us to conclude that the *sindōn* of the *neaniskos* is quite the same as Jesus' shroud: the *neaniskos* participates in baptism as an experience of sharing in the suffering and death of Christ, and wears ritual clothing appropriate for such an experience.

The reference to six days (*kai meth' hēmeras hex,* "six days later," Jesus gives instruction to the *neaniskos,* 2r, 6–7) in the first fragment of *Secret Mark* has provoked a considerable amount of scholarly speculation. This specific reference might be taken to be merely a temporal connective with a designated interval of time;[36] the fact that the immediate context in Mark refers to the resurrection (*meta treis hēmeras* "after three days," 10:34) might also be significant in this regard. Yet a similar Markan reference to a six-day interval of time in 9:2 has prompted additional interpretations of the passage in *Secret Mark.* "Six days later" might be interpreted as communicating an interval of a week; Luke's apparent revision of Mark 9:2 to read *hōsei hēmerai oktō* ("about eight days," 9:28) might indicate as much. Six days could also be understood as symbolizing an appropriate time of preparation and purification before an experience of meeting the divine (e.g., Exod 24:16). According to *Gos. Thom.* 4, "The person old in days will not hesitate to ask a little child seven days old (*oukouei ᵉnšēre šēm efhᵉn sašᵉf ᵉnhoou*) about the place of life, and that person will live." Here the reference to "a little child seven days old" may derive from the Jewish practice of circumcising Jewish boys on the eighth day (cf. Gen 17:12; Phil 3:5). In the *Gospel of Thomas* the child who communicates knowledge is so innocent that he has not yet been circumcised. (In Hippolytus, *Refutatio* 5.7.20, it is said that a gospel according to Thomas refers to children of seven *years*.) Schenke appeals to the well-known theory that the story of the transfiguration originally was a narrative of a post-resurrection appearance of Christ, and connects these two instances of "six days later" or "after six days" in Mark to suggest that both proclaim the resurrection: "Once one imagines the transfiguration functioning as an appearance and glorification of Jesus at the end of Mark, then the correspondence emerges clearly: the phrase 'after six days' connects resurrection and metamorphosis in both cases. The resurrection and initiation of the ideal disciple represent the resurrection and deification of Jesus."[37] Talley, on the other hand, posits an interpretation based upon the Coptic liturgical calendar: "A peculiar aspect of the Coptic tradition is that it identifies the baptismal day, the sixth day of the sixth week, with a tradition which asserted that that was the day on which Jesus baptized his disciples."[38] Hence, Talley concludes, "[W]e can see a pattern which is compellingly suggestive of a course reading of Mark beginning on January 6: the baptism of Jesus on that day, the beginning of the imitation of Jesus' fast on the following day with the continued reading of the gospel during the weeks of the fast so as to arrive at chapter 10 by the sixth week, the reading of the secret gospel inserted into chapter 10 in close conjunction with the conferral of baptism in that sixth week, and the celebration of the entry into Jerusalem with chapter 11 of Mark on the following Sunday."[39]

Secret Mark, *Fragment 2*

The third pericope concerned with the *neaniskos* in Mark is the scene found in the second fragment of *Secret Mark* (2r, 14–16), which Clement states the *Secret Gospel* includes in Mark 10:46. *Secret Mark* 10:46 thus may be reconstructed to read approximately as follows: "And he comes to Jericho. The sister of the youth whom Jesus loved was there, along with his mother and Salome, but Jesus did not receive them (fem.). And as he was leaving Jericho with his disciples and a large crowd, Bartimaeus son of Timaeus, a blind beggar, was sitting by the side of the road." This reference to the *neaniskos* and the women allows for a fuller and more felicitous reading of Mark 10:46, without the brusqueness of the canonical rendering: *kai erchontai eis Ierichō. Kai ekporeuomenou* *autou apo Ierichō*...(And they come to Jericho. And as he was leaving Jericho...). Here canonical Mark gives the impression that the discussion of what transpired in Jericho has been omitted: according to the canonical text, nothing happened in Jericho! Clement's suggestion of the singular *erchetai* (he comes) differs from the plural *erchontai* (they come) in canonical Mark, the only such instance of disagreement between canonical Mark and citations from public Mark in the Mar Saba letter. (Notice should be taken that Luke 18:35 provides a paraphrase of the singular *erchetai* of *Secret Mark* [*egeneto de en tō engizein auton eis Ierichō*..., "And it happened that as he approached Jericho..."], and that B* omits the clause in Mark 10:46 altogether.) The singular *erchetai* reads more naturally with the following *kai ekporeuomenou autou* (And as he was leaving), also in the singular. The mention of Salome in the *Secret Mark* fragment is particularly striking, since in the New Testament writings Salome is mentioned by name only in the Gospel of Mark (15:40; 16:1); she plays a much more prominent role in gnostic and extracanonical sources.[40]

Secret Mark 10:46 reiterates the love of Jesus for the *neaniskos* (cf. Mark 10:21; also *Secret Mark* 2r, 4), and adds a detail significant for our further observations of the interaction between the *neaniskos* and the disciples or women: while Jesus loves the *neaniskos,* he does not accept the women. The description of the *neaniskos* as one *hon ēgapa auton ho Iēsous* (whom Jesus loved) calls to mind at once the Beloved Disciple in John. The contrary statement that Jesus did not "receive" or "accept" the women has prompted Morton Smith to suggest that the original text here has been censored. Smith's careful examination of the vocabulary, phraseology, and grammar of the *Secret Gospel* fragments leads him to conclude that in general these fragments are characteristically and preponderantly Markan;[41] but the use of *apedexato* (he received) is an exception. "In the NT, *apodechomai* is found only in Lk.-Acts," Smith observes,[42] and Clement uses the verb frequently too. Smith posits that the story as transmitted by Clement "has no apparently significant content. There is no miracle, no saying, nothing but Jesus' refusal to receive, on one occasion, three women." What was censored, Smith concludes, was in all likelihood "a conversation with Salome."[43] Crossan concurs with Smith's interpretation.[44] Yet it must be acknowledged that the root verb *dechesthai* (to receive) is used several times in the Gospel of Mark, and often in a sense not unlike that of the *apedexato* of *Secret Mark* (e.g., Mark 6:11; 9:37; 10:15). Further, there may in fact be "significant content" to the pericope as transmitted by Clement. That content will be clarified by the actions of the women in Mark 16:1–8.

Mark 14:51–52

Mark 14:51–52 portrays a *neaniskos* who is dressed in *sindōn* (linen) and is seized at the time of the arrest of Jesus. (The reference to *hoi neaniskoi* in some late texts of Mark seems designed to resolve the enigma of the single *neaniskos;* this attempt at textual clarification need not concern us here.) Just as all the other disciples forsook Jesus and fled, so also the *neaniskos* runs away, leaving his *sindōn* behind and escaping naked. On account of the obvious verbal links between this passage and the fragments of the *Secret Gospel of Mark* (*neaniskos...peribeblēmenos sindona epi gymnou...*, "a youth...wearing a linen shroud over his naked body... "), I interpret the youth of Mark 14:51–52 to be the same paradigmatic disciple as the *neaniskos* in *Secret Mark.* Once dressed in the ritual garment of initiation, he has abandoned his baptismal robes and fled.

Many commentators have attempted interpretations of this intriguing passage, but few of the interpretations are satisfying. Many have suggested that the *neaniskos* was a historical disciple, perhaps an unnamed eyewitness or even Mark inserting himself into the plot of the gospel.[45] Others have sought to derive this reference to the *neaniskos* from Gen 39:12 — Joseph fleeing, *sans* cloak, from Potiphar's wife — or Amos 2:16 — the brave fleeing naked on that Day;[46] Vincent Taylor rightly dismisses such efforts as "desperate in the extreme."[47] Other scholars are probably closer to a correct interpretation in proposing that the figure of the *neaniskos* represents Christ or the Christian: the *neaniskos* prefigures Christ, especially the risen Christ,[48] dramatizes the flight of the disciples,[49] or symbolizes the Christian initiate who becomes like Christ.[50]

In an addendum to their article, Scroggs and Groff discuss these two verses in relation to the *Secret Gospel* material that had just been published, but their discussion is problematic. They suggest that the first *Secret Gospel* fragment could portray "pre-baptismal catechesis, necessarily preceding the actual baptism, which is itself not alluded to until 14:51–52." In Mark 14:51–52, then, "the believer is symbolically baptized," and dies with Christ as he leaves his linen garment behind, only to appear dressed in white baptismal clothing in Mark 16:5.[51] Morton Smith responds to this suggestion by noting sharply, "This interpretation neglects only the main facts: this young man deserted Christ and saved himself."[52] I agree with Smith. Scroggs and Groff rightly recognize the baptismal significance of the Markan passages under discussion, but seem to locate the baptism itself in the wrong pericope! In 14:51–52 the point of the passage is not the baptizing of the *neaniskos* but rather the forsaking of baptismal loyalties: the paradigmatic disciple is scandalized by the suffering of Jesus no less than the other disciples, and even abandons his sacramental clothes symbolizing his participation in Jesus' passion and death. The viability of discipleship itself seems in doubt as the tension builds in Mark 14.

Mark 16:1–8

The final pericope in the story of the *neaniskos* as disciple is Mark 16:1–8. The developing tension concerning discipleship, as observed in the Markan passion narrative, is partly resolved (but only partly resolved) in the scene at Jesus' tomb. The women, including Salome, go to the tomb to anoint the body, but what they see there amazes them. Inside the tomb they see the *neaniskos* himself, wearing clothing once again, now *peribeblēmenon stolēn leukēn* ("wearing a white robe," 16:5). On the basis of this description of the *neaniskos* I interpret this youth in Mark 16 to be the prototypal disciple whose story we have been tracing.[53] There is no compelling reason to consider him an angel; here in Mark the scene is quite different from that in both Matt 28:1–10, where an apocalyptic angel is explicitly mentioned and described, and Luke 24:1–11, where two angelic men (24:4: *andres duo*, "two men"; 24:23: *optasian angelōn*, "a vision of angels") in dazzling clothes inspire fear and awe.

Furthermore, the white robe of the youth must be similar to the ritual *sindōn* he has previously worn and subsequently abandoned. The only substantial difference may be the glory or purity attached to the white robe of chapter 16, which the *neaniskos* wears as he identifies with the dying and rising Christ within the tomb. Scroggs and Groff also understand the *stolē leukē* (white robe) of Mark 16:5 to be "the traditional garment put on the person just emerging from the baptismal waters. It symbolizes the new existence of the believer, in effect, his resurrection."[54] Thus the *neaniskos* is portrayed in the same way as the faithful of the book of Revelation: they are *peribeblēmenous stolas leukas* ("wearing white robes," 7:9, etc.). These white robes reserved for glorified Christians recall the garb of initiates into some of the mystery religions of antiquity: in the mysteries of Isis, those of the Orphics, the Andanian mysteries, and the like, the faithful were commonly dressed in white linen. Since such a use of white linen may be of Egyptian origin, the mystery-religion language and the Alexandrian setting in the Mar Saba letter of Clement become all the more interesting.

The *neaniskos* of Mark 16 has reaffirmed his baptismal loyalties, and proceeds to explain to the visiting women how they and the other disciples may see Christ in Galilee. Yet the women are overcome by fear: they flee away, and say nothing about these remarkable matters. With such a description, I suggest, the Gospel of Mark comes to a close. A full discussion of the conclusion of the Gospel of Mark cannot be undertaken here; I simply suggest that Mark originally ended at 16:8, in spite of the creative and imaginative efforts of scholars to demonstrate that an appearance story (perhaps the transfiguration narrative, Mark 9:2–8) may be taken as the original post-resurrection ending of Mark. According to the Gospel of Mark, previously the twelve (or the eleven) had fled from the arrest of Jesus, and Peter had denied Jesus. Now the women too flee from the tomb in fear; only the youth is left to proclaim the crucified and risen Christ. It is no wonder that, as we have seen earlier, the second fragment of the *Secret Gospel* has Jesus refusing to accept the women who are with the *neaniskos*. They, after all, unlike the *neaniskos* at the end of Mark, do not endure in the life of discipleship.

Lately the interpretation of the role of the women disciples in the Gospel of Mark by Elisabeth Schüssler Fiorenza and Elizabeth Struthers Malbon has presented a different assessment of their role in Mark 16. Fiorenza suggests that "the women disciples flee not from the angel and the resurrection news but from the tomb," and eventually bring the resurrection message "to special designated persons," namely the disciples and Peter, while maintaining silence only to the public. Hence, she concludes, "Despite the extraordinary fear for their lives the women disciples stood with Jesus in his suffering, sought to honor him in his death, and now become the proclaimers of his resurrection."[55] Such an interpretation, attractive as it is, seems to overlook the finality of Mark 16:8 (*oudeni ouden eipan*, "they said nothing to any one"; it does not seem to me that the similar clause in Mark 1:44 mitigates this finality), and minimizes the force of the women disciples' act of flight (*ephygon*, "they fled," also used to describe the flight of the male disciples in 14:50 and that of the *neaniskos* in 14:52). Still it should be noted, with Fiorenza, that the women disciples are present at the crucifixion, as they look on from afar (Mark 15:40–41): "Though the twelve have forsaken Jesus, betrayed and denied him, the women disciples, by contrast, are found under the cross, risking their own lives and safety."[56] The significance of these women disciples at the cross must not be ignored, nor should the roles of such followers as Bartimaeus (Mark 10:52), Simon of Cyrene (15:21), the centurion (15:39), and Joseph of Arimathea (15:43–46). Yet it is also likely that the flight of the women in Mark 16:8 should be seen as the culminating stage in the progressive defection of the disciples. After Judas (Mark 14:43–45), the rest of the male disciples (14:50), the *neaniskos* (14:52), and Peter (14:66–72) all fail to follow Jesus, the women, too, finally flee in fear.[57]

With the abrupt ending of Mark the attention turns to the implied reader, for only he or she can resolve the remaining tensions in the gospel.[58] All the closest followers of Jesus have fled in the face of the cross and the resurrection, but the *neaniskos* has faced the difficulties and challenges of discipleship, and in the end has identified with Christ in death and resurrection. Throughout the Markan subplot about the *neaniskos* we may notice that the *neaniskos* and the disciples commonly are set over against each other for comparison or contrast. Thus the wealthy young man of Mark 10:17–22 turns away from following Jesus, but the disciples counter by insisting, through Peter, that they have left all and followed Jesus (10:28). Again, the wealthy *neaniskos* of the fragments of *Secret Mark* is baptized by Jesus, just as the disciples are to be baptized into the suffering of Jesus (10:38–39); the text of *Secret Mark* goes on to observe that the *neaniskos* is loved by Jesus and returns the love, while the women are not a part of this network of love. Once again, the *neaniskos* of Mark 14:51–52 flees from Jesus, as the other disciples also have done. But in chapter 16 the *neaniskos* alone, in the face of the defection of the other disciples, can challenge the reader of Mark. Will the reader flee from Mark's theology of the cross and resurrection, like the twelve and even the women? Or will the reader see himself or herself in the *neaniskos,* and also take up the costly life of discipleship? With such a challenge the Gospel of Mark abruptly, but fittingly, comes to a conclusion.

Implications

If this thesis concerning the subplot about the *neaniskos* is convincing, then some of the implications for further Markan research are noteworthy. Several questions might be addressed in subsequent discussion. For instance, what is the origin and development of the subplot itself? Did it emerge from an aretalogical source as the miracle story of the raising of a dead youth (understood as the *neaniskos* in *Secret Mark* and Lazarus in John 11), only to be expanded and modified into the subplot on discipleship in the *Secret Gospel of Mark?* Was the subplot once an independent story in the tradition, or did it develop as a series of vignettes projected intermittently into the gospel account? And finally, what does this subplot, intricately woven as it is into the fabric of *Secret Mark,* do to clarify, confuse, or complicate the knotty questions of the niceties of redactional development in the Markan trajectory?

The study of the *Secret Gospel of Mark* may also advance the discussion of the relationship between the Markan and Johannine traditions, and the role of the Beloved Disciple in the Gospel of John. The miracle story of the raising of the *neaniskos* in *Secret Mark* is remarkably similar to the story of Lazarus in John 11, except that the *Secret Gospel* account has features suggesting that it is more primitive than the Johannine account, and that the Johannine account is dependent, directly or indirectly, upon the *Secret Gospel* account (so Smith; Koester; Crossan; F. F. Bruce begs to disagree).[59] The Markan story of the *neaniskos* in the Mar Saba manuscript lacks the details we expect in a more developed tradition and shows no evidence of specifically Johannine traits. The presentation of the *neaniskos* in Mark also bears striking resemblance to the Beloved Disciple in John, as Schenke has noted.[60] The youth *hon ēgapa auton ho Iēsous* ("whom Jesus loved," 2r, 15) resembles the disciple *hon ēgapa ho Iēsous* in the Gospel of John (13:23–26; 19:26–27; 20:2–10; 21:7, 20–23, 24; cf. also *ho mathētēs ho allos,* "the other disciple" / *allos mathētēs,* "another disciple" in 18:15–16; 20:2–10). The Johannine Beloved Disciple has been widely discussed in the scholarly literature and has been identified, variously, as John the son of Zebedee, John Mark, Lazarus (cf. John 11:3, 5, 11, 36), or (since the discovery of the Nag Hammadi codices) as Judas Thomas (cf. *Gospel of Thomas, Book of Thomas*), Mary Magdalene (cf. *Gospel of Philip, Gospel of Mary*), or even James the brother of the lord (cf. *Apocryphon of James*).[61] Finally,

Raymond E. Brown rightly observes, "There is little doubt that in Johannine thought the Beloved Disciple can symbolize the Christian."[62] This
symbolic understanding of the Beloved Disciple, together with the parallels between the raising of the *neaniskos* and the story of Lazarus, brings
us especially close to the interpretation presented here of the *neaniskos*
as a paradigm for discipleship in canonical and *Secret Mark*.

Notes

1. Morton Smith, "Monasteries and Their Manuscripts," *Arch* 13 (1960): 172–
77.

2. Morton Smith, *The Secret Gospel: The Discovery and Interpretation of the
Secret Gospel According to Mark* (New York: Harper & Row, 1973), 12.

3. Isaac Voss, ed., *Epistulae genuinae S. Ignatii Martyris* (Amsterdam: Blaeu,
1646).

4. Cf. Morton Smith, *Clement of Alexandria and a Secret Gospel of Mark* (Cam-
bridge, Mass.: Harvard University Press, 1973), 449, 451, 453; and M. Smith, *The
Secret Gospel*, 38. Now see new photographs in Hedrick, with Olympiou, "Secret
Mark," 3–11, 14–16.

5. M. Smith, *Clement of Alexandria*, 1.

6. Crossan, *Four Other Gospels*, 100.

7. Cf. Quentin Quesnell, "The Mar Saba Clementine: A Question of Evidence,"
CBQ 37 (1975): 48–67; and Quentin Quesnell, "A Reply to Morton Smith," *CBQ*
38 (1976): 200–3.

8. Morton Smith, "On the Authenticity of the Mar Saba Letter of Clement,"
CBQ 38 (1976): 196–99.

9. Per Beskow, *Strange Tales about Jesus: A Survey of Unfamiliar Gospels* (Philadelphia: Fortress, 1983); and Morton Smith, "Regarding *Secret Mark*: A Response
by Morton Smith to the Account by Per Beskow," *JBL* 103 (1984): 624.

10. Thomas Talley, "Liturgical Time in the Ancient Church: The State of
Research," *Studia Liturgica* 14 (1982): 45.

11. 1r may also be referred to as page 1, 1v as page 2, and 2r as page 3 in the
manuscript.

12. M. Smith, *Clement of Alexandria*, 289.

13. Cf. Jude 13; and M. Smith, *Clement of Alexandria*, 8.

14. These texts are conveniently assembled in M. Smith, *Clement of Alexandria*,
20–21.

15. Cf. Ibid., 28.

16. Morton Smith, "Clement of Alexandria and Secret Mark: The Score at the
End of the First Decade," *HTR* 75 (1982): 449–61.

17. M. Smith, "Clement of Alexandria," 450.

18. Ibid., 457.

19. Ibid., 455.

20. Cf. also Helmut Koester, "Tradition and History of the Early Christian Gospel Literature," Shaffer Lectures, Yale University (1980).

21. Koester, "History and Development of Mark's Gospel," 57.

22. Ibid., 56.

23. Ibid.

24. Schenke, "The Mystery of the Gospel of Mark," 67.

25. Ibid., 69.

26. Ibid., 76.

27. Ibid., 77–78.

28. Crossan, *Four Other Gospels,* 108.

29. Ibid., 119; cf. Koester's stage 1a.

30. Cf. Ron Cameron, Review of Crossan, *Four Other Gospels,* in *JBL* 106 (1987): 559.

31. Crossan, *Four Other Gospels,* 108; cf. 119–20.

32. Otto Stählin, ed., *Clemens Alexandrinus 4/1: Register* (ed. Ursula Treu; 2d ed.; GCS; Berlin: Akademie-Verlag, 1980).

33. See M. Smith, *Clement of Alexandria,* 109.

34. Robin Scroggs and Kent I. Groff, "Baptism in Mark: Dying and Rising with Christ," *JBL* 92 (1973): 542.

35. See M. Smith, *Clement of Alexandria;* J. Z. Smith, "The Garments of Shame"; Scroggs and Groff, "Baptism in Mark"; and Crossan, *Four Other Gospels.*

36. Cf. M. Smith, *Clement of Alexandria,* 115.

37. Schenke, "The Mystery of the Gospel of Mark," 80.

38. Talley, "Liturgical Time in the Ancient Church," 44.

39. Ibid., 45–46.

40. See M. Smith, *Clement of Alexandria,* 190–91.

41. Ibid., 123–35.

42. Ibid., 121.

43. Ibid., 122; cf. *Gos. Thom.* 61.

44. Crossan, *Four Other Gospels,* 109.

45. For example, Marie-Joseph Lagrange, *Évangile selon Saint Marc* (*EBib;* Paris: Gabalda, 1929); and Vincent Taylor, *The Gospel According to St. Mark* (London: Macmillan, 1966).

46. For example, C. G. Montefiore, *The Synoptic Gospels* (2 vols.; London: Macmillan, 1927); and Herman Waetjen, "The Ending of Mark and the Gospel's Shift in Eschatology," *ASTI* 4 (1965): 114–31.

47. Taylor, *The Gospel According to St. Mark,* 561.

48. For example, John Knox, "A Note on Mark 14:51–52," in *The Joy of Study: Papers on New Testament and Related Subjects Presented to Honor Frederick Clifton Grant* (ed. Sherman E. Johnson; New York: Macmillan, 1951), 27–30; and Albert Vanhoye, "La fuite du jeune homme nu (Mc 14,51–52)," *Bib* 52 (1971): 401–6.

49. For example, Harry Fleddermann, "The Flight of a Naked Young Man (Mark 14:51–52)," *CBQ* 41 (1979): 412–18.

50. For example, Scroggs and Groff, "Baptism in Mark"; and Schenke, "The Mystery of the Gospel of Mark."

51. Scroggs and Groff, "Baptism in Mark," 548.

52. M. Smith, "Clement of Alexandria," 457.

53. Contra Fleddermann, "The Flight of a Naked Young Man," 418.

54. Scroggs and Groff, "Baptism in Mark," 543.

55. Elisabeth Schüssler Fiorenza, *In Memory of Her: A Feminist Theological Reconstruction of Christian Origins* (New York: Crossroad, 1983), 322.

56. Ibid., 320.

57. Cf. Winsome Munro, "Women Disciples in Mark?" *CBQ* 44 (1982): 239–40.

58. Norman R. Petersen, "When Is the End Not the End? Literary Reflections on the Ending of Mark's Narrative," *Int* 34 (1980): 151–66.

59. F. F. Bruce, *The "Secret" Gospel of Mark* (Ethel M. Wood Lecture; London: Athlone, 1974).

60. Schenke, "The Mystery of the Gospel of Mark," 77.

61. Cf. Hans-Martin Schenke, "The Function and Background of the Beloved Disciple in the Gospel of John," in *Nag Hammadi, Gnosticism, and Early Christianity* (ed. Charles W. Hedrick and Robert Hodgson, Jr.; Peabody, Mass.: Hendrickson, 1986), 111–25.

62. Raymond E. Brown, *The Gospel According to John* (AB 29–29A; Garden City, N.Y.: Doubleday, 1966–70), 924.

8

The Youth in *Secret Mark* and the Beloved Disciple in John

The Discovery

In the summer of 1958, Morton Smith recounts, seventeen years after he had first visited the Greek Orthodox Monastery of Mar Saba in 1941, he made a remarkable discovery there in the Judean desert.[1] Smith reports that he returned to the monastery with the permission of the Patriarch Benedict, in order to study and catalogue the manuscripts housed there. Smith's colorful account of his discovery deserves to be quoted at some length:

> Then, one afternoon near the end of my stay, I found myself in my cell, staring incredulously at a text written in a tiny scrawl I had not even tried to read in the tower when I picked out the book containing it. But now that I came to puzzle it out, it began, "From the letters of the most holy Clement, the author of the *Stromateis*. To Theodore," and it went on to praise the recipient for having "shut up" the Carpocratians. The *Stromateis*, I knew, was a work by Clement of Alexandria, one of the earliest and most mysterious of the great fathers of the Church — early Christian writers of outstanding importance. I was reasonably sure that no letters of his had been preserved. So if this writing was what it claimed to be, I had a hitherto unknown text by a writer of major significance for early Church history. Besides, it would add something to our knowledge of the Carpocratians, one of the most scandalous of the "gnostic" sects, early and extreme variants of Christianity. Who Theodore was, I had no idea. I still don't. But Clement and the Carpocratians were more than enough for one day. I hastened

to photograph the text and photographed it three times for good measure.[2]

Smith's account raises three issues for our consideration.

1. When Smith mentions the question of the authenticity of the Mar Saba letter of Clement ("if this writing was what it claimed to be"), he inadvertently anticipates the controversy that has swirled around this text and the issue of its authenticity. From the well-known statements of Quentin Quesnell[3] to the more recent dispute over insinuations in Per Beskow's *Strange Tales about Jesus*,[4] the scholarly discussions concerning the Mar Saba manuscript have been conducted within the context of expressed doubts and uncertainties about the authenticity of the text. While uncertainties remain, it is noteworthy that a number of scholars increasingly seem inclined to accept the text as an ancient letter of Clement. Smith himself notes, in a review article surveying 150 publications on the letter of Clement and the *Secret Gospel of Mark*, that "most scholars would attribute the letter to Clement, though a substantial minority are still in doubt."[5] At least four scholars (John Dominic Crossan, Helmut Koester, Marvin Meyer, and Hans-Martin Schenke[6]) have gone into print assuming the authenticity of the text. Such an assumption of authenticity is also the "working hypothesis" (the phrase is Crossan's) of the present essay.

2. Smith indicates that he made the discovery by himself, in the privacy of his monastic cell, and for years Smith apparently remained the only scholar who had seen the actual text. At least one other scholar, Thomas Talley, tried to see the text in January of 1980, but he has written that his attempts were frustrated.[7] I heartily agree with the observation of Crossan that a text's authenticity must be confirmed by scholars examining the original carefully and scientifically.[8]

3. Smith writes that he photographed the letter of Clement. His photographs are reproduced in both his scholarly and his popular editions of the texts,[9] and for a long time these personal photographs were the only published facsimiles of the Mar Saba letter of Clement. The adequate publication of the text in facsimile edition also needs to be undertaken, so that scholars may be able to examine the clearest possible reproductions of the document. The accomplishment of this task will not give scholars access to an actual ancient copy, since the copy of the Mar Saba letter seems to have been made about 1750, according to

the scholars who examined the photographs and attempted to date the scribal hand.[10] Yet a facsimile edition of the text at least will allow more scholars to see reproductions of the letter of Clement and draw their own conclusions from the evidence thus presented. This task has been considerably advanced with the recent publication of new photographs of the text.[11]

The Document

The Mar Saba letter attributed to Clement of Alexandria was written in cursive Greek on two-and-a-half pages at the back of a printed edition of the letters of Ignatius of Antioch.[12] As copied, the document preserves only a fragment of the letter of Clement to Theodore. In the letter Clement as heresiologist commends the recipient for his opposition to the gnostic Carpocratians, and the style and contents of the heresiological letter are reminiscent of Clement's *Stromateis* and *Protreptikos pros Hellenas*. While he is exposing the foul deeds of the Carpocratians, Clement declares that they make use of an edition of the Gospel of Mark that Carpocrates falsified. Clement charges that after Carpocrates obtained from a Christian presbyter in Alexandria a copy of the Gospel of Mark ("the secret gospel," *tou mystikou euangeliou*, 1v,6), he interpreted it "according to his blasphemous and carnal opinion" and polluted it by "mixing the most shameless lies with the undefiled and holy words" (1v,7–9). In contrast to this falsified edition, Clement specifies two other editions of Mark that are true and authoritative: the public version of the Gospel of Mark, which seems, from Clement's account, to be identical or nearly identical with the present canonical Gospel of Mark; and the *Secret Gospel of Mark*, an equally authentic version of Mark that functioned as "a more spiritual gospel for the use of those being perfected" (1r, 21–22).[13]

According to Clement, the *Secret Gospel of Mark* is an edition of the gospel that appears to be only slightly longer than public Mark. Clement cites two relatively brief sections found in *Secret Mark* but not in public Mark. Conceivably Clement may have known of other passages peculiar to *Secret Mark* and may have referred to such passages in a portion of his letter that has not survived. Yet in the extant fragment of his letter Clement indicates nothing to support such a possibility, and he seems to be moving away from the discussion of the passages unique

to *Secret Mark* in the final lines of the fragment ("Now then, the inter-pretation that is true and in accordance with the true philosophy...,"
2r,17–18).

The first section of *Secret Mark* quoted by Clement (1v,23–2r,11) is
to be located immediately after Mark 10:34 and reads as follows:[14]

> And they come to Bethany. This woman whose brother had died
> was there. She came and knelt before Jesus and says to him, "Son
> of David, have mercy on me." But the followers rebuked her. Then
> Jesus became angry and went with her into the garden where the
> tomb was. At once a loud voice was heard from the tomb, and Jesus
> went up and rolled the stone away from the door of the tomb. At
> once he went in where the youth (*neaniskos*) was. He reached out
> his hand, took him by the hand, and raised him up. The youth
> looked at Jesus and loved him, and he began to beg him to be with
> him. Then they left the tomb and went into the youth's house, for
> he was rich. Six days later Jesus told him what to do, and in the
> evening the youth comes to him wearing a linen shroud over his
> naked body. He stayed with him that night, for Jesus was teaching
> him the mystery of the kingdom of God. And from there he got up
> and returned to the other side of the Jordan.

The second section of the *Secret Gospel of Mark* (2r,14–16) is to be lo-cated within Mark 10:46. *Secret Mark* 10:46 then may be reconstructed
to read as follows:

> And he comes to Jericho. The sister of the youth whom Jesus loved
> was there, along with his mother and Salome, but Jesus did not
> receive them (fem.). And as he was leaving Jericho with his disciples
> and a large crowd, Bartimaeus son of Timaeus, a blind beggar, was
> sitting by the side of the road.

The recent studies on *Secret Mark* by Crossan, Koester, Meyer, and
Schenke interpret the fragments of the secret gospel in dramatically dif-ferent ways, but they are in agreement on several matters. As noted
above, these studies assume the authenticity of the Mar Saba letter as an
ancient text and direct serious attention to the letter of Clement and the
Markan fragments imbedded within it. Further, these studies are unan-imous in recommending a redaction-critical approach to *Secret Mark*,

in order to evaluate the place of the *Secret Gospel* within the Markan redactional tradition. And these studies also all advocate the priority of the text of *Secret Mark* to that of canonical Mark. As Koester puts it, "The conclusion is unavoidable: Canonical Mark is derived from Secret Mark. The basic difference between the two seems to be that the redactor of canonical Mark eliminated the story of the raising of the youth and the reference to this story in Mk. 10:46."[15] The evidence marshaled by Koester and others to support this contention need not be rehearsed here. Suffice it to say that peculiar redactional traits of canonical Mark are mirrored in the surviving two sections of *Secret Mark*.

Elsewhere I have argued that a careful reading of the *Secret Gospel of Mark* exposes a subplot in *Secret Mark* that is present in only a truncated form in canonical Mark. This subplot features the story of a paradigmatic youth (*neaniskos*), and the story functions to communicate *Secret Mark*'s vision of the life of discipleship as that is exemplified in the career of the youth. Five pericopae (Mark 10:17–22; *Secret Mark,* fragment 1; *Secret Mark,* fragment 2; Mark 14:51–52; Mark 16:1–8), each connected to the others by means of a series of literary links, serve to advance the story of the youth. The elimination of the story of the raising of the youth in the redaction of canonical Mark thus fractured the integrity of the subplot and left the youth fleeing naked (Mark 14:51–51) and the youth in the tomb (Mark 16:1–8) for scholars to worry over.

This story of the youth in *Secret Mark* also brings to mind features of the Gospel of John. Ever since the initial publication of the Mar Saba letter, scholars have noted that the account of the raising of the youth in *Secret Mark* is remarkably similar to the story of the raising of Lazarus in John 11. According to *Secret Mark,* a youth of Bethany (cf. John 11:1) dies, and his sister comes to Jesus and greets him (cf. John 11:20ff.; in John, Martha comes and Mary stays at home). Jesus is angered at the disciples' rebuke (*Secret Mark* 1v,25, *orgistheis;* in John 11:33, 38 forms of the verb *embrimaomai* are used, a verb that commonly functions as a synonym or near-synonym of *orgizō*). Jesus goes to the tomb in a garden (perhaps cf. John 19:41), and there is the call of a loud voice (*phōnē megalē, Secret Mark* 2r,1; in John 11:43 Jesus himself cries with a loud voice, *phonē megalē*). Jesus removes the stone from the door of the tomb (according to John 11:41, "they took away the stone"), and raises the youth (cf. John 11:41ff.).

That there is a relationship between the Markan story of the youth and the Johannine story of Lazarus seems quite evident. Smith has argued that "there can be no question that the story in the longer text of Mk. is more primitive in form than the story of Lazarus in Jn."[16] I am convinced by Smith's argument; other scholars[17] are not. As Smith points out painstakingly, the Markan story of the youth in the Mar Saba text lacks the details we expect in a more developed tradition (personal names, descriptions of features of the miracle, etc.), and shows no evidence of specifically Johannine redactional traits (vocabulary, delay of the miracle, aretalogical self-predication).[18] To Smith's wide-ranging arguments Crossan adds the claim that it is plausible to read the miracle story of *Secret Mark* as a more primitive version of the story than that of John 11, and that John 11 may well manifest a secondary use of three themes: the loud voice, the anger or strong emotion of Jesus, and the garden.[19]

An additional parallel between the Markan and Johannine miracle stories should be highlighted. According to the *Secret Gospel of Mark*, the resurrected youth looked upon Jesus and loved him (*ho de neaniskos emblepsas autō ēgapēsen auton,* 2r,4), and the youth in turn is described as the *neaniskos* "whom Jesus loved" (*hon ēgapa auton ho Iēsous,* 2r,15), a description that compares well with the statement of Mark 10:21 ("And Jesus, looking upon him, loved him," *ho de Iēsous emblepsas autō ēgapēsen auton*). This statement about the rich youth of Mark 10:17–22 seems especially significant: Only here in the Synoptic Gospels is it specifically said that Jesus loves a given disciple or candidate for discipleship; and this pericope, as I have posited, is linked to the other Markan pericopae in the subplot of the youth in *Secret Mark*. In the Gospel of John, Lazarus also is said to be loved by Jesus in four passages: (1) Lazarus is the one "whom" Jesus "loved" (*hon phileis,* 11:3); (2) Jesus "loved" (*ēgapa*) Martha, her sister, and Lazarus (11:5); (3) Jesus calls Lazarus "our friend" (or, "our loved one," *ho philos hēmōn,* 11:11); and (4) those around say of Jesus, "Look how he loved him!" (*ide pōs ephilei auton,* 11:36).

If, then, the Markan figure of the youth and the Johannine figure of Lazarus constitute the one "whom Jesus loved," how do these characters in turn relate to the Johannine figure of the Beloved Disciple? To the issue of the Beloved Disciple we now turn.

The Beloved Disciple in John

A certain disciple loved by Jesus, "another disciple," and unnamed disciples are all mentioned in the Gospel of John, and all have been said to be important for the interpretation of the role of the Johannine Beloved Disciple. Here we shall attempt to gather these three sorts of references and assess their significance for our understanding of the Beloved Disciple.[20]

1. The Beloved Disciple is explicitly referred to in four passages in the Gospel of John. First, in the account of the Last Supper, Jesus announces that one of the disciples will betray him. The disciples in general are uncertain, but one disciple discovers who the betrayer will be: "One of his disciples, whom Jesus loved (*heis ek tōn mathētōn autou . . . hon ēgapa ho Iēsous*), was reclining in the bosom of Jesus. Simon Peter beckons to him to ask who it might be of whom he speaks. Leaning thus on the breast of Jesus, he says to him, 'Lord, who is it?' " (13:23–25). Jesus proceeds to give indication to the confidant that Judas is the one who will betray him (13:26). Secondly, according to the Johannine passion narrative, several women were standing by the cross, as were two others: "Jesus, seeing his mother and the disciple whom he loved (*ton mathētēn . . . hon ēgapa*) standing near, says to his mother, 'Woman, look, your son.' Then he says to the disciple, 'Look, your mother.' And from that hour the disciple took her to his own house" (19:26–27). Thirdly, after the crucifixion, according to John 20:1–2, Mary Magdalene goes to the tomb of Jesus, only to discover that the stone had been moved. "So she runs and comes to Simon Peter and to the other disciple, whom Jesus loved (*ton allon mathētēn hon ephilei ho Iēsous*), and says to them, 'They have taken the lord from the tomb, and we do not know where they have laid him' " (20:2). Peter and "the other disciple" (*ho allos mathētēs*, 20:3) run to the tomb, and although "the other disciple" reaches the tomb before Peter (20:4) and looks within, he himself does not enter until Peter has done so. "Then the other disciple, who came to the tomb first, also entered, and he saw and believed" (20:8).

In the appendix (or epilogue) to the Gospel of John (chapter 21) occurs the fourth passage that refers to "the disciple whom Jesus loved." After the resurrection Jesus reveals himself to his disciples and has direct exchanges with Peter on the theme of love and with the Beloved Disciple. At 21:7 it is the latter who recognizes Jesus: "That disciple whom Jesus loved (*ho mathētēs ekeinos hon ēgapa ho Iēsous*) says to Peter, 'It is the lord.' " Later in the chapter that disciple is identified with the intimate disciple at the Last Supper (13:23–26):

> Peter, turning, sees the disciple whom Jesus loved following, who also was leaning on his breast at the supper, and said, "Lord, who is it that is going to betray you?" Peter, seeing him, says to Jesus, "Lord, what about him?" Jesus says to him, "If I want him to remain until I come, what is that to you? As for you, follow me." So this saying spread to the brothers, that this disciple is not to die, but Jesus did not say to him that he was not to die, but rather, "If I want him to remain until I come, what is that to you?" (21:20–23).

Finally, the author of the appendix writes that this disciple is the witness who stands behind the tradition: "This is the disciple who bears witness concerning these things and who has written these things, and we know that his witness is true" (21:24).

2. In two passages John describes an anonymous disciple as "the other disciple" (*ho mathētēs ho allos*) or "another disciple" (*allos mathētēs*). According to John 18:15 "another disciple" along with Peter followed Jesus; "that disciple was known to the high priest, and he entered the courtyard of the high priest with Jesus." Then "the other disciple" went out and spoke to the maid at the door, so that Peter also could enter (18:16). In John 20:1–10, as noted above, "the disciple whom Jesus loved" is called, in four instances, "the other disciple" (20:2, 3, 4, 8).

3. In two additional passages unnamed disciples are presented in the Gospel of John. In 1:37–42 two of John the baptizer's disciples follow Jesus: One is identified as Andrew, the other is unnamed. As the most reliable reading of John 1:41 puts it, "He (i.e., Andrew) first (*prōton*) finds his own brother Simon. . . . " The inferior reading *prōtos*, supported by the original hand of Codex Sinaiticus and other manuscripts, could allow — or so it has been suggested — the translation, "He (i.e., Andrew) is the first to find his own brother Simon," thus implying that the unnamed disciple (John the son of Zebedee?) also finds his brother (James?).[21] Again, according to John 19:35 an unnamed eyewitness is the guarantor of the truth of the crucifixion account, perhaps in particular the interpretive elements unique to John (blood and water, possibly also no broken bones): "The one who has seen has borne witness."

How might we evaluate these several Johannine references and their significance for our understanding of the Beloved Disciple? We begin with the unnamed disciple of John 1:37–42: That figure may be dismissed immediately from our consideration, since there is very little evidence, and none of it compelling, that would lead us to suppose an identification of the companion of Andrew with the Beloved Disciple. The reference to "the disciple whom Jesus loved" in John 21 clearly seems to be the work of the redactor, who is supremely interested in tying the motif of the Beloved Disciple to the authorship of the gospel. Such a general observation seems safe enough after the seminal work of Rudolf Bultmann.[22] John 19:35 similarly seems to be a redactional gloss (so also Bultmann), for both its apparent intention and its wording resemble John 21:24. In any case, John 19:35 does not describe the eyewitness either as "the disciple whom Jesus loved" or as "the other disciple." Whether "the other disciple" of John 18:15–16 is to be related to the Beloved Disciple is not obvious. The fact that "the other disciple" of John 20:1–10 is equated with "the disciple whom Jesus loved" suggests the plausibility of a similar equation in John 18, as might the additional parallels between John 18:15–16 and John 20:1–10 (in these two passages "the other disciple" is depicted with Peter, precedes Peter, and finally allows Peter to enter the courtyard of the high priest in chapter 18 or the tomb of Jesus in chapter 20). The two other references to the Beloved Disciple (John 13:23–26; 19:26–27) portray a disciple who is intimate with Jesus, close to Jesus in life and in death. Whatever may be the background of the character of the Beloved Disciple, at key points in these chapters this figure is presented in a personalized manner as a model disciple who is near Jesus.

Conclusion

"The figure of the Beloved Disciple is admittedly one of the great puzzles in the mysterious Fourth Gospel."[23] With these words Schenke turns to his own study of the place of "the disciple whom Jesus loved" in John. Many have attempted to identify the Beloved Disciple with a particular historical figure (e.g., John the son of Zebedee, John Mark, John the presbyter, or, in the case of the disciple in John 18:15–16, a disciple with priestly connections); since Bultmann some have suggested that the Beloved Disciple in John 21 (cf. also 19:35) is an authoritative historical figure, in the Johannine school, whom the redactor of John identifies as the eyewitness and author of the gospel. Now Schenke has combed the Nag Hammadi texts for other figures who resemble the Beloved Disciple, and he proposes that Mary Magdalene, James the Just, and Judas Thomas also function as beloved disciples in one way or another in gnostic texts. In the *Gospel of Philip* (NHC II,3), for example, it is said concerning Mary Magdalene that "[Christ loved] her more than [all] the disciples [and used to] kiss her [often] on her [mouth]" (63,34–36; the reconstruction of these lines is made more secure by the well-preserved lines at 64,1–5). Elsewhere in the *Gospel of Philip* Mary Magdalene is termed the "companion" or "consort" (*koinōnos*) of Jesus (e.g., 59,9). Such a relationship between Mary Magdalene and Jesus in gnostic traditions is confirmed by the *Gospel of Mary* (BG 1; cf. 10,1–9; 17,15–18,15). In other gnostic documents James the Just, the brother of Jesus, is said to be especially close to Jesus (cf. the *Apocryphon of James* [NHC I,2], the *First Apocalypse of James* [NHC V,3], the *Second Apocalypse of James* [NHC V,4], and the *Gospel of Thomas* [NHC II,2] logion 12). Most notable for Schenke are the descriptions of Judas Thomas in the *Gospel of Thomas* (cf. logion 13) and the *Book of Thomas* (NHC II,7). In the *Book of Thomas* Jesus addresses Thomas as his brother (*son/san*) three times (138,4, 10, 19), and at 138,7–8 Jesus also calls Thomas "my twin and my true companion (or, friend)," *pasoeiš auō pašb^er^emmēe,* which Schenke translates back into Greek as *sy ei...ho philos mou ho alēthinos,* or, following Johannine syntax, *sy ei hon philō alēthōs* (second person), or *autos estin hon ephilei alēthōs ho Iēsous* (third person).[24]

Schenke concludes, on the Beloved Disciple, that "the Beloved Disciple passages are only a simple fiction of the redactor," and he may very well be right. He continues:

Reference is made to the alleged Beloved Disciple in the same way as the Pastorals refer to Paul. The function of the Beloved Disciple is to ground the Fourth Gospel (and the tradition of the Christian group in which it originates and has its influence) in the eyewitness testimony of one who was especially intimate with Jesus. This kind of deception may find its explanation and, what is more, its justification, only within a particular historical situation of conflict. The circumstances, however, do not point to a conflict within the group, but rather to a confrontation with another Christian (Petrine) tradition.[25]

Schenke's evaluation of the Beloved Disciple passages suggests that they all have been edited by the redactor, not only John 21 but also John 13:23–26 and John 20:1–10 (Schenke also places John 19:35 with these passages). This interpretation rightly acknowledges the way in which the Beloved Disciple usually accompanies and outranks Peter in the Gospel of John.

At 19:26–27, however, the Beloved Disciple does not appear alongside Peter, but rather is described at the cross with the mother of Jesus. Schenke observes, "The intention of 19:26–27 is to have the Beloved Disciple, in the dying-hour of Jesus, appointed his successor on earth."[26] That is accomplished by means of this scene, which allows the Beloved Disciple to be adopted, as it were, into the family of Jesus, so that he becomes the brother of Jesus. This observation, then, allows Schenke to turn to the figure of Judas Thomas as a close disciple and beloved brother of Jesus and to propose that he may have served as the prototype (Schenke uses the term "historical model") for the Johannine Beloved Disciple. If this is the case, then the role of Thomas would be doubled in the Gospel of John, since the figure of Thomas also appears in John 11:16; 14:5, 22(?); 20:24, 26–28; 21:2. Schenke sees no difficulty in such doubling and concludes, "Finally it seems easy to reverse the whole question and to look upon the conspicuous role that Thomas plays in the text of the unrevised Fourth Gospel as created under the influence of the same Syrian Judas Thomas tradition, which, then, would have affected the Fourth Gospel at two stages in its development."[27]

Schenke's basic thesis concerning the fictional character of the Beloved Disciple is persuasive, in a certain way of considering it, and his reconstruction of the function of the Beloved Disciple in John is at least a plausible alternative to Bultmann's, but I find his argument on the background of "the disciple whom Jesus loved" to be weak. To be sure, gnostic documents show that other figures such as Mary Magdalene, James the Just, and Judas Thomas could be singled out, in a general way, as beloved disciples, that is, as disciples judged to have a special role and authority within the Christian tradition. To this extent the motif of the Beloved Disciple may have a fairly wide application within various early Christian communities. In order to identify Judas Thomas as the "historical model" for the Beloved Disciple in John, however, Schenke must engage in what seems to me to be a forced reading and interpretation of texts on Thomas, in particular the opening page of the *Book of Thomas* from the Nag Hammadi library. Further, his insistence upon reading the Beloved Disciple passages "backwards" (i.e., from chapter 21 back to the other passages) allows for an important way of establishing a redactional uniformity to the passages on "the disciple whom Jesus loved," contrary to Bultmann, but it also may prevent him from giving appropriate attention to another passage that will elucidate the background of the Beloved Disciple. That passage is John 11, with its account of Lazarus, the beloved follower of Jesus who, we have seen, seems to be linked literarily with the youth in the *Secret Gospel of Mark*.

Schenke, too, raises the issue of the Markan youth and the Johannine Beloved Disciple, but he dismisses the parallels as being only apparent. He raises three objections,[28] and each may be answered. (1) He emphasizes the difference between the youth's loving Jesus in the first fragment cited from the *Secret Gospel of Mark* and Jesus' loving the Beloved Disciple in John. But Schenke virtually ignores the significance of the second fragment of *Secret Mark* cited by Clement (with its reference to "the youth whom Jesus loved" [*ho neaniskos hon ēgapa auton ho Iēsous*], 2r,15) and also does not recognize the Markan subplot and the place of Mark 10:21 (with its reference to Jesus loving the rich youth) within the subplot. (2) Schenke stresses that the love of Jesus for the Johannine Beloved Disciple has an exclusive quality, while the love for the Markan youth does not. In the *Secret Gospel of Mark*, we might reply, the claims to exclusivity may be subtler, but they still are there. After all, *Secret Mark* characterizes the youth as a disciple of paradigmatic significance and describes him as one "whom Jesus loved" over against the women whom Jesus did not receive. (3) Schenke points out the differences in role between the Markan youth, representative of cultic interests (i.e., baptism and initiation), and the Johannine Beloved Disciple, a more historicized figure. These distinctions are valid (although we should not ignore the cultic interests of John 13), but they stem mainly from the redactional development of the youth in Mark and of the Beloved Disciple in John.

Hence, I propose that the prototype or "historical model" of the Beloved Disciple may best be understood to be the paradigmatic youth who is presented as the *neaniskos* in *Secret Mark* and as Lazarus in

John. By suggesting this thesis I am building, in part, upon the position of Bultmann and others who have asserted that the Beloved Disciple as depicted by the Johannine evangelist (as opposed to the figure developed by the redactor) "is an ideal figure."[29] I am also appreciative of the scholars who previously have seen the clear ties between Lazarus and the Beloved Disciple.[30] Just as the youth in *Secret Mark* embodies Mark's vision of the life of discipleship, so also Lazarus as Beloved Disciple illustrates the ideal of the follower of Christ who has been raised to new life. This symbolic disciple is depicted in a less developed manner in Mark and in a more expanded and historicized fashion in John. Very possibly this idealized figure emerged from an early aretalogical source (cf. pre-Markan miracle stories, or the pre-Johannine *Semeia-Quelle*), and the figure was taken over and adapted by Mark and John. In John the author or redactor not only developed the story of beloved Lazarus to meet the needs of the gospel. The author or redactor (subsequently?) also introduced the Beloved Disciple into several other portions of the evolving gospel, perhaps in more than one stage, the result being an increasingly historicized presentation of the Beloved Disciple as the witness, authority, and even author (cf. 21:24) of the gospel. This presentation discloses an ideal disciple who surpasses Peter and who "saw and believed" at the tomb (20:8) but who in turn is surpassed by the implied readers, who are pronounced blessed as "those who have not seen and yet have believed" (20:29). Thus the youth in the *Secret Gospel of Mark* may shed important new light on the Gospel of John and may encourage us to reevaluate, once again, the place of the Beloved Disciple within that gospel.

Notes

1. This essay was originally published in a volume in honor of James M. Robinson, whose scholarly career, like that of Morton Smith, has featured studies on the Markan tradition, manuscript discoveries and reconstructed stories of manuscript discoveries, and suggestions about the impact of newly discovered documents upon our knowledge of Christian origins.

2. M. Smith, *The Secret Gospel*, 12–13.

3. Cf. Quesnell, "The Mar Saba Clementine," and "A Reply to Morton Smith," as well as M. Smith, "On the Authenticity of the Mar Saba Letter."

4. Cf. M. Smith, "Regarding *Secret Mark*."

5. M. Smith, "Clement of Alexandria," 451.

6. Crossan, *Four Other Gospels,* 89–121; Koester, "History and Development of Mark's Gospel"; Meyer, "The Youth in the *Secret Gospel of Mark*"; and Schenke, "The Mystery of the Gospel of Mark."

7. Talley, "Liturgical Time in the Ancient Church," 45.

8. Crossan, *Four Other Gospels,* 100.

9. M. Smith, *Clement of Alexandria,* 449, 451, 453; and *The Secret Gospel,* 38.

10. M. Smith, *Clement of Alexandria,* 1.

11. See Hedrick, with Olympiou, "Secret Mark."

12. Voss, *Epistulae genuinae.*

13. 1r may also be referred to as page 1, 1v as page 2, and 2r as page 3 of the manuscript.

14. Here and elsewhere the translation is mine, based upon the Greek text in M. Smith, *Clement of Alexandria,* 448, 450, 452.

15. Koester, "History and Development of Mark's Gospel," 56.

16. M. Smith, *Clement of Alexandria,* 156.

17. Cf. Raymond E. Brown, "The Relation of 'The Secret Gospel of Mark' to the Fourth Gospel," *CBQ* 36 (1974): 466–85; Bruce, *The "Secret" Gospel of Mark.*

18. M. Smith, *Clement of Alexandria,* 148–63.

19. Crossan, *Four Other Gospels,* 105–6.

20. The bibliography on the Beloved Disciple is extensive. Cf. the sources listed in R. Brown, *The Gospel According to John;* Schenke, "Function and Background."

21. Cf. R. Brown, *The Gospel According to John,* 75–76.

22. Rudolf Bultmann, *The Gospel of John: A Commentary* (trans. G. R. Beasley-Murray, R. W. N. Hoare, and J. K. Riches; Philadelphia: Westminster, 1971), esp. 483–86.

23. Schenke, "Function and Background," 114.

24. Ibid., 123.

25. Ibid., 119.

26. Ibid.

27. Ibid., 125.

28. Ibid., 120–21.

29. Bultmann, *The Gospel of John,* 484. Cf. also R. Brown, *The Gospel According to John,* xciv–xcv, also 924: "There is little doubt that in Johannine thought the Beloved Disciple can symbolize the Christian."

30. For example, Floyd V. Filson, "Who Was the Beloved Disciple?" *JBL* 68 (1949): 83–88.

9

The Naked Youths
in the Villa of the Mysteries,
Canonical Mark, and *Secret Mark*

On the walls of a triclinium in a suburban villa at Pompeii is a famous painted mural, or frieze, with brilliant scenes illustrating Dionysian
themes.[1] The mural features depictions of mortal women and patholog-
ical characters, and one young mortal male is to be seen. He is shown,
in a scene adjacent to a door of the triclinium, nude except for boots,
and he is reading from a scroll, with a look of apparent wonderment on
his face. He is in the company of several mature women, one of whom
is helping him keep his place in the scroll with a stylus she is holding.
Although a great deal of attention has been given by scholars of religion,
classicists, and art historians to this naked youth, his place and identity
remain a mystery.

Another naked youth, equally elusive, streaks through the pages of an
ancient Christian text, the Gospel of Mark. There, in the account of the
arrest of Jesus, an unnamed youth, wearing only a linen shroud, is briefly

Villa of the Mysteries,
frescoes in the triclinium:
The naked youth in scene 1.

apprehended, but when grabbed he abandons his linen garment and flees naked. The role of this youth in Mark is made more interesting and more challenging by the discovery of the *Secret Gospel of Mark,* which includes in its lines a description of a similar youth — the same youth? — dressed in a similar fashion and associated with Jesus. Exegetes have provided creative and sometimes peculiar interpretations to elucidate who this youth may be in the Gospel of Mark, but his place and identity, too, remain an enigma.

The present essay seeks to address this mystery and enigma, to explore whether the mystery may clarify the enigma, and vice versa.

Villa of the Mysteries

Just outside the Porta Ercolano at Pompeii lies the Villa of the Mysteries, a large suburban villa that is in a good state of preservation and contains, in addition to more modest decorations elsewhere in the villa, a cubiculum and a triclinium (or oecus) (rooms 4 and 5) with beautiful wall paintings or frescoes.[2] The mural in the triclinium represents the Second Style of Pompeian painting, and it qualifies as a masterpiece of classical art. The mural most likely was created in the middle of the first century B.C.E., and, I suggest, specifically for this room. The several scenes in the mural fit the architectural features and contours of the room so well that it is hard to imagine, as sometimes has been done, that the Roman painting in the Villa of the Mysteries is a copy of a Greek original.[3] Of course, my suggestion is not meant to deny the likelihood that artistic themes and motifs from an earlier day are represented in the Roman painting.[4] The scenes in the mural cover the walls of the triclinium, though the scenes are interrupted by two doors and a large window. As a result, the triclinium and the scenes in the mural must have been accessible and visible to the people who passed through the villa.

Amedeo Maiuri, the excavator of the Villa of the Mysteries, identified ten scenes in the mural of the triclinium, and that convention of numbering ten scenes is maintained here.[5] The actual background of the mural is green, and Pompeian red panels are painted around the mural in order to give the visual impression of private space enclosed by panels. The individual scenes of the mural are linked together by means of artistic conventions: the movement of figures, the direction of glances, the lines created by figures in the painting. Upper borders — one with a floral design and Bacchic motifs, another with a geometric design and meander pattern — also bring unity to the room and movement through the scenes. Further, the individual scenes are sequenced, and they form a cycle of scenes, but there is disagreement about how the sequence and cycle are to be read. Roger Ling prefers "a centralised reading, in which the divine couple, situated at the centre of the wall opposite the main entrance, just like the cult-image in a temple, constitutes a focus for the remaining scenes, which balance across the room."[6] The strength of Ling's reading is that it emphasizes the divine couple as the center-piece of the composition. The weakness of his reading is that the door to the cubiculum and the large window interrupt the presentation of the scenes and destroy any real chance for the scenes to "balance across the room." I, with others, prefer a clockwise reading of the mural, beginning with the scene of the naked youth near the door to the cubiculum and continuing on to the scene of the woman seated on the bed.

Such a clockwise reading of the scenes in the mural is assumed in the detailed discussion of the ten scenes that follows.

The first scene, on the north wall of the triclinium, presents the youthful male, naked except for fawnskin boots. He is holding a scroll, from which he appears to be reading, and he looks surprised or astonished. With him are three adult women. One, veiled, moves to the right — clockwise — from the area of the door. A second woman, unveiled and seated in the middle, rests her right hand on the boy's shoulder and points to the scroll with a stylus. Her gesture and touch communicate a sense of tenderness. In her left hand she holds another scroll, and on the ring finger of her left hand she wears a ring, thereby indicating that she is married. The third woman, on the right, is looking back while stepping to the right and out of the scene. She is wearing bracelets on her right arm and a garland in her hair, and she is carrying a silver tray with something on it, cakes perhaps, while holding a floral branch or stalk in her right hand. Clearly she is pregnant. The direction of her movement carries her, and the viewer, into the second scene.

The second scene shows three women gathered around a table. The woman on the left bends over and holds a tray partially covered with a purple cloth. The woman in the center is seated with her back to the viewer. Her position is deliberately calculated to conceal what is taking place on the table and the tray. With her left hand she raises the purple cloth covering the tray, and in her right hand, toward which she looks,

Villa of the Mysteries, frescoes in the triclinium: Scenes 1–4.

she holds greenery over a bowl. The woman on the right has a garland in her hair, and she is pouring liquid from a small jug over the greenery. Something, possibly another scroll, is tucked into her garment. The right leg of the silenus from scene three extends back in front of the woman on the right in the present scene, and this provides a visual transition to the next scene.

The third scene includes a silenus, a satyr, and a satyress in a pastoral setting. The silenus leans against a pedestal as he plays a lyre. In his right hand he holds an object, maybe a pick for playing the lyre. His clothes are falling off his body, and his enraptured gaze seems to be directed toward the scene that may be the centerpiece of the entire mural, the divine couple of scene six. The satyr, seated on a rock, plays the syrinx (panpipes) and watches while the satyress, also seated on a rock, nurses a young goat or a similar young animal. Another animal stands in front, looking out into the room. The satyress nursing the young animal recalls the familiar Dionysian scene described in Euripides' *Bacchae:*

Villa of the Mysteries, frescoes in the triclinium: Scenes 5–7.

Breasts swollen with milk,
new mothers who had left their babies behind at home
nestled gazelles and young wolves in their arms,
suckling them. Then they crowned their hair with leaves,
ivy and oak and flowering bryony (698–702).[7]

The fourth scene depicts a frightened and fleeing woman, and as such it stands in dramatic contrast with the preceding pastoral scene. The woman flees in apparent alarm, her garment flying around her and behind her. Her eyes look across the room, most likely toward the flagellation in scenes seven and eight.

The fifth scene, around the northeast corner and on the east wall of the triclinium, has a silenus and two satyrs with a bowl and a mask.[8] The silenus is seated and garlanded, and his glance back toward the previous scene helps with the transition around the corner to the new scene on the new wall. The silenus holds a bowl in his hands, and one of the satyrs leans over and peers into the bowl. We may surmise that the bowl (with or without liquid inside) functions as a mirror (if without liquid, a concave mirror), and that the satyr sees a reflection in the bowl, either of himself or of something else. The expression on the face of the satyr suggests that he is startled by what he sees, and he has eyes wide open. The other satyr is standing and holding a mask, a silenus mask, behind the head of the first satyr. From this we may understand the emotion on the face of the peering satyr: he looks into a mirror and beholds not his own image, as he would anticipate, but rather that of a silenus. We might speculate that he sees himself not as the young satyr that he is but as the old silenus that he will become, after a lifetime of living the Dionysian life.[9]

The sixth scene, at the center of the east wall and arguably at the center of the mural, presents the divine couple. As the fates would have it, the painting is somewhat damaged here, but much of the scene remains visible. A garlanded male reclines voluptuously across the lap of a seated female. His leg extends into the previous scene and serves as a bridge to the present scene. His clothes, like those of the silenus before, are falling off his body, and a thyrsus, or Dionysian staff, lies across his lap. He is *monosandalos,* one sandal off and one sandal on, in the tradition of Jason and warriors. (About Jason Apollodorus writes that the oracle warned Pelias to watch out for "the man with the single sandal [*ton monosandalon*]," and Pindar likewise has the oracle warn about "the man with the single shoe [*ton monokrēpida*]," while other classical authors describe warriors in similar terms.[10]) The top portion of the head of the male is missing, but most of the face is preserved, including the eyes, which look up in passion and devotion into the face of the female. The female is seated — we might almost say she is enthroned — in a chair that is slightly raised. Her right arm rests gently, even lovingly, around the neck of the reclining male, and in her left hand she holds an object. On the ring finger of her left hand she wears a ring. The identification of this divine couple has prompted considerable scholarly debate.[11] I believe, with others, that the divine couple is Dionysos (or Bacchos) and Ariadne. Such is intimated by the posture of the couple and the ring on her finger, and by the similar portrayals of these divine lovers in other works of art. Some scholars prefer to identify the male figure as Liber and the female as Libera, using the names of Italian deities identified with Dionysos and Ariadne, while other scholars see the female figure as Aphrodite or Venus, with whom Dionysos is sometimes connected. A more problematical identification of the female figure is Semele, the mother of Dionysos, for although the female figure is seated above Dionysos in apparent dignity and honor, as may befit a mother, the obvious intimacy between the two suggests a lover rather than a mother.

The seventh scene features a theme well known from the mysteries of Dionysos: the unveiling of the object in the liknon, or winnowing basket. Here a woman kneels or crouches before a liknon, which contains a tall, erect object covered by a purple cloth, and she is about to uncover the hidden object. The shape of the object under the cloth is somewhat columnar, judging from how the cloth hangs. From other artwork with Dionysian themes we know what the tall object in the liknon represents. It is an erect phallus, the Dionysian symbol of male vitality and fertility. Over the kneeling woman's shoulder is a thyrsus (or perhaps a torch or pole), and behind her are figures that are difficult to identify, partly because of the damage to the painting. Ling sees two figures, one of which carries a plate with something like pine twigs on it.[12] Standing to the right of the kneeling woman is a winged female figure, wearing boots and miniskirt, and threatening with a whip. Her position relates artistically to the woman uncovering the liknon, but her head and body are turned so that the threatening whip is aimed toward a figure in the next scene, around the corner of the room. The winged female has been identified variously, but her large wings, her dark demeanor, and her menacing pose suggest a supernatural female on a mission of flagellation or punishment, akin to a demoness or goddess. Karl Kerényi names her Aidos, goddess of shame, who may protect the sanctity of the phallic symbol of Dionysos.[13] Similar images of winged female figures are known in Greco-Roman art, and while some twenty divine names have been used by scholars to identify this mysterious winged figure from Pompeii — "from Artemis to Telete," Jessica M. Davis summarizes — no positive identification has been made.[14]

The eighth scene, around the southeast corner and on the south wall of the triclinium, shows four women who may exemplify the agony and the ecstasy of the Dionysian life. One woman kneels with her back exposed, about to receive the blows of the whip wielded in the previous scene. Another, seated, holds and supports the cringing woman, and she looks back at the figure with whip and boots. Her glance is yet another example

Villa of the Mysteries, frescoes in the triclinium: Scene 8.

of the employment of a visual transition to help the viewer move from
scene to scene in the mural. A third woman holds a thyrsus and watches
from the background. A fourth whirls in dance, her clothes in disarray
and cymbals in her hands. In her wild dance of one seemingly possessed,
this fourth woman acts like a maenad, a woman filled with the mania of
the god Dionysos.

After a large window in the south wall interrupts the painting, the
mural resumes with scene nine, which is located on both the south and
west walls in the southwest corner of the triclinium. This scene presents
a young bride, recognizable from her coiffure, with a female attendant
and two cupids. One cupid holds a mirror, and the other cupid, on the
other wall, leans on a pillar and observes. The reflection of the young
bride's face is visible in the mirror. She is arranging her hair, with the
help of her attendant, who is looking down at the cupid with the mirror.
The bride, meanwhile, looks out toward the triclinium and the scenes in
the mural.

Villa of the Mysteries, frescoes in the triclinium: Scene 9.

On the other side of the main door in the west wall, the tenth and concluding scene is painted in the corner of the west wall, and this scene extends to the very end of the wall by the small door to the cubiculum. A mature woman, veiled and seated upon a bed or couch, is shown resting her head on her right hand and gazing out on the scenes presented in the mural. The expression on her face may suggest that she is thinking, pondering, musing. She wears bracelets on her arms and a ring on the ring finger of her left hand. A tablet rests on the bed; this tablet has been interpreted as a marriage document.[15] The bed extends, visually, into and through the wall and hence into the adjoining cubiculum. This scene, then, accentuates and completes the clockwise reading of the cycle of scenes in the triclinium and ushers the viewer, visually, through the small door into the cubiculum.

Within the cubiculum there are more individual wall paintings with Dionysian themes. Several paintings throughout the cubiculum present typical Dionysian figures and motifs — an inebriated Dionysos being

Villa of the Mysteries,
frescoes in the triclinium:
Scene 10.

helped by a silenus, a silenus also being helped, a dancing and leering
satyr, dancing women or maenads, a woman with shoulder exposed and
apparently holding a scroll in her left hand, a scene with figures who may
bear offerings — but one painting above that of the inebriated Dionysos
is particularly noteworthy. This small painting is framed with painted
shutters, and it shows, with shutters open, a scene in a grotto, with a
bearded man carrying a torch and a cupid leading a garlanded pig to a
rock or altar on which a Priapos herm is placed, along with flowers and
fruit. Both the man and the cupid glance backward, but their movement,
like that of the pig, is toward Priapos on the rock.

How these frescoes in these two rooms of the Villa of the Mysteries are to be interpreted remains mysterious. Here I mean to suggest basic interpretive directions I consider appropriate for an understanding of these paintings, and I do so with an eye toward the naked youth in the triclinium. I assume that the thematic and artistic unity between the paintings in the triclinium and the cubiculum recommends an interpretation that takes into account both rooms in the Villa of the Mysteries.

Hence, I suggest that these paintings in these rooms present an obscure sequence of scenes of Dionysian content concerned with a domesticated view of sexuality that emphasizes the place of women.

1. The paintings are obscure, and deliberately so. The composition is created and the figures are positioned so as to obscure rather than reveal. The viewer is given a peek, even a playful peek, into the mysteries of Dionysos, but the figures, cloths, and veils preserve the secrets.

2. The paintings in the triclinium in particular are given in sequence, though it appears not to be precisely a narrative sequence. Rather, the eye of the viewer is directed around the triclinium through the Dionysian scenes and eventually through the door into the cubiculum, where the conclusion and the culmination of the scenes are to be located. And if in fact the triclinium is a room for dining and entertaining and the cubiculum is a bedroom (points still debated among scholars), then the resolution of the Dionysian mystery may be found in the bedroom.[16]

3. The paintings present Dionysian scenes that capture images, many well known, from the myths and mysteries of Dionysos. That does not mean, however, that formal ceremonial initiation into the mysteries of Dionysos took place here in the triclinium, before the gods and everybody, in an open room. Rather, the decorative scenes simply depict aspects of the Dionysian mysteries and the Dionysian life.

4. In particular, the paintings focus upon sexuality, which is thoroughly within the domain of Dionysos, but here sexuality is embraced in a domesticated way. This is Dionysos in the affluent suburbs. This artistic vision of sexuality includes pain and pleasure, to be sure, and mystery, but everything is relatively proper. Several

female figures, including Ariadne, are married, one is about to be
married, one is pregnant, and the conclusion of it all seems to be
that the Dionysian mysteries are enjoyed in the master bedroom.
This domesticated vision of sexuality seems removed from the more
scandalous stories of Dionysian ecstasies, excesses, and orgies recounted, for example, in Livy, which led the Roman Senate to enact
a decree, *Senatus Consultum de Bacchanalibus,* which outlawed the
practice of the mysteries of Dionysos, in the early second century
B.C.E.[17]

5. The paintings, especially in the triclinium, feature mortal women
   interacting with immortals and mythological characters in the mysteries of sexuality. As depicted, the same women may appear several
   times in several scenes. These women seem to be in charge of sexual matters and enlightened in sexual mysteries. The only mortal
   male in the room is the naked young man, who apparently is being
   introduced to — we might say initiated into — sexual mysteries. As
   his expression indicates, the lad is excited and surprised by what
   he is learning about sexuality from the women.

Secret Gospel of Mark

In 1958, while studying in the library of the Greek Orthodox monastery of Mar Saba (Hagios Sabbas, in Greek), near Jerusalem, Morton
Smith claimed he discovered a portion of a *Secret Gospel* (or Spiritual
or Mystical Gospel, *mystikon euangelion*) *of Mark.* Two short passages
from the *Secret Gospel of Mark* are included in a letter of Clement of
Alexandria to a person named Theodore, and the letter was copied in
Greek into the back of an early (1646) printed edition of the letters of
Ignatius of Antioch. Smith published two editions of the *Secret Gospel
of Mark* in 1973, a critical edition and a popular edition, and since then
the scholarly community has debated the authenticity and significance of
the letter of Clement and the *Secret Gospel of Mark.*[18] That debate con-
tinues, but increasingly scholars are conceding that the letter of Clement
is most likely authentic and that the passages from the *Secret Gospel of
Mark* may be of considerable importance for our understanding of the
Gospel of Mark and the Markan tradition. The study of the letter of
Clement and the *Secret Gospel of Mark* has been aided by the recent

publication of new and better photographs of the pages of Clement's letter.[19]

Elsewhere I have presented my interpretation of the *Secret Gospel of Mark* within the Markan tradition.[20] Here it suffices to indicate that I begin with the assumption that the passages from the *Secret Gospel of Mark* are authentic and early, and that they reflect an edition of the Gospel of Mark that antedates the canonical Gospel of Mark. These passages describe a youth (*neaniskos*), who lives with his sister in Bethany, and who dies and is raised back to life by Jesus. It is said that the youth loves Jesus and Jesus loves him. In the evening the youth, "wearing a linen shroud over his naked body" (*peribeblēmenos sindona epi gymnou*, 3,8), comes to Jesus, and Jesus proceeds to teach him "the mystery of the kingdom of God" (*to mystērion tēs basileias tou theou*, 3,10). Not only is this account of the *neaniskos* in the *Secret Gospel of Mark* strongly reminiscent of the story of Lazarus (and the Beloved Disciple) in the Gospel of John. It also recalls features of the *neaniskos* in the canonical Gospel of Mark, specifically the youth fleeing naked on the occasion of the arrest of Jesus according to Mark 14:51–52: "And a youth (*neaniskos tis*) followed him, wearing a linen shroud over his naked body (*peribeblēmenos sindona epi gymnou*). They seized him, but he left the linen shroud behind and ran away naked."

I propose, then, that when the passages of the *Secret Gospel of Mark* are restored to their original position, it is possible to discern a subplot that presents the *neaniskos* as paradigmatic disciple in the Gospel of Mark. The *neaniskos* is not a historical figure, but rather a mythological or literary figure in a story. Evidence for the subplot may be found in the account of the rich young man (Mark 10:17–22), the two passages in *Secret Mark* (2,23–3,11 and 3,14–16), the account of the naked youth (Mark 14:51–52), and the story of the youth in the empty tomb of Jesus (Mark 16:1–8). The subplot about the *neaniskos* describes the circumstances of the life of discipleship, and with the abrupt conclusion of the Gospel of Mark, the final verses leave the implied hearer or reader with the choice of fleeing with the other disciples from the cross or hearkening to the *neaniskos* in the tomb. In the Johannine tradition the Markan figure of the *neaniskos* must have been known, and he has been adapted, and secondarily historicized, as Lazarus and the Beloved Disciple. Fundamental to this figure of the *neaniskos* is his death and resurrection, his instruction in the mystery of the kingdom, and his naked and clothed status. He is said, variously, to be clothed only in a linen shroud, to be naked, or to be clothed in a white robe in the tomb, where he is practically identified with Jesus.

In his book *The Homeric Epics and the Gospel of Mark*, Dennis Mac-Donald has maintained that the author of the Gospel of Mark imitates or emulates Homeric stories by adapting them to the story of Jesus.[21] In the case of the Markan account of the *neaniskos*, MacDonald cites parallels between Mark and Homer that indicate, he says, Mark's textual dependence upon the Homeric story of Odysseus's dinner with Circe prior to his journey to Hades. The story is about a certain youth named Elpenor. According to *Odyssey* book 10, Elpenor drank too much at Circe's dinner:

> There was a certain (*tis*) Elpenor, the youngest (*neōtatos*) in our
>   ranks,
> none too brave in battle, none too sound in mind.
> He'd strayed from his mates in Circe's magic halls
> and keen for the cool night air,
> sodden with wine he'd bedded down on her roofs.
> But roused by the shouts and tread of marching men,
> he leapt up with a start at dawn but still so dazed
> he forgot to climb back down again by the long ladder —
> headfirst from the roof he plunged, his necked snapped
> from the backbone, his soul flew down to Death (552–60).[22]

Thus Elpenor's soul departs to Hades. As MacDonald observes with regard to Mark's youth in chapter 14 and Homer's Elpenor in the *Odyssey*, "The garment the youth left behind thus may symbolize the flight of the naked soul from the body; if so, it corresponds to the flight of Elpenor's soul to Hades."[23] Homer's Elpenor also resembles Luke's Eutychus in the Acts of the Apostles, perhaps even more, as Eutychus falls to his death and is raised back to life (20:7–12). MacDonald also mentions an artistic depiction of Elpenor on a vase at the Boston Museum of Fine Arts, on which Elpenor, a soul without a body, is portrayed as a naked youth.[24] Later, in *Odyssey* book 11, Odysseus goes to Hades to see the blind seer Tiresias, and while there he visits the soul of Elpenor and promises to burn Elpenor's body on a funeral pyre, give it a proper burial, and mount an oar upon the burial mound (59–83). This Odysseus does, on a certain day at dawn, and the comrades all weep (book 12,

8–15). This story prompts MacDonald to think of Mark 16, and he concludes, on the *neaniskos* and on Eutychus, "Mark did not just imitate Elpenor, he emulated him, and his reasons for doing so were similar to Luke's, namely, to symbolize resurrection."[25]

MacDonald's thesis is thought-provoking, his presentation fascinating, and his accumulation of evidence impressive. His book merits a careful reading, and some of his examples of suggested imitation or emulation will doubtless have an impact upon biblical studies. I remain somewhat skeptical about his overall approach and the implications of that approach, and I have misgivings about his specific interpretation of the story of the *neaniskos* in Mark as an imitation or emulation of the story of Elpenor in Homer. The basic interpretation seems forced, the evidence does not convince. Yet MacDonald is surely correct in seeing parallels between these youths in Mark and Homer, both of whom are caught up in experiences of death and life. But after MacDonald we are left with enigmatic naked youths, even more than we had before, in canonical Mark, *Secret Mark*, Homer, and on vases such as the one in Boston.

Naked Youths

At the conclusion of this essay I offer some preliminary thoughts to help clarify the mystery and the enigma we have been examining.

The lad shown in the Villa of the Mysteries at Pompeii, the *neaniskos* in canonical and *Secret Mark*, and, for that matter, Elpenor in Homer's *Odyssey* all function as naked youths, and the place and role of youths and children in religious contexts and of ritual nudity in a variety of religious traditions need not be rehearsed here.[26] These three youths are different from each other in many respects, but they all have one crucial thing in common. They all are, in some sense of the word, initiates — candidates for the mysteries, understood in different ways. The youth in the triclinium of the Villa of the Mysteries is portrayed as one being indoctrinated in the sexual mysteries of Dionysos. Even though it is unlikely that any secret initiation ceremonies took place in this room, the images on the walls recall Dionysian rituals. The *neaniskos* in the Markan tradition is described as one being introduced to the life of Christian discipleship. He is not depicted as undergoing baptism per se, but his nudity and his clothing bring to mind baptismal practices in the church.[27] As the *Secret Gospel of Mark* puts it, this introduction to the life of discipleship is instruction in "the mystery of the kingdom of God," and the language of the mysteries continues to be employed in the description of Christian baptism, to the present day. Elpenor in the *Odyssey* is said to be one who passes from life to death, and the last wish of his soul is realized in the proper disposition of his body. Deprived of his body in death, Elpenor is a naked soul, confined to Hades, hoping only for the honorable treatment of his corpse and for others to remember him from his burial mound, surmounted by the oar he used when he rowed during his life.

Initially Elpenor may not be perceived as an initiate, but as one who dies he stands in some relationship to initiates, and initiates like the Pompeian youth and the Markan *neaniskos* stand in some relationship to a person, like Elpenor, who dies. According to fragment 178 attributed to Plutarch in Stobaeus's *Anthologion,* the experience of death is like that of initiation into the mysteries.[28] Plutarch was probably thinking first and foremost of the great mysteries of Demeter and Kore at Eleusis in his comments, but his description may apply more broadly to other mysteries as well. Throughout the mysteries motifs of living, dying, rising, and being reborn come to expression in many ways, and being clothed and unclothed may accompany the experience of dying and being reborn. Throughout the mysteries, and beyond, the experience of dying was thought to entail removing the clothing of the body, and the experience of living was thought to involve putting on the clothing of the body. This is the very issue — that the body is the clothing of the soul — that leads Paul to offer his own opinion, a contrary one, on the matter of the clothing of souls: "[W]e do not want to be unclothed but to be clothed the more, so that the mortal may be swallowed up by life" (2 Cor 5:4). Paul is too committed to the resurrection of the body to be very happy with naked youths and naked souls of the dead.[29]

Plutarch compares death to initiation. He notes that even the verbs *teleutan* (to die) and *teleisthai* (to be initiated) are similar. He goes on to describe initiation into the mysteries in these terms:

At first there is wandering, and wearisome roaming, and fearful traveling through darkness with no end to be found. Then, just before the consummation, there is every sort of terror, shuddering and trembling and perspiring and being alarmed. But after this a marvelous light appears, and open places and meadows await, with voices and dances and the solemnities of sacred utterances and holy visions. In that place one walks about at will, now perfect and initiated and free, and wearing a crown, one celebrates religious rites, and joins with pure and pious people. Such a person looks over the uninitiated and unpurified crowd of people living here, who are packed together and trample each other in deep mud and murk, but who hold onto their evil things on account of their fear of death, because they do not believe in the good things that are in the other world.

So it is for Elpenor, as described in Homer, and so it is, in ways that are apparent from the art of the Villa of the Mysteries and the text of Mark, for the youths from Pompeii and Mark.

Finally, the naked youths in the Villa of the Mysteries, canonical Mark, and *Secret Mark* — along with Elpenor in the *Odyssey* — may indeed bring some clarity to what it means to be initiates, followers of divine mysteries, in the traditions of Homer, Dionysos, and Christ.

Notes

1. This paper was presented in an earlier version at the meeting of the Pacific Coast Region of the SBL, Claremont, Calif., March 2001, and in a lecture at Calvin College, Grand Rapids, Mich., February 2002. I thank my colleagues for their comments on those occasions and since. I also acknowledge the support of the Griset Chair in Bible and Christian Studies at Chapman University, which enabled me to visit Pompeii and the Villa of the Mysteries during the summers of 2001 and 2002.

2. The bibliography on the Villa of the Mysteries (Villa Item) and the paintings within is huge. Fortunately, a substantial and up-to-date bibliography is provided in Elaine K. Gazda, ed., *The Villa of the Mysteries in Pompeii: Ancient Ritual, Modern Muse* (Ann Arbor, Mich.: The Kelsey Museum of Archaeology and the University of Michigan Museum of Art, 2000), 250–61.

3. See several essays in Gazda, ed., *The Villa of the Mysteries,* especially Jessica M. Davis, "The Search for the Origins of the Villa of the Mysteries Frieze," 83–95.

4. Kenneth D. Bratt of Calvin College has suggested to me, in a private communication, that the Roman painting in the Villa of the Mysteries may reflect the artistic conventions of the painted scenes employed earlier in the Greek theatre. Such a suggestion may be made more plausible by the focus upon Dionysos, divine patron of drama, in the painting in the Villa of the Mysteries, and the dramatic masks depicted in the Villa painting.

5. Amedeo Maiuri, *Pompeii* (Rome: Istituto Poligrafico dello Stato, 1954), 95–101.

6. Roger Ling, *Roman Painting* (Cambridge: Cambridge University Press, 1991), 104.

7. William Arrowsmith, trans., *Euripides: V*, in *The Ancient Mysteries: A Source-book of Sacred Texts* (ed. Marvin Meyer; Philadelphia: University of Pennsylvania Press, 1999), 76.

8. For similar motifs compare the marble statue of a silenus with a young Dionysian figure and a mask on his shoulders, in the National Archaeological Museum of Athens.

9. On the similar use of bowls with liquids for divinatory purposes, compare, for example, *PGM* 3209–54, a spell for the divination of Aphrodite: "Having kept oneself pure for 7 days, take a white saucer, fill it with water and olive oil.... Let it rest on the floor and looking intently at it, say, 'I call upon you, the mother and mistress of nymphs, ILAOUCH OBRIE LOUCH TLOR; [come] in, holy light, and give answer, showing your lovely shape....' " (Hans Dieter Betz, ed., *The Greek Magical Papyri in Translation* (2nd ed.; Chicago and London: University of Chicago Press, 1992), 100.

10. Apollodorus, *Bibliotheke (Library)* 1.9.16; Pindar, *Pythionikai (Pythian Odes)* 4.75. On other references to warriors with a single sandal, see the note by James George Frazer in the LCL edition of Apollodorus, 1.94–95. Additional examples of the use of such a figure include the bronze krater from Derveni (Grave *Beta*), in the Archaeological Museum of Thessalonike, with various Dionysian themes, including a young Dionysos lounging with Ariadne, and a bearded *monosandalos* figure with spears and sword.

11. Compare several essays in Gazda, ed., *The Villa of the Mysteries*, including Catherine Hammer, "Women, Ritual, and Social Standing in Roman Italy," 38–49; Drew Wilburn, "The God of Fertility in Room 5 of the Villa of the Mysteries," 50–58; and Brenda Longfellow, "Liber and Venus in the Villa of the Mysteries," 116–28.

12. Ling, *Roman Painting*, 101.

13. Karl Kerényi, *Dionysos: Archetypal Image of Indestructible Life* (trans. Ralph Manheim; Bollingen Series 65.2; Princeton: Princeton University Press, 1976), 359.

14. Davis, "The Search for the Origins of the Villa," 90.

15. Compare K. Kerényi, *Dionysos*, 361.

16. Compare, for example, Brenda Longfellow, "A Gendered Space? Location and Function of Room 5 in the Villa of the Mysteries," in Gazda, *The Villa of the Mysteries*, 24–37.

17. Livy, *Ab Urbe Condita (History of Rome)* 39.8–19; see Meyer, *The Ancient Mysteries*, 81–93.

18. M. Smith, *Clement of Alexandria*; M. Smith, *The Secret Gospel*; M. Smith, "Clement of Alexandria," 449–61. Recent studies on the Secret or Mystical Gospel of Mark are mentioned in Meyer, "The Youth in Secret Mark," 94–105; and Meyer, "The Youth in the *Secret Gospel of Mark*," 129–53. To the studies mentioned there may be added the following, which relate directly or indirectly to the

Secret Gospel of Mark: Scott G. Brown, "The More Spiritual Gospel: Markan Literary Techniques in the Longer Gospel of Mark" (Ph.D. diss., University of Toronto, 1999); Howard M. Jackson, "Why the Youth Shed His Cloak and Fled Naked: The Meaning and Purpose of Mark 14:51–52," *JBL* 116 (1997): 273–89; Steven R. Johnson, "The Identity and Significance of the Neaniskos in Mark," *FF Forum* 8 (1992): 123–39; Philip Sellew, "Secret Mark and the History of Canonical Mark," in *The Future of Early Christianity: Essays in Honor of Helmut Koester* (ed. Birger A. Pearson; Minneapolis: Fortress, 1991), 242–57.

19. Hedrick, with Olympiou, "Secret Mark," 3–11, 14–16.

20. See Meyer, "The Youth in the *Secret Gospel of Mark*"; and Meyer, "The Youth in Secret Mark."

21. Dennis R. MacDonald, *The Homeric Epics and the Gospel of Mark* (New Haven and London: Yale University Press, 2000).

22. Robert Fagles, trans., *The Odyssey,* in MacDonald, *The Homeric Epics and the Gospel of Mark,* 128–29.

23. MacDonald, *The Homeric Epics and the Gospel of Mark,* 129.

24. Ibid.

25. Ibid., 167.

26. See, for instance, Howard Clark Kee, " 'Becoming a Child' in the *Gospel of Thomas,*" *JBL* 82 (1963): 307–14; Meyer, *The Ancient Mysteries;* Martin P. Nilsson, *The Dionysiac Mysteries of the Hellenistic and Roman Age* (Skrifter Utgivna av Svenska Institutet i Athen [8°] 5; Lund: Gleerup, 1957; reprinted New York: Arno, 1975); Scroggs and Groff, "Baptism in Mark," 531–48; J. Z. Smith, "The Garments of Shame," 217–38, reprinted in Jonathan Z. Smith, *Map Is Not Territory: Studies in the History of Religions* (Studies in Judaism in Late Antiquity 23; Leiden: E. J. Brill, 1978), 1–23; entries in Pauly-Wissowa, *Realencyclopädie der classischen Altertumswissenschaft* (Stuttgart: Alfred Druckenmuller, 1894–).

27. Compare Scroggs and Groff, "Baptism in Mark."

28. Stobaeus, *Anthologion (Anthology)* 4.52.49; translation and discussion in Meyer, *The Ancient Mysteries,* 8–9.

29. Compare also 1 Cor 15 on the resurrected body: Paul states, ἐγείρεται ἐν ἀφθαρσίᾳ (15:42), ἐν δόξῃ and ἐν δυνάμει (15:43), and it is σῶμα πνευματικόν (15:44); δεῖ γάρ, he proclaims, τὸ φθαρτὸν τοῦτο ἐνδύσασθαι ἀφθαρσίαν καὶ τὸ θνητὸν τοῦτο ἐνδύσασθαι ἀθανασίαν (15:53; compare also 15:54). The *Treatise on the Resurrection* and the *Gospel of Philip,* both Valentinian gnostic texts from the Nag Hammadi library (NHC I,4 and II,3), include similar reflections on being naked, being clothed, and the resurrected body.

Taking Up the Cross
and Following Jesus

Discipleship in the Gospel of Mark
and *Secret Mark*

If any people would come after me, let them deny themselves, take
up their cross, and follow me. For those who would save their lives
will lose them, and those who would lose their lives for my sake
and the gospel's will save them.   —Mark 8:34–35[1]

The youth looked at Jesus and loved him, and he began to beg him
to be with him.   —*Secret Gospel of Mark* (following 10:34)[2]

The theme for this scholarly meditation has significance and power for
any day, but doubtless it has a particular significance for our own. The
theme we address is that of discipleship, specifically discipleship in the
Gospel of Mark, including *Secret Mark*.[3] I choose Mark as the gospel
upon which to focus for three reasons.

1. I find the Gospel of Mark to be an engaging gospel — the most
   engaging New Testament gospel, in fact — on account of its early
   date (I am convinced that a version of Mark was the first canonical
   gospel composed),[4] its rapid and reckless pace (everything happens
   at once, immediately, as Jesus races through the sixteen chapters
   on his way to Jerusalem),[5] and its profound theology of the cross
   presented in Greek that is oftentimes not so profound.[6]

2. The theme of discipleship is a particularly poignant one in the Gospel of Mark, in the light of the strong emphasis upon discipleship
   in Mark combined with the famed fickleness of Mark's male and

female disciples and the enigmatic presence, if only for a moment, of the shadowy disciple fleeing naked at the time of Jesus' arrest.[7]

3. The theme of discipleship in Mark is linked to bearing the cross, taking up the cross and following Jesus. Mark's theological perspective, I shall attempt to demonstrate, questions a theology of success and proclaims that the life of discipleship is lived with the reality of the cross. We all know about the popularity of the book entitled *The Prayer of Jabez,* which offers a Judeo-Christian mantra to be recited in order to achieve a blessed life of being healthy, wealthy, and wise.[8] We also know of Christian churches that preach what may be called a theology of success — from possibility thinking to the "be happy attitudes."[9] I hear the Gospel of Mark proclaiming the life of discipleship in remarkably different tones.

We consider, then, five passages from Mark's gospel that are germane to the issue of discipleship in the Gospel of Mark.

First, Mark 1:1, the incipit: *Archē tou euangeliou Iēsou Christou,* "The beginning of the good news of Jesus Christ." Some manuscripts add here *huiou theou,* "son of God"; the textual evidence for the inclusion or exclusion of the phrase leaves little room for certainty.[10] Whether or not we take this additional phrase to reflect the original reading, certainly Mark means to announce that Jesus is to be understood as son of God. Just a bit later in chapter 1, at the occasion of the baptism of Jesus, the *bat qol* or heavenly voice says as much.[11] Exactly what it means, for Mark, that Jesus is to be understood as son of God is another matter altogether — the central matter in the Gospel of Mark.

As with many an incipit, so also here: if we really understand the incipit, we understand the text as a whole. The opening words claim to introduce Mark as a text of good news, *euangelion,* with a messianic figure Jesus who may be proclaimed, we are told in the incipit or soon thereafter, as son of God.

Yet what does that actually mean? What is not stated explicitly in the incipit is what we know all too well — painfully well — as did some of the first hearers of the gospel. And if they did not know when the incipit was read, they found out soon enough. This text of good news apparently has bad news, not *euangelion* but *dysangelion,* painful news, deadly news. Mark is, as it has been put aptly, a passion narrative with a long introduction.[12] The good news is the bad news, and the bad news is the good news: the news of the cross, the suffering Messiah and son of God, and the suffering followers of the Messiah and son of God.

Second, Mark 8:22–33. At Bethsaida a blind man is brought to Jesus for the healing touch. Jesus spits and touches, and the man then can see, but with poor focus. "I see people, but they look like trees walking about," he says. So Jesus touches the man again, and now the man sees everything clearly.

This miracle story is used in Mark to put into context the story of the discussion among Jesus and his disciples on the road to Caesarea Philippi about who Jesus is. Like the blind man at Bethsaida, the disciples too need to be restored in their vision. They need to be transformed from a lack of clarity to a sharper focus on who Jesus is. Is he John the baptizer, Elijah, a prophet? Peter offers the correct answer, at least in a general way: *sy ei ho christos,* "You are the Christ." Yet at the end of both the miracle story and the scene placed on the road to the north of Galilee, Mark adds variations upon the command used to emphasize the messianic secret: tell no one who I am.[13]

I take my place as a traveler on the Wredestraße when I suggest that Mark's messianic secret is part of Mark's theology and has nothing to do with the historical Jesus.[14] Mark employs a goodly number of miracle stories in his gospel, but comparatively few sayings. Mark's Jesus is a strong, quiet figure who is potent in his deeds but does not say much. We need not fault Mark for this. Mark did not use Q materials in his gospel in the manner of Matthew and Luke.[15] Mark most likely did use a small collection of miracle stories in the compilation of his gospel, after the fashion of John the evangelist and his Signs Source.[16] Yet Mark typically concludes his miracle stories with a command of silence from Jesus — tell no one who I am.

Such a command to secrecy flies in the face of the usual form and function of miracle stories in early Christian and Greco-Roman sources.[17] Miracle stories typically mean to elicit a response, belief, applause. Mark seems self-consciously to manipulate the form, or "bend the genre,"[18] of his miracle stories by stifling the applause through the messianic secret.

For Mark the applause — and the belief — that come from the spectacular deeds of the miracle stories are insufficient for true discipleship. To confess Jesus as just another Greco-Roman divine man and son of God, remarkable from birth and outstanding in deeds of power, is not enough for Mark. To applaud Jesus for healings, exorcisms, and the like is easy — too easy. To follow Jesus through health, wealth, and success is also easy — too easy. To follow Jesus to the cross is much more difficult. This very point is underscored in Mark 8:31–33, where Mark has Jesus announce that the son of man, the child of humankind — *ho huios tou anthrōpou* — will suffer, die, and rise.[19] Jesus says this, at last, with no thought of a messianic secret: *parrēsia ton logon elalei*, "he said this clearly." Jesus finally speaks clearly and openly when he discusses suffering. Peter, who put it correctly before, now gets it quite wrong, because he refuses to accept the suffering, and for his response he needs, as it were, to be exorcised: *hypage opisō mou, satana*, "Get behind me, Satan."

The point being made becomes crucial because Mark presents the theme of suffering linked not only to Jesus, the suffering Christ and son of God as son of man, but also to discipleship and the suffering followers of Jesus. "If any people would come after me," Jesus says, "let them deny themselves, take up their cross, and follow me. For those who would save their lives will lose them, and those who would lose their lives for my sake and the gospel's will save them."[20] Mark's theology and christology are no abstractions. Mark's theology and christology are closely connected to following Jesus and living the life of discipleship — suffering discipleship.

Third, Mark 14:51–52, the passage about the *neaniskos*, or youth: *kai neaniskos tis synēkolouthei autō peribeblēmenos sindona epi gymnou, kai kratousin auton, ho de katalipōn tēn sindona gymnos ephygen*, "And a youth followed him, wearing a linen shroud over his naked body. They seized him, but he left the linen shroud behind and ran away naked." These two verses have proved to be an interpretive conundrum to scholars. Some have even suggested that the figure of the streaker is the figure of the evangelist who introduces himself, à la Alfred Hitchcock in his films, into the story line as a minor character.[21]

I propose that the resolution of this problem of Mark 14:51–52 may well rest with the text of the letter of Clement to Theodore and the extracts of the so-called *Secret* or *Mystical Gospel of Mark* contained therein.[22]

During his life Morton Smith embraced the secrets of the *Secret Gospel* he found at the Mar Saba monastic library in the Judean desert, and he took secrets with him into his grave. All things considered, I conclude that the two fragments of *Secret Mark* in the letter of Clement are probably authentic fragments from the Markan tradition, and very early fragments, and that they help present a subplot on the life of discipleship in the Gospel of Mark.[23]

The two fragments of *Secret Mark* read as follows.[24] The first fragment is to be located after Mark 10:34:

> And they come to Bethany. This woman whose brother had died was there. She came and knelt before Jesus and says to him, "Son of David, have mercy on me." But the disciples rebuked her. Then Jesus became angry and went with her into the garden where the tomb was. At once a loud voice was heard from the tomb, and Jesus went up and rolled the stone away from the door of the tomb. At once he went in where the youth[25] was. He reached out his hand, took him by the hand, and raised him up. The youth looked at Jesus and loved him, and he began to beg him to be with him. Then they left the tomb and went into the youth's house, for he was rich. Six days later Jesus told him what to do, and in the evening the youth comes to him wearing a linen shroud over his naked body. He stayed with him that night, for Jesus was teaching him the mystery of the kingdom of God. And from there he got up and returned to the other side of the Jordan.

The second fragment is to be located after Mark 10:46a: "The sister of the youth whom Jesus loved was there, along with his mother and Salome, but Jesus did not receive them."[26]

When the fragments of *Secret Mark* are returned to their appropriate places in the text, a story about the *neaniskos* — a disciple, any disciple, you or me — emerges. And that *neaniskos,* like us, will eventually face the tomb of Jesus with the decision placed before him or her: Will you still follow Jesus?

In his book *The Homeric Epics and the Gospel of Mark,* Dennis MacDonald discusses the *neaniskos* in Mark in the light of his theories regarding Mark.[27] MacDonald argues that Mark imitates or emulates Homer by adopting and adapting Homeric motifs. His assemblage of data is prodigious. With regard to the concerns of this meditation, Mac-Donald hypothesizes that Homer's story of Elpenor, recounted in books 10 and 12 of the *Odyssey,* becomes the basis for the story of the youth, the *neaniskos,* in canonical and *Secret Mark.* According to Homer's story, Elpenor, a young man in Odysseus's crew, drank too much, dozed off, took a fall, and died and went to Hades, where he was, of course, stripped of his body. Later, after Odysseus visited him in Hades, he was given a proper burial. (The similarities to the story of Eutychus in the Acts of the Apostles are also clear, and are not missed by MacDonald.[28])

MacDonald's thesis is interesting and provocative, but I do not agree with him on some of his most significant points. The similarities between the portrayals of the Markan youth and Homeric Elpenor — along with other figures, for example the young male initiate depicted in the triclinium of the Villa of the Mysteries near Pompeii[29] — most likely stem from their roles as initiates, or disciples, of one sort or another, in their respective religious traditions.

Fourth, Mark 15:39, the culmination of the crucifixion account in the passion narrative: "And when the centurion who stood facing him — Jesus — saw that he thus breathed his last, he said, *alēthōs houtos ho anthrōpos huios theou ēn*, 'In truth this man was son of God.' " After Mark, Matthew redacts the passage to say that the centurion was awestruck and offered his confession when he saw the earthquake and other apocalyptic events that Matthew imports into the account. Who would not call Jesus son of God in the middle of an apocalypse?[30] Luke redacts the passage to indicate that the centurion praised God — a good Christian should offer a hymn of praise on such an occasion, according to Luke — and pronounced Jesus innocent. Luke thus has the centurion, a representative of Rome, declare Jesus to be a blameless martyr, much like the other victims in the early church, such as Stephen and the apostles. In Luke Jesus is the first in a long line of innocent Christian martyrs of God.[31]

Among the synoptic authors only Mark retains a truly creative tension in the confession of the centurion. Mark has discouraged the confession that Jesus is son of God, in the miracles that have been performed, by means of his application of the messianic secret. But here, when Jesus is suffering and dying, the centurion, a Gentile like so many early Christians, confesses what is hard to confess, what is a paradox of confession. Jesus is son of God in his suffering, he is powerful in his weakness, he is God with us in his death. In Mark the centurion says so clearly and openly, just as Jesus had said so on the road to Caesarea Philippi when he was discussing his own suffering as son of man. Peter did not like it then, and we may not like it now. There is nothing easy about this confession. There is nothing cheap about this grace, nor about this life.

Fifth, Mark 16:8. At the time of the arrest and crucifixion of Jesus, the disciples progressively defect. They rarely seemed to understand Jesus during his life, and now they are not up to the challenge of following Jesus. Judas betrays Jesus, Peter denies Jesus, the male disciples run for their lives, and even the youth dashes away. The women disciples are somewhat more courageous; they at least linger at the cross and come to the tomb.[32]

But here, at Mark 16:8, in an awkward Greek sentence, the gospel concludes with a description that is both syntactically and theologically hard. This is what comes after the confrontation of the women with the youth — the *neaniskos* — in the tomb: *Kai exelthousai ephygon apo tou mnēmeiou, eichen gar autas tromos kai ekstasis, kai oudeni ouden eipan, ephobounto gar,* "And they left and fled from the tomb, for they were trembling and beside themselves. And they said nothing to no one [*sic*], for they were afraid." The Greek negation in the final sentence could not be more strongly put. The Gospel of Mark also ends with a dangling conjunction, *gar,* and with the fear of the disciples, here the female disciples. The *gar* is left hanging at the end of Mark, and so are we.

The copyists of Mark and the other synoptic evangelists tried to deal with the awkwardness of the conclusion of Mark's gospel in a couple of ways. Over the years several longer endings were appended to the Gospel of Mark — a long ending, a shorter ending, the Freer logion, with variations — and while these later endings might resolve some of the uneasiness of readers of the Gospel of Mark, they are clearly secondary in character and derived from the other gospel accounts. The codices Sinaiticus and Vaticanus know nothing of these longer accounts.[33]

Further, in his gospel Matthew makes the youth in the tomb into an apocalyptic angel, and the disciples do meet Jesus in Galilee and are commissioned by him there: "Go then and make disciples of all nations, baptizing . . . teaching . . . I am with you always, to the end of the age" (Matt 28:19–20). In his gospel Luke transforms the *neaniskos* into two angels, and after the disciples remark about what Jesus said while he was still in Galilee, they stay around Jerusalem until they are sent, spirit-filled, from Jerusalem and Judea to the ends of the earth — or at least to Rome, with Paul, at the end of the Acts of the Apostles, Luke's second scroll.[34]

At the end of the Gospel of Mark as it was composed, at Mark 16:8, there is no easy resolution to the tension created. On the one hand, most of the male and female disciples have fled in fear and dismay, in the face of the scandal of the cross and the demands of the cross on their lives. On the other hand, the voice of the youth, who now is in the tomb of Jesus, continues to cry out. I suggest that in Mark this youth is the same youth who earlier was raised to life by Jesus, was taught by Jesus, and yet ran away from Jesus when Jesus was arrested. In Mark 16 the youth has come back to Jesus in his death; he identifies with Jesus in the tomb, and he even looks and sounds rather like Jesus: "Do not be alarmed. You are looking for Jesus of Nazareth, who was crucified. He has risen, he is not here. Look at the place where they laid him. But go, tell his disciples and Peter [who may yet get his understanding of Jesus correct] that he is going before you to Galilee. There you will see him, as he told you."[35]

Only the hearer, the implied hearer or reader, can resolve the tension so deliberately and ingeniously created at the conclusion of the gospel. It is perhaps too much to propose that an altar call is needed at the end of Mark, but something similar is implied.[36]

Only the hearer and reader — finally that is you and I — can resolve the tension at the end of Mark. How shall we respond to the cross of Christ? Shall we, like so many disciples, flee from the cross and the tomb, or shall we, like the youth, be counted with Jesus in the tomb? Are we ready to take up the cross and follow Jesus into the Galilee of our lives, into a world that is suffering, into a life of discipleship that entails dying and living with Christ? Today, in the world after September 11, 2001, the Galilee of our lives may be New York City, Washington, D.C., Israel, Palestine, Afghanistan, our neighborhoods — wherever the suffering and living Jesus is to be found. Are we ready to affirm — and to live out of our affirmation — that in following Jesus there is strength in weakness and life in death? The call to discipleship is given in Mark; it is up to you and me to hear it, respond to it, and live it.

Notes

1. εἴ τις θέλει ὀπίσω μου ἀκολουθεῖν, ἀπαρνησάσθω ἑαυτὸν καὶ ἀράτω τὸν σταυρὸν αὐτοῦ καὶ ἀκολουθείτω μοι. ὃς γὰρ ἐὰν θέλῃ τὴν ψυχὴν αὐτοῦ σῶσαι ἀπολέσει αὐτήν· ὃς δ' ἂν ἀπολέσει τὴν ψυχὴν αὐτοῦ ἕνεκεν ἐμοῦ καὶ τοῦ εὐαγγελίου σώσει αὐτήν.

2. ὁ δὲ νεανίσκος ἐμβλέψας αὐτῷ ἠγάπησεν αὐτὸν καὶ ἤρξατο παρακαλεῖν αὐτὸν ἵνα μετ' αὐτοῦ ᾖ.

3. This essay was originally presented as a scholarly meditation at a convocation in honor of three retired professors of New Testament studies whose contributions to Calvin Theological Seminary and the church have been magnificent: Andrew Bandstra, David Holwerda, and Bastiaan Van Elderen. Subsequently the meditation was published in an issue of *Calvin Theological Journal* dedicated to these professors and friends. As I noted in the meditation as presented at the convocation and as published in *Calvin Theological Journal,* the theme of discipleship seemed particularly well suited to the occasion. These three professors have shown in their teaching and have modeled in their living what it means to follow Jesus and live a life of discipleship.

4. In other words, I affirm a version of the two-source hypothesis, and I date the Gospel of Mark to around 70 c.e. The issue of the date of Mark is made more complex, however, by the discovery and interpretation of the *Secret Gospel of Mark.* See Koester, "History and Development of Mark's Gospel."

5. The adverb εὐθύς, "at once, immediately," occurs forty-one times in the Gospel of Mark (C. E. B. Cranfield, *The Gospel According to Saint Mark* [Cambridge Greek Testament Commentary; Cambridge: Cambridge University Press, 1959], calls it a "favourite adverb in Mk" [52]).

6. On the Greek of the Gospel of Mark, see Cranfield, *The Gospel According to Saint Mark,* 20–21.

7. Mark 14:51–52, discussed below.

8. Bruce H. Wilkinson, *The Prayer of Jabez: Breaking Through to the Blessed Life* (Sisters, Ore.: Multnomah Publishers, 2000).

9. Compare Robert H. Schuller, *The Be Happy Attitudes: 8 Positive Attitudes That Can Transform Your Life* (New York: Bantam Books, 1987).

10. The phrase is absent in the original hand of Codex Sinaiticus and other manuscripts, and present in the first correction of Codex Sinaiticus and in Codex Vaticanus, Codex Bezae, and other manuscripts; a few additional manuscripts read υἱοῦ τοῦ θεοῦ or υἱοῦ τοῦ κυρίου.

11. Mark 1:11: σὺ εἶ ὁ υἱός μου ὁ ἀγαπητός, ἐν σοὶ εὐδόκησα.

12. Martin Kähler, *Der sogenannte historische Jesus und der geschichtliche, biblische Christus* (Munich: Chr. Kaiser, 1956), 60.

13. On the messianic secret, see especially William Wrede, *Das Messiasgeheimnis in den Evangelien: Zugleich ein Beitrag zum Verständnis des Markusevangeliums* (Göttingen: Vandenhoeck & Ruprecht, 1901).

14. On the Wredestraße and the Schweitzerstraße (and the Autobahn), see N. T. Wright, *Jesus and the Victory of God* (vol. 2 of *Christian Origins and the Question of God;* Minneapolis: Fortress, 1996).

15. On Q, see especially John S. Kloppenborg, *Excavating Q: The History and Setting of the Sayings Gospel* (Minneapolis: Fortress, 2000); Robinson et al., *The Critical Edition of Q.*

16. On the Signs Source, see especially Robert T. Fortna, *The Fourth Gospel and Its Predecessor: From Narrative Source to Present Gospel* (Philadelphia: Fortress, 1988), and *The Gospel of Signs: A Reconstruction of the Narrative Source Underlying the Fourth Gospel* (Society for New Testament Studies Monograph Series 11; New York and London: Cambridge University Press, 1970).

17. On the form of miracle stories, see Rudolph Bultmann, *The History of the Synoptic Tradition* (trans. John Marsh; New York: Harper & Row, 1963), 209–44.

18. This phrase was used by Harold W. Attridge in his Society of Biblical Literature presidential address, "Genre Bending in the Fourth Gospel," presented during November 2001 in Denver, Colo., and published in *JBL* 121 (2002): 3–21.

19. On the range of meanings for son of man, or child of humankind, see Gerhard Kittel and Gerhard Friedrich, ed., *Theological Dictionary of the New Testament,* vol. 8 (trans. Geoffrey W. Bromiley; Grand Rapids, Mich.: Wm. B. Eerdmans, 1972), 400–77.

20. Mark 8:34–35. Here (and above) I translate the third person singular masculine pronouns of the Greek text with third person plural English pronouns for the sake of inclusivity.

21. See Taylor, *The Gospel According to St. Mark,* 562.

22. On the *Secret Gospel of Mark,* see M. Smith, *Clement of Alexandria,* and *The Secret Gospel.*

23. See Meyer, "The Youth in the *Secret Gospel of Mark,*" 129–53.

24. For the Greek text, see M. Smith, *Clement of Alexandria,* 445–54; good photographs are now available in Hedrick, with Olympiou, "Secret Mark," 3–11, 14–16.

25. The Greek word used for "youth," here and elsewhere in the text, is νεανίσκος.

26. On "the youth whom Jesus loved" and the Beloved Disciple — and Lazarus — in the Gospel of John, see Meyer, "The Youth in Secret Mark," 94–105.

27. MacDonald, *The Homeric Epics and the Gospel of Mark,* 124–30, 162–68.

28. Compare Acts 20:7–12.

29. The young male initiate from Pompeii is the only mortal male depicted in the triclinium of the Villa of the Mysteries. See the recent discussions in Gazda, *The Villa of the Mysteries.*

30. Matt 27:54: Ὁ δὲ ἑκατόνταρχος καὶ οἱ μετ' αὐτοῦ τηροῦντες τὸν Ἰησοῦν ἰδόντες τὸν σεισμὸν καὶ τὰ γενόμενα ἐφοβήθησαν σφόδρα, λέγοντες· ἀληθῶς θεοῦ υἱὸς ἦν οὗτος.

31. Luke 23:47: Ἰδὼν δὲ ὁ ἑκατοντάρχης τὸ γενόμενον ἐδόξαζεν τὸν θεὸν λέγων· ὄντως ὁ ἄνθρωπος οὗτος δίκαιος ἦν.

32. See Fiorenza, *In Memory of Her,* 321–23.

33. See Bruce M. Metzger, *The Text of the New Testament: Its Transmission, Corruption, and Restoration* (New York and Oxford: Oxford University Press, 1992), 226–29, along with page 57. Additional issues on the longer endings to the Gospel of Mark are discussed in the literature, including the debated issue of blank space left after Mark 16:8 in the manuscript tradition and the possible implications for the ending of the gospel. See, for example, Paul Mirecki, "Mark 16:9–20: Composition, Tradition and Redaction" (Th.D. diss., Harvard Divinity School, 1986).

34. Like the Gospel of Mark, the Acts of the Apostles also has an open-ended conclusion: Ἐνέμεινεν δὲ διετίαν ὅλην ἐν ἰδίῳ μισθώματι καὶ ἀπεδέχετο πάντας τοὺς εἰσπορευομένους πρὸς αὐτόν, κηρύσσων τὴν βασιλείαν τοῦ θεοῦ καὶ διδάσκων τὰ περὶ τοῦ κυρίου Ἰησοῦ Χριστοῦ μετὰ πάσης παρρησίας ἀκωλύτως (28:30–31).

35. Mark 16:6–7. The particular mention made of Peter here recalls his forthright role as the disciple who is initially right and then wrong in his assessment of Jesus in Mark 8:27–33. Note the further amplification of the role of Peter in Matt 16:13–20.

36. Compare Meyer, "The Youth in the *Secret Gospel of Mark*," 148. In a study that is in preparation, Jonathan J. Meyer of Calvin College suggests that the account of discipleship in the Gospel of Mark is presented with two sets of framed sections, the first introduced by the story of the "rich young ruler" (Mark 10:17–22) and closed by the first fragment of the *Secret Gospel of Mark*, the second introduced by the story of the *neaniskos* fleeing naked (Mark 14:51–52) and closed by the youth in the tomb of Jesus (Mark 16:1–8), both proclaiming, in a parallel and escalating fashion, the suffering life of discipleship. (Scott G. Brown, "The More Spiritual Gospel," sees the fragment of *Secret Mark* and the story of the youth in the tomb — both resurrection stories — as framing stories for the passion of Jesus, which in turn is divided into two parts by the account of the fleeing *neaniskos*.)

Bibliography

Arrowsmith, William, trans. *Euripides: V.* Pages 67–81 in *The Ancient Mysteries: A Sourcebook of Sacred Texts.* Edited by Marvin Meyer. Philadelphia: University of Pennsylvania Press, 1999.

Asin y Palacios, Michael. *Logia et Agrapha Domini Jesu apud Moslemicos Scriptores.* Patrologia orientalis 13.3, 335–431; 19.4, 531–624. Paris: Firmin-Didot, 1919, 1926; Turnhout, Belgium: Brepols, 1974.

Attridge, Harold W. "The Greek Fragments." Pages 95–128 in vol. 1 of *Nag Hammadi Codex II,2–7 Together with XIII,2*, Brit. Lib. Or. 4926(1), and P. Oxy. 1, 654, 655.* Edited by Bentley Layton. Nag Hammadi Studies 20. Leiden: E. J. Brill, 1989.

———. "'Seeking' and 'Asking' in Q, *Thomas,* and John." Pages 295–302 in *From Quest to Q: Festschrift James M. Robinson.* Edited by Jon Ma. Asgeirsson, Kristin De Troyer, and Marvin W. Meyer. Bibliotheca Ephemeridum Theologicarum Lovaniensium 146. Leuven: Peeters/Leuven University Press, 1999.

Baarda, Tjitze. "Jesus Said: Be Passers-By; On the Meaning and Origin of Logion 42 of the Gospel of Thomas." Pages 179–205 in *Early Transmission of Words of Jesus: Thomas, Tatian, and the Text of the New Testament.* Edited by J. Helderman and S. J. Noorda. Amsterdam: VU Boekhandel/Uitgeverij, 1983.

Badham, F. P., and F. C. Conybeare. "Fragments of an Ancient (? Egyptian) Gospel Used by the Cathars of Albi." *Hibbert Journal* 11 (1913): 805–18.

Baer, Richard A. *Philo's Use of the Categories Male and Female.* Leiden: E. J. Brill, 1970.

Baker, Aelred. "Fasting to the World." *Journal of Biblical Literature* 84 (1965): 291–94.

Barnstone, Willis, and Marvin Meyer, eds. *The Gnostic Bible.* Boston: Shambhala Publications (forthcoming).

Beskow, Per. *Strange Tales about Jesus: A Survey of Unfamiliar Gospels.* Philadelphia: Fortress, 1983.

Betz, Hans Dieter. *Galatians.* Hermeneia. Philadelphia: Fortress, 1979.

———, ed. *The Greek Magical Papyri in Translation.* 2d ed. Chicago and London: University of Chicago Press, 1992.

Bianchi, Ugo, ed. *Le Origini dello Gnosticismo.* Leiden: E. J. Brill, 1967.

Böhlig, Alexander. "Der jüdische und judenchristliche Hintergrund in gnostischen Texten von Nag Hammadi." Pages 109–40 in *Le Origini dello Gnosticismo.* Edited by Ugo Bianchi. Leiden: E. J. Brill, 1967.

Brown, Peter. *The Body and Society: Men, Women, and Sexual Renunciation in Early Christianity.* New York: Columbia University Press, 1988.

Brown, Raymond E. *The Gospel According to John.* Anchor Bible 29–29A. Garden City, N.Y.: Doubleday, 1966–70.

———. "The Relation of 'The Secret Gospel of Mark' to the Fourth Gospel." *Catholic Biblical Quarterly* 36 (1974): 466–85.

Brown, Scott G. "The More Spiritual Gospel: Markan Literary Techniques in the Longer Gospel of Mark." Ph.D. diss., University of Toronto, 1999.

Bruce, F. F. *The "Secret" Gospel of Mark.* Ethel M. Wood Lecture. London: Athlone, 1974.

Buckley, Jorunn Jacobsen. *Female Fault and Fulfillment in Gnosticism.* Chapel Hill and London: University of North Carolina Press, 1986.

———. "An Interpretation of Logion 114 in *The Gospel of Thomas.*" *Novum Testamentum* 27 (1985): 245–72.

Bultmann, Rudolf. *The Gospel of John: A Commentary.* Translated by G. R. Beasley-Murray, R. W. N. Hoare, and J. K. Riches. Philadelphia: Westminster, 1971.

———. *The History of the Synoptic Tradition.* Translated by John Marsh. New York: Harper & Row, 1963.

Cameron, Ron. Review of Crossan, 1985. *Journal of Biblical Literature* 106 (1987): 558–60.

———, ed. *The Other Gospels: Non-Canonical Gospel Texts.* Philadelphia: Westminster, 1982.

Castelli, Elizabeth. " 'I Will Make Mary Male': Pieties of the Body and Gender Transformation of Christian Women in Late Antiquity." Pages 29–49 in *Body Guards: The Cultural Politics of Gender Ambiguity.* Edited by Julia Epstein and Kristina Straub. London and New York: Routledge, 1991.

Clark, Henry. *The Ethical Mysticism of Albert Schweitzer: A Study of the Sources and Significance of Schweitzer's Philosophy of Civilization.* Boston: Beacon, 1962.

Cranfield, C. E. B. *The Gospel According to Saint Mark.* Cambridge Greek Testament Commentary. Cambridge: Cambridge University Press, 1959.

Crim, Keith, ed., et al. *The Interpreter's Dictionary of the Bible.* Nashville: Abingdon, 1962.

Crossan, John Dominic. *The Birth of Christianity: Discovering What Happened in the Years Immediately After the Execution of Jesus.* San Francisco: HarperSanFrancisco, 1998.

———. *Four Other Gospels: Shadows on the Contours of Canon.* Minneapolis: Winston [Seabury], 1985.

Dart, John. *The Jesus of Heresy and History: The Discovery and Meaning of the Nag Hammadi Gnostic Library.* San Francisco: Harper & Row, 1988.

Davies, Stevan L. *The Gospel of Thomas and Christian Wisdom.* New York: Seabury, 1983.

Davis, Jessica M. "The Search for the Origins of the Villa of the Mysteries Frieze." Pages 83–95 in *The Villa of the Mysteries in Pompeii: Ancient Ritual, Modern Muse.* Edited by Elaine K. Gazda. Ann Arbor, Mich.: The Kelsey Museum of Archaeology and the University of Michigan Museum of Art, 2000.

DeConick, April D., and Jarl Fossum. "Stripped before God: A New Interpretation of Logion 37 in the *Gospel of Thomas.*" *Vigiliae christianae* 45 (1991): 123–50.

Delcourt, Marie. *Hermaphrodite: Myths and Rites of the Bisexual Figure in Classical Antiquity.* London: Studio Books, 1961.

Dewey, Arthur J. "A Passing Remark: Thomas 42." *Foundations and Facets Forum* 10 (1994): 69–85.

Döllinger, I. *Beiträge zur Sektengeschichte des Mittelalters.* Darmstadt: Wissenschaftliche Buchgesellschaft, 1968.

Dunderberg, Ismo. "Thomas' I-sayings and the Gospel of John." Pages 33–64 in *Thomas at the Crossroads.* Edited by Risto Uro. Edinburgh: T. & T. Clark, 1998.

Dunkerley, Roderic. *Beyond the Gospels.* Harmondsworth, Eng.: Penguin, 1957.

Eliade, Mircea. *Mephistopheles and the Androgyne.* New York: Sheed & Ward, 1965.

Emmel, Stephen. "A Fragment of Nag Hammadi Codex III in the Beinecke Library: Yale Inv. 1784." *Bulletin of the American Society of Papyrologists* 17 (1980): 53–60.

The Facsimile Edition of the Nag Hammadi Codices. Published under the auspices of the Department of Antiquities of the Arab Republic of Egypt, in conjunction with UNESCO. Leiden: E. J. Brill, 1972–84.

Fallon, Francis T., and Ron Cameron. "The Gospel of Thomas: A Forschungsbericht and Analysis." Pages 4195–251 in vol. 2.25.6 of *Aufstieg und Niedergang der römischen Welt: Geschichte und Kultur Roms im Spiegel der neueren Forschung.* Edited by H. Temporini and W. Haase. Berlin and New York: De Gruyter, 1988.

Filson, Floyd V. "Who Was the Beloved Disciple?" *JBL* 68 (1949): 83–88.

Fiorenza, Elisabeth Schüssler. *In Memory of Her: A Feminist Theological Reconstruction of Christian Origins.* New York: Crossroad, 1983.

Fitzmyer, Joseph A. "The Oxyrhynchus Logoi of Jesus and the Coptic Gospel According to Thomas." Pages 355–433 in *Essays on the Semitic Background of the New Testament.* Edited by Joseph A. Fitzmyer. London: Chapman, 1971.

Fleddermann, Harry. "The Flight of a Naked Young Man (Mark 14:51–52)." *Catholic Biblical Quarterly* 41 (1979): 412–18.

Foerster, Werner. *Gnosis.* Oxford: Clarendon, 1972.

Fortna, Robert T. *The Fourth Gospel and Its Predecessor: From Narrative Source to Present Gospel.* Philadelphia: Fortress, 1988.

———. *The Gospel of Signs: A Reconstruction of the Narrative Source Underlying the Fourth Gospel.* Society for New Testament Studies Monograph Series 11. New York and London: Cambridge University Press, 1970.

Fuller, Reginald H. *Longer Mark: Forgery, Interpolation, or Old Tradition?* Center for Hermeneutical Studies in Hellenistic and Modern Culture, Colloquy 18. Edited by Wilhelm H. Wuellner. Berkeley: Center for Hermeneutical Studies, 1976.

Gärtner, Bertil. *The Theology of the Gospel of Thomas.* Translated by Eric J. Sharpe. London: Collins/New York: Harper, 1961.

Gazda, Elaine K., ed. *The Villa of the Mysteries in Pompeii: Ancient Ritual, Modern Muse.* Ann Arbor, Mich.: The Kelsey Museum of Archaeology and the University of Michigan Museum of Art, 2000.

Giversen, Søren. "The Palaeography of Oxyrhynchus Papyri 1 and 654–655." Paper presented at the annual meeting of the SBL. Boston, November 1999.

Gourgues, Michel. "A propos du symbolisme christologique et baptismal de Marc 16.5." *New Testament Studies* 27 (1981): 672–78.

Grant, Robert M. "The Mystery of Marriage in the Gospel of Philip." *Vigiliae christianae* 15 (1961): 129–40.

Grant, Robert M., and David Noel Freedman. *The Secret Sayings of Jesus, with an English Translation of the Gospel of Thomas by William R. Schoedel*. Garden City, N.Y.: Doubleday/London: Collins, 1960.

Grenfell, B. P., and A. S. Hunt. *Logia Iesou: Sayings of Our Lord*. London: Henry Frowde, 1897.

Guillaumont, Antoine, et al. *The Gospel According to Thomas: Coptic Text Established and Translated*. New York: Harper & Row, 1959.

Haenchen, Ernst. "Die Anthropologie des Thomas-Evangeliums." Pages 207–27 in *Neues Testament und christliche Existenz: Festschrift für Herbert Braun*. Edited by H. D. Betz and L. Schottroff. Tübingen: J. C. B. Mohr [Paul Siebeck], 1973.

———. *Die Botschaft des Thomas-Evangeliums*. Theologische Bibliothek Töpelmann 6. Berlin: Töpelmann, 1961.

Hammer, Catherine. "Women, Ritual, and Social Standing in Roman Italy." Pages 38–49 in *The Villa of the Mysteries in Pompeii: Ancient Ritual, Modern Muse*. Edited by Elaine K. Gazda. Ann Arbor, Mich.: The Kelsey Museum of Archaeology and the University of Michigan Museum of Art, 2000.

Harl, M. "A propos des Logia de Jésus: Le sens du mot *monachos*." *Revue des études grecques* 73 (1960): 464–74.

Hedrick, Charles W., and Paul A. Mirecki. *Gospel of the Savior: A New Ancient Gospel*. California Classical Library. Santa Rosa, Calif.: Polebridge, 1999.

Hedrick, Charles W., with Nikolaos Olympiou. "Secret Mark: New Photographs, New Witnesses." *The Fourth R* 13 (2000): 3–11 and 14–16.

Hock, Ronald F., and Edward N. O'Neil. *The Chreia in Ancient Rhetoric*, vol. 1: *Progymnasmata*. Society of Biblical Literature Texts and Translations 27, Graeco-Roman Religion 9. Atlanta: Scholars, 1985.

Hofius, Otfried. "Das koptische Thomasevangelium und die Oxyrhynchus-Papyri Nr. 1, 654 und 655." *Evangelische Theologie* 20 (1960): 21–42, 182–92.

Horsley, G. H. R. *New Documents Illustrating Early Christianity: A Review of Greek Inscriptions and Papyri Published in 1977*. North Ryde, N.S.W., Australia: Ancient History Documentary Research Centre, Macquarie University, 1982.

———. *New Documents Illustrating Early Christianity: A Review of Greek Inscriptions and Papyri Published in 1978*. North Ryde, N.S.W., Australia: Ancient History Documentary Research Centre, Macquarie University, 1983.

Jackson, Howard M. *The Lion Becomes Man: The Gnostic Leontomorphic Creator and the Platonic Tradition*. Society of Biblical Literature Dissertation Series 81. Atlanta: Scholars, 1985.

———. "Why the Youth Shed His Cloak and Fled Naked: The Meaning and Purpose of Mark 14:51–52." *Journal of Biblical Literature* 116 (1997): 273–89.

James, Montague Rhodes. *The Apocryphal New Testament*. Oxford: Clarendon, 1953.

Janssens, Yvonne. "L'Évangile selon Thomas et son caractère gnostique." *Muséon: Revue d'études orientales* 75 (1962): 301–25.

Jeremias, Joachim. *Unbekannte Jesusworte*. 3d ed. Gütersloh: Gerd Mohn, 1963.

Johnson, Steven R. "The Identity and Significance of the Neaniskos in Mark." *Foundations and Facets Forum* 8 (1992): 123–39.

Jonas, Hans. *The Gnostic Religion*. Boston: Beacon, 1963.

Kähler, Martin. *Der sogenannte historische Jesus und der geschichtliche, biblische Christus*. Munich: Chr. Kaiser, 1956.

Kasser, Rodolphe. *L'Évangile selon Thomas: Présentation et commentaire théologique*. Bibliothèque théologique. Neuchâtel: Delachaux & Niestlé, 1961.

Kee, Howard Clark. " 'Becoming a Child' in the *Gospel of Thomas*." *Journal of Biblical Literature* 82 (1963): 307–14.

Kees, Hermann. *Aegypten. Religionsgeschichtliches Lesebuch*. Edited by A. Bertholet. Tübingen: J. C. B. Mohr [Paul Siebeck], 1928.

Kerényi, K. *Dionysos: Archetypal Image of Indestructible Life*. Translated by Ralph Manheim. Bollingen Series 65.2. Princeton: Princeton University Press, 1976.

———. *Eleusis*. New York: Schocken, 1977.

Kermode, Frank. *The Genesis of Secrecy: On the Interpretation of Narrative*. Cambridge, Mass.: Harvard University Press, 1979.

Keuls, Eva C. *The Reign of the Phallus: Sexual Politics in Ancient Athens*. Berkeley: University of California Press, 1993.

Khalidi, Tarif. *The Muslim Jesus: Sayings and Stories in Islamic Literature*. Convergences: Inventories of the Present. Cambridge, Mass., and London: Harvard University Press, 2001.

King, Karen L. "Kingdom in the Gospel of Thomas." *Foundations and Facets Forum* 3 (1987): 48–97.

Kittel, Gerhard, and Gerhard Friedrich, ed. *Theological Dictionary of the New Testament*. Translated by Geoffrey W. Bromiley. Grand Rapids, Mich.: Wm. B. Eerdmans, 1972.

Klausner, Joseph. *Jesus of Nazareth*. New York: Macmillan, 1925.

Klijn, A. F. J. "The 'Single One' in the Gospel of Thomas." *Journal of Biblical Literature* 81 (1962): 271–78.

Kloppenborg, John. "City and Wasteland: Narrative World and the Beginning of the Sayings Gospel (Q)." Pages 145–60 in *Semeia 52: How Gospels Begin*. Edited by Dennis E. Smith. Atlanta: Scholars, 1990.

———. *Excavating Q: The History and Setting of the Sayings Gospel*. Minneapolis: Fortress, 2000.

———. *The Formation of Q: Trajectories in Ancient Wisdom Collections*. Studies in Antiquity and Christianity. Philadelphia: Fortress, 1987.

———. *Q Parallels: Synopsis, Critical Notes, and Concordance*. Foundations and Facets. Sonoma, Calif.: Polebridge, 1988.

Knox, John. "A Note on Mark 14:51–52." Pages 27–30 in *The Joy of Study: Papers on New Testament and Related Subjects Presented to Honor Frederick Clifton Grant*. Edited by Sherman E. Johnson. New York: Macmillan, 1951.

Koester, Helmut. "History and Development of Mark's Gospel (From Mark to Secret Mark and 'Canonical' Mark)." Pages 35–57 in *Colloquy on New Testament Studies: A Time for Reappraisal and Fresh Approaches*. Edited by Bruce Corley. Macon, Ga.: Mercer University Press, 1983.

————. *History and Literature of Early Christianity*. Vol. 2 of *Introduction to the New Testament*. Philadelphia: Fortress, 1982.

————. "Tradition and History of the Early Christian Gospel Literature." Shaffer Lectures, Yale University, 1980.

————. "Überlieferung und Geschichte der frühchristlichen Evangelienliteratur." Pages 1463–1542 in vol. 2.25.2 of *Aufstieg und Niedergang der römischen Welt: Geschichte und Kultur Roms im Spiegel der neueren Forschung*. Edited by H. Temporini and W. Haase. Berlin and New York: De Gruyter, 1984.

Koester, Helmut, and Elaine Pagels. Introduction to *Nag Hammadi Codex III,5: The Dialogue of the Savior*. Edited by Stephen Emmel. Nag Hammadi Studies 26. Leiden: E. J. Brill, 1984.

LaGrand, James. "How Was the Virgin Mary 'Like a Man'?" *Novum Testamentum* 22 (1980): 97–107.

Lagrange, Marie-Joseph. *Évangile selon Saint Marc. Études bibliques*. Paris: Gabalda, 1929.

Laqueur, Thomas. *Making Sex: Body and Gender from the Greeks to Freud*. Cambridge, Mass.: Harvard University Press, 1990.

Layton, Bentley. "Bulletin: Gnosticisme." *Revue biblique* 83 (1976): 458–69.

————. *A Coptic Grammar, with Chrestomathy and Glossary, Sahidic Dialect*. Porta Linguarum Orientalium, Neue Serie 20. Wiesbaden: Harrassowitz, 2000.

————. *The Gnostic Scriptures*. Garden City, N.Y.: Doubleday, 1987.

————, ed. *Nag Hammadi Codex II,2–7, Together with XIII, 2*, Brit. Lib. Or. 4926(1), and P. Oxy. 1, 654, 655*. Vol. 1. Nag Hammadi Studies 20. Leiden: E. J. Brill, 1989.

Leipoldt, Johannes. *Das Evangelium nach Thomas: Koptisch und Deutsch*. Texte und Untersuchungen 101. Berlin: Akademie-Verlag, 1967.

Ling, Roger. *Roman Painting*. Cambridge: Cambridge University Press, 1991.

Longfellow, Brenda. "A Gendered Space? Location and Function of Room 5 in the Villa of the Mysteries." Pages 24–37 in *The Villa of the Mysteries in Pompeii: Ancient Ritual, Modern Muse*. Edited by Elaine K. Gazda. Ann Arbor, Mich.: The Kelsey Museum of Archaeology and the University of Michigan Museum of Art, 2000.

————. "Liber and Venus in the Villa of the Mysteries." Pages 116–28 in *The Villa of the Mysteries in Pompeii: Ancient Ritual, Modern Muse*. Edited by Elaine K. Gazda. Ann Arbor, Mich.: The Kelsey Museum of Archaeology and the University of Michigan Museum of Art, 2000.

MacDonald, Dennis R. *The Homeric Epics and the Gospel of Mark*. New Haven and London: Yale University Press, 2000.

————. *There Is No Male and Female: The Fate of a Dominical Saying in Paul and Gnosticism*. Harvard Dissertations in Religion 20. Philadelphia: Fortress, 1987.

Mack, Burton L. *A Myth of Innocence: Mark and Christian Origins*. Philadelphia: Fortress, 1988.

Maiuri, Amedeo. *Pompeii*. Rome: Istituto Poligrafico dello Stato, 1954.

Malbon, Elizabeth Struthers. "Fallible Followers: Women and Men in the Gospel of Mark." *Semeia* 28 (1983): 29–48.

Marcovich, M. "Textual Criticism on the *Gospel of Thomas*." *Journal of Theological Studies*, New Series 20 (1969): 53–74.

Margoliouth, D. S. "Christ in Islam: Sayings Attributed to Christ by Mohammedan Writers." *Expository Times* 5 (1893–94): 59, 107, 177–78, 503–4, 561.

McGuire, Anne. "Women, Gender, and Gnosis in Gnostic Texts and Traditions." Pages 257–99 in *Women and Christian Origins*. Edited by Ross S. Kraemer and Mary R. D'Angelo. New York and Oxford: Oxford University Press, 1999.

Meeks, Wayne A. "The Image of the Androgyne: Some Uses of a Symbol in Earliest Christianity." *History of Religions* 13 (1974): 165–208.

Metzger, Bruce M. *The Text of the New Testament: Its Transmission, Corruption, and Restoration*. New York and Oxford: Oxford University Press, 1992.

Meyer, Marvin. "Affirming Reverence for Life." Pages 22–36 in *Reverence for Life: The Ethics of Albert Schweitzer for the Twenty-First Century*. Edited by Marvin Meyer and Kurt Bergel. Albert Schweitzer Library. Syracuse: Syracuse University Press, 2002.

———. "Albert Schweitzer and the Image of Jesus in the *Gospel of Thomas*." Pages 72–90 in *Jesus Then and Now: Images of Jesus in History and Christology*. Edited by Marvin Meyer and Charles Hughes. Harrisburg, Pa.: Trinity Press International, 2001.

———. *The Ancient Mysteries: A Sourcebook of Sacred Texts*. Philadelphia: University of Pennsylvania Press, 1999.

———. "The Beginning of the Gospel of Thomas." Pages 161–73 in *Semeia 52: How Gospels Begin*. Edited by Dennis E. Smith. Atlanta: Scholars, 1990.

———. " 'Be Passersby': *Gospel of Thomas* Saying 42, Jesus Traditions, and Islamic Literature." In essays on the Gospel of Thomas. Edited by Jon Ma. Asgeirsson and Risto Uro. Leiden: E. J. Brill (forthcoming).

———. "Did Jesus Drink from a Cup? The Equipment of Jesus and His Followers in Q and al-Ghazzali." Pages 143–56 in *From Quest to Q: Festschrift James M. Robinson*. Edited by Jon Ma. Asgeirsson, Kristin De Troyer, and Marvin W. Meyer. Bibliotheca Ephemeridum Theologicarum Lovaniensium 146. Leuven: Peeters/Leuven University Press, 1999.

———. *The Gospel of Thomas: The Hidden Sayings of Jesus*. San Francisco: HarperSanFrancisco, 1992.

———. "*Gospel of Thomas* Logion 114 Revisited." Pages 101–11 in *For the Children, Perfect Instruction: Studies in Honor of Hans-Martin Schenke on the Occasion of the Berliner Arbeitskreis für koptisch-gnostische Studien's Thirtieth Year*. Edited by Hans-Gebhard Bethge, Stephen Emmel, Karen L. King, and Imke Schletterer. Nag Hammadi and Manichaean Studies 54. Leiden: E. J. Brill, 2002.

———. *The Letter of Peter to Philip: Text, Translation, and Commentary*. Society of Biblical Literature Dissertation Series 53. Atlanta: Scholars, 1981.

———. "Making Mary Male: The Categories 'Male' and 'Female' in the *Gospel of Thomas*." *New Testament Studies* 31 (1985): 544–70.

———. "The νεανίσκος in Canonical and Secret Mark." Paper presented at the 119th annual meeting of the SBL, Dallas, Tex., December 19–22, 1983.

———. *The Secret Teachings of Jesus: Four Gnostic Gospels.* New York: Random House, 1984.

———. "Seeing or Coming to the Child of the Living One? More on *Gospel of Thomas* Saying 37." *Harvard Theological Review* 91 (1998): 413–16.

———. "Taking Up the Cross and Following Jesus: Discipleship in the Gospel of Mark." *Calvin Theological Journal* 37 (2002): 230–38.

———. *The Unknown Sayings of Jesus.* San Francisco: HarperSanFrancisco, 1998.

———. "The Youth in the *Secret Gospel of Mark.*" Pages 129–53 in *Semeia 49: The Apocryphal Jesus and Christian Beginnings.* Edited by Ron Cameron. Atlanta: Scholars, 1990.

———. "The Youth in Secret Mark and the Beloved Disciple in John." Pages 94–105 in *Gospel Origins and Christian Beginnings: In Honor of James M. Robinson.* Edited by Jack T. Sanders, Charles W. Hedrick, and James E. Goehring. Sonoma, Calif.: Polebridge, 1990.

Mirecki, Paul. "Mark 16:9–20: Composition, Tradition and Redaction." Th.D. diss., Harvard Divinity School, 1986.

Montefiore, C. G. *The Synoptic Gospels.* 2 vols. London: Macmillan, 1927.

Morrice, William G. *Hidden Sayings of Jesus: Words Attributed to Jesus Outside the Four Gospels.* Peabody, Mass.: Hendrickson, 1997.

Munro, Winsome. "Women Disciples in Mark?" *Catholic Biblical Quarterly* 44 (1982): 225–41.

Neirynck, Frans. "La fuite du jeune homme en Mc 14,51–52." *Ephemerides Theologicae Lovanienses* 55 (1979): 43–66.

Nilsson, Martin P. *The Dionysiac Mysteries of the Hellenistic and Roman Age.* Skrifter Utgivna av Svenska Institutet i Athen [8°] 5. Lund: Gleerup, 1957; reprinted New York: Arno, 1975.

Nugent, Georgia. "The Sex Which Is Not One: Deconstructing Ovid's Hermaphrodite." *Differences* 2 (1990): 160–85.

Pagels, Elaine H. "Exegesis of Genesis 1 in the Gospels of Thomas and John." *Journal of Biblical Literature* 118 (1999): 477–96.

———. *The Gnostic Gospels.* New York: Random House, 1979.

———. "What Became of God the Mother? Conflicting Images of God in Early Christianity." *Signs* 2 (1976): 293–303.

Parrinder, Geoffrey. *Jesus in the Qur'an.* New York: Oxford University Press, 1977.

Patterson, Stephen J. "The *Gospel of Thomas*: Introduction." Pages 77–123 in *Q — Thomas Reader.* Edited by John S. Kloppenborg, Marvin W. Meyer, Stephen J. Patterson, and Michael G. Steinhauser. Sonoma, Calif.: Polebridge, 1990.

———. *The Gospel of Thomas and Jesus.* Foundations and Facets. Sonoma, Calif.: Polebridge, 1993.

———. "Understanding the *Gospel of Thomas* Today." Pages 33–75 in *The Fifth Gospel: The Gospel of Thomas Comes of Age.* Edited by Stephen J. Patterson, James M. Robinson, and Hans-Gebhard Bethge. Harrisburg, Pa.: Trinity Press International, 1998.

———. "Wisdom in Q and Thomas." Pages 187–221 in *In Search of Wisdom: Essays in Memory of John G. Gammie*. Edited by Leo G. Perdue, Bernard Brandon Scott, and William Johnston Wiseman. Louisville: Westminster/John Knox, 1993.

Pauly-Wissowa. *Realencyclopädie der classischen Altertumswissenschaft*. Stuttgart: Alfred Druckenmuller, 1894–.

Pearson, Birger A. *Nag Hammadi Codices IX and X*. Nag Hammadi Studies 15. Leiden: E. J. Brill, 1981.

Perkins, Pheme. *The Gnostic Dialogue*. New York: Paulist, 1980.

———. "Peter in Gnostic Revelation." Pages 1–13 in vol. 2 of *Society of Biblical Literature: 1974 Seminar Papers*. Edited by G. W. MacRae. Cambridge, Mass.: Society of Biblical Literature, 1974.

Petersen, Norman R. "When Is the End Not the End? Literary Reflections on the Ending of Mark's Narrative." *Interpretation* 34 (1980): 151–66.

Preisendanz, Karl, ed. *Papyri Graecae Magicae: Die griechischen Zauberpapyri*. 2 vols. 2d ed. Edited by Albert Henrichs. Stuttgart: B. G. Teubner, 1973.

Puech, Henri-Charles. "The Gospel of Thomas." Pages 278–307 in vol. 1 of *New Testament Apocrypha*. Edited by E. Hennecke and W. Schneemelcher. Philadelphia: Westminster, 1963.

Quesnell, Quentin. "The Mar Saba Clementine: A Question of Evidence." *Catholic Biblical Quarterly* 37 (1975): 48–67.

———. "A Reply to Morton Smith." *Catholic Biblical Quarterly* 38 (1976): 200–3.

Quispel, Gilles. "Gnosticism and the New Testament." *Vigiliae christianae* 19 (1965): 65–85.

———. "The *Gospel of Thomas* Revisited." Pages 218–66 in *Colloque internationale sur les Textes de Nag Hammadi*. Edited by B. Barc. Quebec: L'Université Laval, 1981.

———. "L'Évangile selon Thomas et les origines de l'ascèse chrétienne." Pages 98–112 in vol. 2 of *Gnostic Studies*. Leiden: Nederlands Historisch-Archaeologisch Instituut te Istanbul, 1975.

———. *Makarius, das Thomasevangelium und das Lied von der Perle*. Novum Testamentum, Supplement 15. Leiden: E. J. Brill, 1967.

ur-Rahim, Muhammad 'Ata. *Jesus, Prophet of Islam*. Elmhurst, N.Y.: Tahrike Tarsile Qur'an, 1991.

Rengstorf, K. H. "Urchristliches Kerygma und 'gnostische' Interpretation in einigen Sprüchen des Thomasevangeliums." Pages 563–74 in *Le Origini dello Gnosticismo*. Edited by Ugo Bianchi. Leiden: E. J. Brill, 1967.

Resch, Alfred, ed. *Agrapha: Aussercanonische Schriftfragmente*. 2d ed. Texte und Untersuchungen zur Geschichte der altchristlichen Literatur 15,3–4. Leipzig: J. C. Hinrichs/Darmstadt: Wissenschaftliche Buchgesellschaft, 1967.

Riley, Gregory J. "A Note on the Text of the *Gospel of Thomas* 37." *Harvard Theological Review* 88 (1995): 179–81.

Robinson, James M. Foreword to *Q — Thomas Reader*. Edited by John S. Kloppenborg, Marvin W. Meyer, Stephen J. Patterson, and Michael G. Steinhauser. Sonoma, Calif.: Polebridge, 1990.

————. "The Image of Jesus in Q." Pages 7–25 in *Jesus Then and Now: Images of Jesus in History and Christology*. Edited by Marvin Meyer and Charles Hughes. Harrisburg, Pa.: Trinity Press International, 2001.

————. Introduction to *The Nag Hammadi Library in English*. Leiden: E. J. Brill/ San Francisco: Harper & Row, 1977; paperback edition, 1981.

————. "LOGOI SOPHON: On the Gattung of Q." Pages 71–113 in *Trajectories Through Early Christianity*. Edited by James M. Robinson and Helmut Koester. Philadelphia: Fortress, 1971.

————, ed. *The Nag Hammadi Library in English*. Leiden: E. J. Brill/San Francisco: Harper & Row, 1977; paperback edition, 1981.

Robinson, James M., Paul Hoffmann, and John S. Kloppenborg. *The Critical Edition of Q*. Hermeneia. Philadelphia: Fortress; Leuven: Peeters, 2000.

Robson, James. *Christ in Islam*. New York: E. P. Dutton, 1930.

Ropes, James Hardy. "Agrapha." Pages 343–52 in *A Dictionary of the Bible*, extra vol. Edited by James Hastings. New York: Scribner's; Edinburgh: T. & T. Clark, 1904.

Rousseau, John J., and Rami Arav. *Jesus and His World: An Archaeological and Cultural Dictionary*. Minneapolis: Fortress, 1995.

Rudolph, Kurt. "Der gnostische 'Dialog' als literarisches Genus." Pages 85–107 in *Probleme der koptischen Literatur*. Edited by Peter Nagel. Wissenschaftliche Beitrage, K2. Halle-Wittenberg: Martin-Luther-Universität, 1968.

Schenke, Hans-Martin. "The Function and Background of the Beloved Disciple in the Gospel of John." Pages 111–25 in *Nag Hammadi, Gnosticism, and Early Christianity*. Edited by Charles W. Hedrick and Robert Hodgson, Jr. Peabody, Mass.: Hendrickson, 1986.

————. "The Mystery of the Gospel of Mark." *Second Century* 4 (1984): 65–82.

Schippers, R. "Het evangelie van Thomas een onafhankelijke traditie? Antwoord aan professor Quispel." *Gereformeerd theologisch tijdschrift* 61 (1961): 46–54.

Schmidt, Carl, and Violet MacDermot. *Pistis Sophia*. Nag Hammadi Studies 9. Leiden: E. J. Brill, 1978.

Scholer, David M. *Nag Hammadi Bibliography 1948–1969*. Nag Hammadi Studies 1. Leiden: E. J. Brill, 1971.

Schuller, Robert H. *The Be Happy Attitudes: 8 Positive Attitudes That Can Transform Your Life*. New York: Bantam Books, 1987.

Schweitzer, Albert. *Out of My Life and Thought: An Autobiography*. Translated by Antje Bultmann Lemke. Baltimore: Johns Hopkins University Press, 1998.

————. *The Philosophy of Civilization*. Translated by C. T. Campion. Buffalo: Prometheus, 1987.

————. *The Quest of the Historical Jesus: A Critical Examination of Its Progress from Reimarus to Wrede*. Translated by W. Montgomery. Baltimore: Johns Hopkins University Press, 1998.

————. *Reverence for Life*. Translated by Reginald H. Fuller. New York: Irvington/ Harper & Row, 1969.

Scroggs, Robin, and Kent I. Groff. "Baptism in Mark: Dying and Rising with Christ." *Journal of Biblical Literature* 92 (1973): 531–48.

Sellew, Philip. "Secret Mark and the History of Canonical Mark." Pages 242–57 in *The Future of Early Christianity: Essays in Honor of Helmut Koester.* Edited by Birger A. Pearson. Minneapolis: Fortress, 1991.

Singer, June. *Androgyny: Toward a New Theory of Sexuality.* Garden City, N.Y.: Anchor Press/Doubleday, 1976.

Smith, Jonathan Z. "The Garments of Shame." *History of Religions* 5 (1966): 217–38.

———. *Map Is Not Territory: Studies in the History of Religions.* Studies in Judaism in Late Antiquity 23. Leiden: E. J. Brill, 1978.

Smith, Morton. *Clement of Alexandria and a Secret Gospel of Mark.* Cambridge, Mass.: Harvard University Press, 1973.

———. "Clement of Alexandria and Secret Mark: The Score at the End of the First Decade." *Harvard Theological Review* 75 (1982): 449–61.

———. "Monasteries and Their Manuscripts." *Archaeology* 13 (1960): 172–77.

———. "On the Authenticity of the Mar Saba Letter of Clement." *Catholic Biblical Quarterly* 38 (1976): 196–99.

———. "Regarding *Secret Mark:* A Response by Morton Smith to the Account by Per Beskow." *Journal of Biblical Literature* 103 (1984): 624.

———. *The Secret Gospel: The Discovery and Interpretation of the Secret Gospel According to Mark.* New York: Harper & Row, 1973.

Stählin, Otto, ed. *Clemens Alexandrinus 4/1: Register.* 2d ed. Edited by Ursula Treu. Die griechische christliche Schriftsteller der ersten Jahrhunderte. Berlin: Akademie-Verlag, 1980.

Stone, Michael E., and John Strugnell, trans. *The Books of Elijah: Parts 1–2.* Society of Biblical Literature Texts and Translations 18, Pseudepigrapha 8. Missoula, Mont.: Scholars, 1979.

Talley, Thomas. "Liturgical Time in the Ancient Church: The State of Research." *Studia Liturgica* 14 (1982): 34–51.

Tannehill, Robert C. "The Disciples in Mark: The Function of a Narrative Role." *Journal of Religion* 57 (1977): 386–405.

Taylor, Vincent. *The Gospel According to St. Mark.* London: Macmillan, 1966.

Torjesen, Karen. "Wisdom, Christology, and Women Prophets." Pages 186–200 in *Jesus Then and Now: Images of Jesus in History and Christology.* Edited by Marvin Meyer and Charles Hughes. Harrisburg, Pa.: Trinity Press International, 2001.

Tripp, David H. "The Aim of the 'Gospel of Thomas.'" *Expository Times* 92 (1980–81): 41–44.

Turner, John D. *The Book of Thomas the Contender from Codex II of the Cairo Gnostic Library from Nag Hammadi (CG II,7).* Society of Biblical Literature Dissertation Series 23. Missoula, Mont.: Scholars, 1975.

Vaage, Leif E. *Galilean Upstarts: Jesus' First Followers According to Q.* Harrisburg, Pa.: Trinity Press International, 1994.

Valantasis, Richard. *The Gospel of Thomas.* New Testament Readings. London and New York: Routledge, 1997.

Vanhoye, Albert. "La fuite du jeune homme nu (Mc 14,51–52)." *Biblica* 52 (1971): 401–6.

Vermaseren, Maarten J. *Cybele and Attis: The Myth and the Cult.* London: Thames & Hudson, 1977.

Voss, Isaac, ed. *Epistulae genuinae S. Ignatii Martyris.* Amsterdam: Blaeu, 1646.

Waetjen, Herman. "The Ending of Mark and the Gospel's Shift in Eschatology." *Annual of the Swedish Theological Institute* 4 (1965): 114–31.

Wallace, Donna Kennon. "Androgyny as Salvation in Early Christianity." Ph.D. diss., Claremont Graduate University, 2000.

Wilburn, Drew. "The God of Fertility in Room 5 of the Villa of the Mysteries." Pages 50–58 in *The Villa of the Mysteries in Pompeii: Ancient Ritual, Modern Muse.* Edited by Elaine K. Gazda. Ann Arbor, Mich.: The Kelsey Museum of Archaeology and the University of Michigan Museum of Art, 2000.

Wilkinson, Bruce H. *The Prayer of Jabez: Breaking Through to the Blessed Life.* Sisters, Ore.: Multnomah Publishers, 2000.

Williams, Michael A. *Rethinking "Gnosticism": An Argument for Dismantling a Dubious Category.* Princeton: Princeton University Press, 1996.

Wilson, R. McL. "Jewish Christianity and Gnosticism." *Recherches de science religieuse* 60 (1972): 261–72.

Wisse, Frederik. "Gnosticism and Early Monasticism in Egypt." Pages 431–40 in *Gnosis: Festschrift für Hans Jonas.* Edited by B. Aland. Göttingen: Vandenhoeck & Ruprecht, 1978.

———. "Die Sextus-Sprüche und das Problem der gnostischen Ethik." Pages 55–86 in *Zum Hellenismus in den Schriften von Nag Hammadi.* Edited by A. Böhlig and F. Wisse. Wiesbaden: Otto Harrassowitz, 1975.

Wrede, William. *Das Messiasgeheimnis in den Evangelien: Zugleich ein Beitrag zum Verständnis des Markusevangeliums.* Göttingen: Vandenhoeck & Ruprecht, 1901.

Wright, N. T. *Jesus and the Victory of God.* Vol. 2 of *Christian Origins and the Question of God.* Minneapolis: Fortress, 1996.

Zolla, Elémire. *The Androgyne: Reconciliation of Male and Female.* New York: Crossroad, 1981.

Index